Subjection &

Thinking Gender
Edited by Linda Nicholson

Also published in the series

Subjection
& Subjectivity

PSYCHOANALYTIC FEMINISM
& MORAL PHILOSOPHY

Diana Tietjens Meyers

ROUTLEDGE   NEW YORK   LONDON

Published in 1994 by
Routledge
29 West 35th Street
New York, NY 10001

Published in Great Britain by
Routledge
11 New Fetter Lane
London EC4P 4EE

Library of Congress Cataloging-in-Publication Data

Meyers, Diana T.
      Subjection and subjectivity : psychoanalytic feminism and moral
   philosophy / Diana Tietjens Meyers.
            p.   cm. — (Thinking gender)
         Includes bibliographical references (pp. 185–193) and index.
         ISBN 0-415-90471-4 — ISBN 0-415-90508-7 (pbk.)
         1. Feminist ethics.   2. Psychoanalysis and feminism.   3. Subjectivity
   I. Title.   II. Series.
   BJ1395.M48   1994
   176'.082—dc20   94-20584
                                                                          CIP

For Lewis

Contents

Acknowledgments

I am deeply grateful to many people who have read and commented on different parts of this book at different stages of development. I want to take this opportunity to thank Sandra Bartky, Susan Brison, Jennifer Church, Nancy Fraser, Kathryn Jackson, Eva Feder Kittay, Joel Kupperman, Larry May, Lewis Meyers, Linda Nicholson, Sara Ruddick, Margaret Urban Walker, Margaret Whitford, and the members of my graduate seminars on feminist ethics and psychoanalytic feminism. In the course of writing this book, I have presented pieces of it in many forums where I have received helpful suggestions. I want to acknowledge, as well, the contributions of audiences at Wesleyan University, the University of Washington, New York University, St. Mary's College (Notre Dame), the University of Dayton Conference on the Fragmented Self, the Canadian Society for Women in Philosophy (meeting at the University of Calgary), the New Jersey Philosophical Association (meeting at Hoboken, NJ), Amintaphil (meeting at Allentown, PA), and the Eastern Division of the Society for Women and Philosophy (both at regional meetings and at a meeting in conjunction with the APA). Also, I want to express my profound gratitude to Maureen MacGrogan, my editor at Routledge and previously my editor at Columbia University Press. I am indebted to her for supporting my work over many years.

Others have contributed to this project by furnishing indispensable funding. Thanks to a Provost's Fellowship awarded by the Provost of the University of Connecticut and a sabbatical leave granted by the University of Connecticut, I have enjoyed the luxury of a year-long leave in which to write. I am also grateful to the Rockefeller Foundation for an idyllic residency at the Villa Serbelloni in Bellagio, Italy. Finally, I thank the University of Connecticut Research Foundation for grants that supported my research in France and my travel to Italy.

Parts of this book have been published before and are used here with permission. I would like to thank Indiana University Press for permission to use parts of "The Subversion of Women's Agency in Psychoanalytic Feminism: Chodorow, Flax, Kristeva," which first appeared in *Revaluing French Feminism* edited by Nancy Fraser and Sandra Bartky, *Law and Philosophy* for permission to use parts of "Social Exclusion, Moral Reflection, and Rights," and *Hypatia* for permission to use parts of "Moral Reflection: Beyond Impartial Reason."

1

Difference:
The Challenge to Moral Reflection

Over the years, I have gradually and, I confess, somewhat reluctantly become convinced that the classic philosophical project of setting out an account of justice that anticipates a comprehensive social ideal is misguided. It seems to me that ideal theories—theories of the principles that perfectly just societies would implement—often distract attention from pressing social problems and that, when these problems are addressed through ideal theories, the ideals they commend are too stringent to be helpful for purposes of devising feasible solutions in a profoundly nonideal world. Abstracting from the realities of pervasive and persistent injustice and historical animosity between social groups, ideal theory overlooks the problems of entrenched domination and oppression, offers (at best) vague guidance for eliminating those evils, and even obstructs social change by locking in place ostensibly neutral standards that in fact disadvantage some social groups.

In view of these deficiencies, it is doubtful that ideal theory should be moral and political philosophy's paramount concern. Instead, it seems to me best to scale back our philosophical ambitions and to try to understand the process through which moral insight may be gained and through which practices and policies designed to rectify injustice can be defended. Thus, I have turned to problems concerning moral subjectivity and moral reflection. In my judgment, however, the most prominent contemporary philosophical treatments of these topics remain too much in thrall to the traditions of impartial

1

reason. As a result, they ignore important dimensions of experience that are conventionally tagged feminine, and they fail to provide an adequate basis for defining and defending feminist objectives.

One way to understand these failings is to trace them to the lingering influence of logical positivism. Early in the twentieth century, the logical positivists—partly out of outrage over Nazi propagandistic abuses—prosecuted a vigorous and thoroughgoing campaign of philosophical purification. They sought to purge philosophy of ambiguity, to cast its arguments in certifiably valid forms, and thereby to ensure the soundness of its claims. Stylistic flourish and figurative language were regarded as suspect and consigned to the disdained category of poetry. Thought to be devoid of cognitive content, such uses of language were dismissed as merely emotive. Indeed, normative ethics itself did not fare well under the positivist juggernaut. Having reduced prescriptive and proscriptive claims to expressions of emotion, positivism banished them from philosophy proper. Only metaethics—that is, theory about the nature of normative statements—was deemed amenable to rational analysis and argument and therefore within the ken of philosophy.

It took the civil rights movement and the anti-Vietnam War movement and the urgency of the issues they raised to prick philosophy's collective professional conscience and spark a revitalization of philosophical treatments of public policy questions. Around the same time, John Rawls published *A Theory of Justice* (1971), the first major work of systematic political philosophy to appear in this century, and the topic of social justice regained a spot on the philosophical agenda. Since then, normative ethics and political philosophy have remained philosophically respectable.

Yet, normative ethics and political philosophy remain deeply tradition-bound. Kantianism and utilitarianism dominate debate both as contenders for acceptance as general theories and also as ways of addressing timely issues. Curiously, Kantianism and utilitarianism defend themselves against positivist skepticism by conceding a great deal to it. Moral subjects are construed as rational deliberators—either checking their beliefs for consistency or devising ways to maximize social welfare. In short, these views seem to enable normative moral and political philosophy to proceed without "betraying" reason and descending into the "nether world" of emotion and rhetoric.

Despite the undeniable importance of this body of work, I believe that normative ethics and political philosophy have been stunted by this aversion to the realm of affect and expressiveness. Indeed, it seems to me that emotion and rhetoric are pivotal in nonideal theory, for prejudice against members of some social groups and systematic misconstrual of their needs, desires, and aspirations often block solutions to urgent social problems. In my judgment, when Kantianism and utilitarianism do not simply bypass these aspects of moral reality, they treat them superficially.

This study aims to remedy the oversights of standard accounts of moral subjectivity and moral reflection and to do so in a way that accommodates feminist critique and feminist demands. I begin by clarifying the political challenge that contemporary accounts of moral subjectivity and moral reflection face. Since systematic group-based social exclusion is one of the most pressing, pervasive, and seemingly intractable injustices, I contend that an account of moral subjectivity and moral reflection that cannot fruitfully address this wrong should be rejected. I then argue that philosophy's unitary rational subject is ill-equipped to address this problem and that it is necessary to look beyond philosophy for a realistic and rich view of moral subjectivity. In psychoanalytic feminism, I have found a salutary corrective to philosophy's monistic moral subject. Unlike most philosophers, psychoanalytic feminists appreciate the role of culturally transmitted imagery in shaping people's moral perception, the contribution of empathy to moral reflection, and the potential of a complex moral identity to enhance moral insight. Thus, I propose to mine this literature in order to set forth a view of moral reflection designed to handle the sort of serious, real-world social problems that feminists and many other social activists raise.

1. The Problem of Difference

Until recently, the problem of unjust social exclusion was commonly construed as the problem of prejudice or bigotry—mass contempt for and concerted discrimination against individuals simply because they belong to a minority or powerless social group. But thinking of social exclusion solely in terms of the prejudice of the excluders reduces the problem to the despicable attitudes of a dominant group and leaves out two important dimensions of the problem: (1) the institutionalization of exclusion, and (2) the viewpoint of the excluded. Recasting the wrong of group-based social exclusion as the problem of difference acknowledges the role of prejudice in perpetuating this injustice, but this reformulation has the advantage of bringing out these added complexities.

The problem of difference is partly a problem about how we think about people. Instead of noticing individuals, we consign people to exclusionary categories organized by sex, race, sexual orientation, disability, ethnicity, religion, and so forth, and then we dismiss the people thus classified—for example, women, African-Americans, lesbians and gays, and Muslims—as inherently defective. In this way, difference—the neutral fact that people look different, act different, and choose different affiliations—degenerates into "difference"—the censorious freighting of the facts of difference.

Yet, prejudice by no means exhausts the problem of difference, for "difference" is memorialized in entrenched social practices. When established institutions and the policies they implement are taken to be natural and fair, any change that accommodates "different" people will disrupt the settled expectations of members of the dominant group—the people for whom these arrangements were designed and who accept them. As a result, such change will appear to interfere with these individuals' freedom and will be regarded as departing from neutrality in bestowing undeserved benefits on a new group of claimants. Yet, the status quo is not neutral for members of socially excluded groups—their free choice and prospects for self-realization are obstructed by the very institutions and policies that serve others so well.

When unilateral ascriptions of "difference" are institutionalized in this way, the double bind that Martha Minow calls the "dilemma of difference" arises. As Minow points out, "[t]he stigma of difference may be recreated both by ignoring and by focusing on it" (Minow, 1990, 20). A society trapped in the dilemma of difference seems to be without resources to rectify unjust social exclusion. By ignoring difference and treating everyone as the same, government may "freeze in place the past consequences of difference," but, by creating programs that acknowledge difference, government "make[s] those differences matter and thus symbolically reinforces them" (Minow, 1990, 42). Neutral policies often perpetuate the subordinate status of "different" social groups, and difference-sensitive policies often catalyze backlashes.

By pretending that women in the United States today are no different from men, equal opportunity guarantees that many women who regard having and raising children as a core project and who take time off to fulfill this goal will be left behind in their careers. They have chosen, goes the familiar rationale, to put family ahead of professional advancement and thus to sacrifice work experience, which is, after all, a legitimate factor in promotion decisions. However, if government were to provide affirmative action for women who leave career tracks to care for preschool children and who later wish to rejoin the workforce (Held, 1984, 19), the cri de QUOTA would be raised. Women would be stigmatized as freeloaders—taking "vacations" to raise kids and returning to unearned advantages in the workplace. Either way, women who become mothers in the context of traditional relations with men lose. As equals, they do not measure up; as recipients of special favors, they would be despised and resented.

What is to be done? Minow suggests two ways in which the dilemma of difference can be resolved. One possibility is to "expand the definition of who is the same"—that is, to recognize excluded others as persons, too (Minow, 1990, 95). Another possibility is to "broaden the definition of difference"—that is, to recognize that one is oneself different from the standpoint of excluded others (Minow, 1990, 95). These two strategies—accepting universal humanity and accepting diversity—correspond to two forms that the dilemma of difference takes.

In one form, blindness to commonality where it exists or where it could exist creates artificial boundaries between groups of people that work to the detriment of all but the most powerful of those groups. In Chapter 2, I shall argue that this form of the dilemma of difference can be resolved through more skillful and imaginative use of Kantian impartial reason—the approach to moral reflection that figures most prominently in judicial reasoning and in public policy debate in the United States. By including purportedly different people in established moral categories or by creating more inclusive moral categories, impartial reason can identify and justify policies that break down unjust social and economic exclusion.

However, Kantian impartial reason is no panacea. In Chapter 2, I shall also argue that this approach to moral reflection is not capable of addressing the second form of the dilemma of difference. Here contempt for self-ascribed and cherished difference or irremediable and non-negligible difference is invoked to justify a powerful group's indifference to or exploitation of others. Broadening the definition of difference presupposes recognizing difference as such and appreciating it.

But since the logic of social reform based on Kantian impartial reason is a logic of conceptual, and sometimes behavioral, assimilation, this approach to moral reflection fails to accord due respect to individuals who regard their difference as central to their identity and to individuals who suffer from disabilities that few others share. In these cases, impartial reason's universal categories negate differences that demand direct moral attention and thwart moral recognition of diversity.

In my estimation, an account of moral reflection and moral subjectivity that is incapable of addressing the second form of the dilemma of difference is untenable, for this kind of group-based social exclusion is among the most glaring and widespread injustices confronting societies today. Now, it seems to me that the intractability of this form of the dilemma of difference is an artifact of routinized, unidimensional moral reflection coupled with a monistic, rationalistic conception of the moral subject. Thus, it is my objective to develop an account of moral reflection that endows moral subjects with resources adequate to the task of resolving this form of the dilemma of difference.

2. The Problem of the Moral Subject

The view of the moral subject that currently dominates discussion in moral and political philosophy is a legalistic view—one preoccupied with the distribution of social goods and with accountability. To frame the problem of social distribution in manageable terms, individual idiosyncracies, deep interpersonal bonds, and cultural affiliations are set aside, and a set of universal human interests that can be equitably satisfied is enumerated. Hence, people are conceived as fundamentally homogeneous. Moreover, since the concern with accountability dictates treating the moral subject as a locus of control, those influences that people do not recognize or that are too powerful to resist are discounted. Hence, the self is seen as largely independent, transparent, and rational. But this conception of the moral subject bears little resemblance to the people we know and value. Our vital, baffling, fascinating friends are reduced to ciphers in a social order of rationally certified rights and duties.

A related problem with much work in applied ethics is that the positions taken and the arguments supporting these positions typically reprise rival traditional moral theories—that is, they draw out the implications of the author's preferred moral theory with respect to a current issue. To find such an argument persuasive, one must already endorse the tenets of the moral theory that anchors it. But since these theories are themselves controversial, the arguments derived from them seldom convince a broad audience.

Indeed, the power of impartial reason to settle moral questions has often been exaggerated. In *A Theory of Justice*, for example, John Rawls proclaims his interpretation of the original position to be the "philosophically favored" one, and he maintains that the parties to the original position would decisively reject utilitarianism and perfectionism and opt for a rights-based welfare state (Rawls, 1971, 17–18, 22). But it was not long before Robert Nozick invoked impartial reason to defend a libertarian vision of justice (Nozick, 1974). Since then, the challenges to Rawls's theory have multiplied, and Rawls eventually weakened his claims about the conclusiveness of his earlier arguments (Rawls, 1985, 224).[1] Impartial reason's record so far hardly warrants according it exclusive sway over the problem of social justice. There is little reason to think that impartial reason will ever bring the debate over social justice to an end or, for that matter, that controversy over the nature of justice will ever cease. Furthermore, the Rawls-Nozick debate testifies to the malleability of impartial reason in the hands of skilled practitioners and thus to its susceptibility to manipulation that merely rationalizes the status quo. There is no assurance, then, that impartial reason will detect unjust social policies and practices and prescribe needed remedies.

This quandary suggests that there is an acute need to examine the pretheoretical resources available to moral reflection. In other words, our conception of the moral subject needs to undergo a corrective naturalization. As everyone who is not a professional philosopher knows, people are endowed with an array of moral capacities that they bring to bear on their moral perplexities (for helpful discussion of the role of interpersonal skills in moral reflection, see M. Walker, 1989, 1991; for an account of autonomy competency, see Meyers, 1987b). Likewise, people typically endorse a variety of values. Indeed, it hardly seems likely that privileging a single moral capacity, such as rationality, or privileging a single moral value, whether fairness or happiness, will lead to better moral judgments. Moreover, since both interpersonal forces and intrapersonal forces belie the unity of the subject, there is reason to think that a nonunitary moral subject should displace the rational monolith of the Kantian tradition.

Still, acknowledging the pluralistic, heterogeneous, multiskilled nature of the moral subject generates a novel set of problems. Pulled hither and yon by disparate, possibly incoherent influences, people may seem incapable of critical moral judgment and firm moral conviction. However, I shall urge that, on the contrary, the nonunitary moral subject renders basic social critique and far-reaching social change morally defensible.

To help me with this project, I have turned to recent psychoanalytic feminist theory, for I believe that intimations of a more convincing view of moral subjectivity and moral reflection are to be found in this literature. First, these theorists are specifically concerned with dimensions of moral subjectivity that are conventionally coded as feminine, such as emotion and the unconscious. Thus, they highlight capacities and concerns that philosophers have by and large ignored. Second, the psychoanalytic feminist literature is serving as a laboratory for experimenting with the medium of figurative language for purposes of critiquing and reconstituting gender. Thus, psychoanalytic feminist theory includes precisely what I miss in moral and political philosophy. This book is not, then, a work of psychoanalytic feminism. It is, rather, an attempt to correct and expand moral and political philosophy with the assistance of psychoanalytic feminism. I believe that this unorthodox juxtaposition of disciplines yields a radical and felicitous reconceptualization of moral reflection and moral subjectivity.

3. Psychoanalytic Feminism and Moral Reflection

Since its inception, psychoanalysis has played a controversial role in intellectual history. A revolutionary doctrine from the start—some thought it obscene, and few were not shocked—it soon came under attack in positivistic circles and fell into disrepute. Yet, it is clear that in many respects psychoanalytic precepts have been incorporated into our folk psychology. People's explanations of their own and others' conduct often rely on the assumption that nonconscious forces are at work. Likewise, people commonly assume that dreams, parapraxes, and similar phenomena are meaningful and interpretable (for related discussion, see Sachs, 1989, 362–368; Nagel, 1994, 34–36). The questionability of Freud's theory of gender notwithstanding, it seems to me that only the most intransigent empiricists and skeptics fail to see the power of his mythic, eroticized tale of the unformed infant coming into the world and embarking upon the travail of personality consolidation, with its attendant torments and triumphs.

It is not surprising, then, that with the recent rise in interest in problems concerning gender, Freud's brainchild has regained prominence. Nevertheless, the conjunction of psychoanalysis with feminism is perplexing, for Freud was no friend of feminism, and he gave a notoriously insulting account of femininity (see Chapter 4, Section 1). In view of this checkered history, it might seem that feminists must eschew psychoanalysis, but many have not.

Arguing that Freud's treatment of femininity denigrates women and locks them in their traditional domestic role, feminists have produced withering critiques of his account. Still, Freud's hidebound conservativism regarding gender has not deterred feminists from capitalizing on the emancipatory potential of psychoanalysis that is embedded in its rich account of intrapsychic forces and interpersonal dynamics. Psychoanalytic views of the interaction between conscious and unconscious mental life, of the contribution of empathy in building trusting, collaborative interpersonal relationships, and of the therapeutic efficacy of interpreting and emotionally working through repressed materials are evanescent in spirit and assume a potential for salubrious transformation. Although psychoanalysis has been the site of some of the most reactionary and misogynist attempts to suppress feminist aims, it has also been the inspiration for sharp feminist challenges to the status quo—both feminist reconstructions of gender and also feminist proposals for changes in social practices and policies.

Couching their work in the stirring rhetoric of psychoanalysis and drawing on the plot line that Freud expounds, psychoanalytic feminists contest gender norms in a distinctive way. Indeed, the imaginativeness and the subtlety of their oppositional methods initially attracted me to this literature and led me to consider whether this literature might suggest a less divisive approach to the dilemma of difference.

I claimed above that resolving the dilemma of difference by broadening the definition of difference presupposes recognizing difference as such and appreciating it. However, appreciating difference is no easy matter. Indeed, I believe that diversity will continue to seem threatening and that the obstacles to morally responding to difference will remain insuperable unless we augment our repertory of moral skills. In particular, intersubjective channels of communication and understanding must be opened through empathy (see Chapter 2). Now, underscoring the need for empathy across the boundaries of contending social groups might seem to dwell needlessly on an obvious truism. However, this modest suggestion raises a number of difficult theoretical questions—questions that, for the most part, moral philosophy and political philosophy ignore, but that, in contrast, psychoanalytic feminism brings to the fore. Broadly, then, my strategy in this study is to appropriate feminist reformulations of psychoanalysis to enrich moral and political philosophy in ways that will facilitate resolutions of seemingly intractable forms of the dilemma of difference.

In this regard, I have found the work of three psychoanalytic feminists, Julia Kristeva, Nancy Chodorow, and Jessica Benjamin, particularly helpful, and, in this book, I propose to consider the moral capacities and strategies that their scholarship features. For Julia Kristeva, the subject is decentered—unconscious drives and repressed material unsettle people's speech and action. Since these disruptions trouble the subject who longs for seamless unity, they activate defense mechanisms that become the binding force behind xenophobia. Thus, the question of how the pernicious social consequences of the decentered self's defenses can be mitigated is central to Kristeva's thought, and I shall explore her work on aesthetic practices and its implications for a politics of counterfiguration in Chapters 3–5. In contrast, Nancy Chodorow and Jessica Benjamin examine the process of internalizing emotionally charged relationships and the social self to which it gives rise. Focusing on the role of empathy in nurturance and the importance of reciprocity in caring relationships, their work calls attention to problems in moral reflection stemming from deficient sensitivity to others or from a weak sense of self. In Chapters 6 and 7, I shall address their views regarding intersubjectivity and individual identity. My contention is that our account of moral reflection will be impoverished unless it embraces the dissident linguistic capacities to which Kristeva's account of the decentered self alerts us along with the empathic capacities that Chodorow and Benjamin discern in the social self. Though overlooked in the philosophical literature, the moral capacities that Kristeva, Chodorow, and Benjamin identify are integral to moral reflection.

Before proceeding, however, it is important to acknowledge that psychoanalytic feminism does not provide a comprehensive explanation of the problem of male dominance. Psychoanalytic feminism has been justly criticized both for its insensitivity to differences among women and also for its neglect of the economic arrangements through which differential power relations between women and men are maintained (Kuykendall, 1984, 270–271; Young, 1984, 139; Grimshaw, 1986, 57–65; Spelman, 1988, 80–113; Leland, 1989, 87–89;

but for discussion of fruitful African-American feminist and working-class feminist appropriations of psychoanalysis, see Abel, 1990). These objections are devastating if psychoanalytic feminism is viewed as a universal empirical account of childhood development or as a complete feminist theory eclipsing other types of social analysis and criticism.

However, psychoanalytic feminist narratives need not be read in this way. They can be read as theories about the nature of subjectivity and the meaning of gender, as opposed to speculative developmental psychology. If these narratives are construed as dissident counterfigurations of gender, and if they are interpreted as riveting attention on moral capacities that philosophers have sidelined, there is good reason for feminists and moral philosophers to heed this body of work. Not only does psychoanalytic feminist imagery exhibit the emotional significance of gender while at the same time probing gender as no other theory can, but also it foregrounds relational capacities that have traditionally been associated with maternal caregiving and that have been peremptorily dismissed, perhaps for that highly dubious reason.

A. Difference and Figuration

In Chapter 3, I take up a major obstacle to empathy with people from social groups different from one's own—that is, the problem of culturally normative prejudice. Attempts to empathize with members of socially excluded groups often fail because emotionally entrenched, unconscious prejudice distorts empathic understanding, and this pseudoempathic "insight" is invoked to rationalize seriously defective moral judgments. I argue that prejudice is not merely a result of individual cognitive malfunction, but that it is culturally encoded and transmitted through figurations of socially excluded groups, including emblematic characters in stories and myths as well as pictorial imagery. These cultural figurations are exceedingly difficult to dislodge. Both because they enhance the self-esteem of members of the dominant group, and also because they are implicated in the culture's overarching worldview, prejudicial figurations are inaccessible to critiques based on impartial reason.

In view of the immunity of culturally normative prejudice to rational criticism, I consider Julia Kristeva's call for developing rhetorical strategies designed to counteract it. Some forms of psychopathology are sustained by self-defeating systems of figurations that structure the individual's self-understanding as well as the individual's inter-pretations of social relations. Just as freeing individual patients from the grip of such psychopathology requires supplanting these figura-tions with therapeutic figurations that are conducive to a more satis-fying life, so freeing social policy from the ills of culturally normative prejudice requires supplanting figurations that crystallize and per-petuate negative stereotypes of socially excluded groups with emanci-patory figurations. Insofar as prejudicial figurations shape moral perception, empathic understanding of the members of socially ex-cluded groups will be distorted, and this "dysempathy" will under-mine public discussion of the problem of difference.

Chapters 4 and 5 explicate and defend a politics of counterfigura-tion as a method of dislodging culturally normative prejudice. Follow-ing Kristeva's observations about the links between political dissent and this practice of emancipatory counterfiguration, I call this discur-sive politics "dissident speech." To clarify the role of figuration in cul-turally normative prejudice, I begin Chapter 4 with an examination of a powerful prejudicial figuration of gender—Freud's account of femi-ninity. Then, to indicate what is involved in the production of feminist counterfigurations, I survey a selection of provocative counterfigura-tions taken from the work of four psychoanalytic feminists—Jessica Benjamin, Nancy Chodorow, Julia Kristeva, and Luce Irigaray.

Each of these psychoanalysts advances a theory of gender—a the-ory of cultural standards and expectations regarding femininity and masculinity.[2] Yet, there is often ambiguity about what a psychoana-lytic theory of gender does. My discussion in Chapter 4 is premised on a view of the metatheoretical status of psychoanalytic accounts of gender that does not hearken to Freud's empiricist, medical self-understanding.

Some psychoanalytic feminists join with Freud and present their work as an explanatory account of the psychological development and dispositions of gendered women and men—as a rival, that is, to behaviorism and cognitive development theory (Chodorow, 1978, 32–39, 53; Benjamin, 1988, 108). On this literalist, scientistic view, penis envy, whether it is understood as a desire to have a penis or a desire to enjoy the social advantages of men, names a desire that, it is claimed, first arises during women's preadolescent years and that helps to explain how their personalities are structured and why they are motivated as they are when they reach adulthood. However, other psychoanalytic feminists regard Freud's theory of gender as a figurative rendition of cultural gender norms that expresses the emotional significance that people commonly attach to gender (Kristeva, 1987a, 276). On this symbolist view, penis envy becomes a metaphor that captures culturally regulative beliefs, attitudes, and feelings regarding heterosexuality and femininity. Correlatively, psychoanalytic feminist gender theories are seen as counterfigurations of gender—either counterfigurations that exhibit the harm done by traditional gender norms or counterfigurations that proffer alternative visions of gender. In other words, the symbolist view assigns psychoanalytic feminism the task of discursively ambushing gender norms.

Few psychoanalytic feminists ever furnish anything more than cursory and cryptic metatheoretical comments, and most appear to vacillate between the alternatives I have sketched. It seems to me, however, that the literalist reading credits psychoanalytic feminist theories of gender with the wrong sort of theoretical power. In light of widespread and, to my mind, justified skepticism about psychoanalysis as a competing developmental psychology, I want to emphasize that adopting the symbolist view and rejecting the literalist view does not strip psychoanalytic feminism of interest. From the standpoint of feminist social critique and from the standpoint of moral and political philosophy, I submit, psychoanalytic accounts of gender are most profitably understood as expressive and normative. The family romances that psychoanalytic feminists narrate figuratively reinterpret and reassess established gender norms, or they figuratively recast gender and invite us to embrace these novel conceptions.

Admittedly, it is hard to avoid lapsing into thinking of psychoanalytic feminist theories of gender as explanatory theories. Since psychoanalytic theory projects its figurative narrative onto the adult's largely forgotten past, it is virtually impossible to write about psychoanalysis without leaving the impression that one is chronicling actual childhood events. Nevertheless, resisting the temptation to read psychoanalytic feminism as a social scientific explanation of the genesis of gender and instead reading it as an oppositional rhetorical strategy repays the effort. On the symbolist interpretation, the corpus of psychoanalytic feminism furnishes many and sundry examples of dissident speech without establishing a canonical counterfiguration of gender. Moreover, this reading makes it evident that psychoanalytic feminists have contributed substantially to the critique and reconfiguration of gender that originated in the women's movement, without shackling feminist dissident speakers to the imagery or narrative setting that is character-

istic of psychoanalytic discourse (for skepticism about some psychoanalytic feminist figurations, see Meyers, 1992 and Chapter 5, Section 1).
Finally, in illustrating how counterfiguration can circumnavigate entrenched emotional responses and inveterate patterns of thought
regarding women, the symbolist view demonstrates the relevance of
psychoanalytic feminism to the dilemma of difference and thus to
moral and political philosophy. One need not be persuaded, then, that
psychoanalysis accurately describes the course of childhood development, nor need one be persuaded that psychoanalytic feminists have
unfailingly produced figurations that women should embrace to see
the value of psychoanalysis to feminist theory.

Still, the examples of psychoanalytic figurations of gender that I
present in Chapter 4 and the heated debates surrounding them raise
the question of how emancipatory figurations can be distinguished
from repressive ones. Chapter 5 addresses this issue. Julia Kristeva
and Martha Nussbaum maintain that love is the emotional spring
that nourishes emancipatory imagery, and Maria Lugones maintains
that love is necessary for women from different social groups to
travel to one another's "worlds." However, to stress the political
nature of dissident speech, I urge that emancipatory counterfigurations arise from solidarity among members of socially excluded
groups. Still, candidate counterfigurations must be tested in practice,
for a novel figuration that seems attractive to the members of a
socially excluded group may prove to shape moral perception in
unforeseen and undesirable ways. A critical test of the viability of a
counterfiguration is its impact on empathy and on interaction in
which people are guided by their empathic understanding of others.
Whereas prejudicial figurations obstruct empathic understanding of
others, emancipatory figurations facilitate empathic understanding.
Thus, emancipatory figurations support the expansion of well-
placed trust and mutually beneficial collaboration, while reducing
debilitating anxiety about oneself and others and poor coordination
between oneself and others. In short, emancipatory figurations are
ones that the members of a socially excluded group can identify with
without becoming complicit in their own subordination.[3]

It is necessary for the members of socially excluded groups to take
control over the figurations through which they are perceived and
through which experience is interpreted. Important though the production of emancipatory counterfigurations is, however, I stress that
this project must be part of a comprehensive political struggle.

Without tangible economic and political gains, counterfigurations will never take root in the dominant culture; but, without resymbolization of socially excluded groups, culturally normative prejudice will always threaten material advances. Although it would be disastrous for socially excluded groups to rely solely on the dissemination of emancipatory counterfigurations to overcome economic and political subordination, it would also be disastrous for these groups to neglect the power of prejudicial figurations to sustain social exclusion.

B. Empathy and Moral Judgment

Dissident speech provides an antidote for culturally normative prejudice and clears the way for empathy between members of different social groups. Yet, moral reflection requires more than understanding other people. It requires making judgments about how one ought to behave toward them. Some might hold that all that remains, once one has empathized with another, is to feed empathically obtained information into Kantian impartial reason or into utilitarian calculation of the social welfare. However, I contend that neither of these approaches is adequate to the task of resolving the dilemma of difference. Considering this dead end, I take up Nancy Chodorow's and Jessica Benjamin's work on empathy and mutual recognition, and, in Chapters 6 and 7, I use it to develop empathy-based approaches to moral and political reflection.

In Chapter 6, I turn from psychoanalytic feminist theories of gender to two psychoanalytic feminist theories of the constitution of subjectivity. Chodorow maintains that empathy enables caregivers to grasp children's needs and desires without psychologically fusing with them—that is, to recognize children's separate existence. Moreover, Benjamin maintains that children consolidate their identities when caregivers recognize their needs in this way and when they, in turn, recognize the independent needs of their caregivers—that is, when there is mutual recognition. Now, to recognize a child, a caregiver must decide which of a child's desires to satisfy and which to frustrate and must decide when and how to go about satisfying or frustrating a child's desires. In other words, caregivers must exercise independent judgment. Although their theories provide a framework for developing an account of independent judgment, I believe that neither Chodorow nor Benjamin gives sufficient attention to this problem. Drawing out the implications of their views, I present an account of self-recognition—that is, directing care to oneself—and I explain how self-recognition structures empathy-based decision-making.

Here, it is worth noting that, since Chodorow's and Benjamin's theories of the constitution of subjectivity concern parent-child relations at the earliest stages of development, and since mothers or other women commonly serve as primary caregivers, their theories are inextricable from gender issues. Thus, the interpersonal skills and the interdependent relationships that Chodorow and Benjamin describe carry distinctly feminine connotations. Indeed, this association with femininity together with the cultural devaluation of femininity may explain why these capacities and this form of interaction have generally been marginalized. Jane Flax points out the close resemblance between the tasks of the psychotherapist and the tasks of the mother, and she diagnoses Freud's repudiation of maternal caregiving as a model of psychoanalytic clinical practice and his reliance on military imagery to characterize therapeutic relationships as a flight from femininity (Flax, 1986, 334, 340–343). Likewise, despite the seemingly obvious need for empathy in moral reflection as well as the seemingly obvious relevance of people's experience with family, friends, and other associates to their moral outlook, moral philosophy has devoted little attention to this moral capacity and this source of moral values.

The psychoanalytic feminist project of revaluing the mother and maternal caregiving helps to neutralize the stigma attaching to being influenced as a result of one's emotional ties, the stigma attaching to knowledge gained through emotional insight into others, and the stigma attaching to nonunitary identity. Thus, psychoanalytic feminists have helped to clear away barriers to expanding our repertory of moral capacities and to enriching our account of the moral subject. In the remainder of Chapter 6, I apply Chodorow's and Benjamin's views to the problem of moral reflection and defend an account of critical moral reflection that situates empathic understanding of others in a context structured by the values of mutual recognition and self-recognition.

I believe that this approach to moral reflection is already implicit in a familiar deliberative prompt—that is, a query that serves as a reminder of a salient moral consideration and that focuses moral reflection. Two well-known deliberative prompts express the Kantian and the utilitarian forms of impartial reason respectively—"How would you like to be treated that way?" and "Would such-and-such be best for all?" But another vernacular prompt—"Do you want to be the sort of person who would do such-and-such?"—adumbrates an approach to moral reflection that few philosophers have taken seriously. Instead of seeing moral reflection as the application of an overriding, philosophically approved criterion of right and wrong to a set of available options, the latter view sees moral judgment as a process of interpreting the moral significance of various courses of conduct that one might undertake both in light of one's own values and capabilities and also in light of one's understanding of others' needs and circumstances.

Posing the question of what sort of person would choose a particular option spurs people to think about who they are and who they aspire to be. This approach to moral reflection presupposes that one has a moral identity and that one should try not to betray one's moral identity. But it does not presuppose that one's moral identity is fixed or that everyone's moral identity is the same. A moral identity consists of a realistic moral ideal—that is, a set of values that one believes one should live up to and that takes into account one's capacities and limitations. Thus, there is room for individual variation in the selection and the weighting of values, and there is room for change as one discovers new values or reassesses the importance of familiar ones. By focusing attention on one's moral identity and on how it can be enacted (or how it would be betrayed), asking whether one wants to be the sort of person who would act in a certain way makes self-recognition central to moral reflection.

Nevertheless, this approach to moral reflection does not authorize people to indulge in some sort of moral solipsism, for finding a way to enact one's moral identity depends on understanding one's interpersonal context. Uttering a certain sentence or making a certain gesture does not retain the same moral significance regardless of context. Thus, fulfilling one's moral ideal requires recognizing others, and, since recognizing others requires understanding them, this approach to moral reflection requires that people become adept at empathizing with others. On this view, moral judgment synthesizes empathic understanding of others with understanding of one's personal moral ideal and one's knowledge of one's options. To stress both the key role that empathy with different others plays in this type of moral reflection and also its demand that moral subjects not abrogate responsibility for independent judgment, I call this approach to moral reflection "empathic thought." I close Chapter 6 by applying empathic thought to a practical problem of gender difference, namely, parenting. Here, I urge that this empathy-friendly approach to moral reflection is much more likely to succeed in convincing reluctant fathers to coparent than arguments based on impartial reason and that this promise is a good reason to adopt this view of moral reflection.

Chapter 7 takes up the question of the feasibility of empathic thought in the political arena. An empathic and improvisational approach to moral reflection, empathic thought might seem too particularized or too mercurial to address public policy issues. However, I urge that this approach to moral reflection can be adapted to politics and also that it is capable of grounding rights. Indeed, I argue that construing a society's moral identity so narrowly that its values are limited to those certified by Kantian impartial reason or utilitarian impartial reason—that is, fairness or social welfare—impairs the society's ability to acknowledge difference morally and to resolve the dilemma of difference. Rights derived from empathic thought do not submerge difference in universal human interests, nor do they create the impression of undue favoritism when the special needs of members of socially excluded groups are accommodated. Thus, this approach to moral reflection justifies rights that facilitate, rather than obstruct, mediation of the dilemma of difference.

Apart from the emphasis that empathic thought places on empathy with others and on moral interpretation of possible actions, the chief innovation it introduces is its view of moral subjects. Whether the individual moral subject making choices at the interpersonal level or the social moral subject making policy at the political level, the moral subject of empathic thought is nonunitary. The unidimensional moral subject—the monistic impartial reasoner—is replaced by a pluralistic, heterogeneous moral subject—a subject whose perception may be structured by culturally normative prejudice and who needs dissident speech to overcome prejudice and empathize with different others and also a subject who embraces diverse values and who seeks to reconcile them in practice. Of course, many people and many societies number the values of Kantian and utilitarian impartial reason among those they endorse. Thus, my defense of empathic thought is not a repudiation of impartial reason. Rather, it is a plea to regard impartial reason as part of a repertory of reflective strategies, to regard the skills of the impartial reasoner as part of a repertory of reflective skills, and to regard the values of impartial reason as components of a moral identity that includes other values.

For those who think of impartial reason as preeminent and as defining the moral point of view, my nonunitary moral subject may seem to entail a bewildering demotion of impartial reason. Yet, alone, impartial reason is not a satisfactory approach to moral reflection. In the real world of systematic misperceptions, competing interests, festering resentments, and so forth, emancipatory refiguration of socially excluded groups and empathic understanding of the members of these groups make a vital contribution to moral and political judgment. Taking the problem of unjust, systematic social and economic exclusion—that is, the dilemma of difference—as a key test of the adequacy of accounts of moral reflection shows that moral reflection would be shallow, if not seriously warped, without the involvement of these moral capacities. As long as impartial reason is captivated by a rigid set of categories and as long as impartial reason preempts empathic thought, difference will be despised and penalized. The dilemma of difference will persist, then, until empathic thought joins with dissident speech to pierce the cocoon of contempt. Only then will people be able to explicitly honor human diversity in their moral thinking and to shape public policy to respond to actual social contingencies. I grant that my inclusive view of the resources available to moral reflection does not yield tidy moral theory. It does, however, render sensitive, complex, and dynamic moral reflection—moral reflection that is undertaken in the midst of deeply perplexing and troubling circumstances—intelligible.

2

Difference, Empathy, and Impartial Reason

Since the Enlightenment, justice and the rights through which liberal democracies guarantee justice have been linked indissolubly to impartial reason. Classically, basic rights are characterized as rights that one has simply in virtue of being a person, and violating basic rights is considered a grave injustice, for doing so denies a person's humanity. Some utilitarians have defended a rights-based conception of justice, but both in the history of ideas and in the legal systems of liberal democracies this view of justice rests primarily on the account of impartial reason that is threaded through contractarian moral and political theory and that Kant crystallized in the categorical imperative.

Whether codified in the Golden Rule, in Kant's refinement of it, or in social contract theory, impartial reason holds moral reflection to consistency. Asking whether you would be willing to have others treat you as you propose to treat them, impartial reason bars conscious bias in favor of yourself or your kind along with conscious bias against others. But deliberate partiality is hardly the only form of moral pathology. People can be so insensitive to others or so oblivious to their own emotional dispositions that exercises in impartial reason yield morally grotesque judgments. For this reason, it has been suggested that impartial reason needs to be supplemented by empathy. In this chapter, I shall review some of the roles that defenders of Kantian impartial reason (hereafter, impartial reason) have assigned to empathy, and I shall raise some doubts about relying on empathy to save impartial reason from its critics.

As we have seen, the problem of difference and group-based social exclusion reflects historical patterns of domination and subordination (Chapter 1, Section 1). Seeking to rectify these injustices, societies commonly find themselves oscillating between inaugurating reforms that provoke a backlash, on the one hand, and clinging to principles that perpetuate the status quo, on the other. I shall argue that impartial reason is capable of addressing some versions of the dilemma of difference, but not others (for an alternative critique of impartial reason that stems from the morality of close interpersonal relationships, see Blum, 1980). In the cases where impartial reason falters, I shall urge that empathic understanding of the members of unjustly excluded social groups is missing from moral reflection. In the course of my discussion, I shall distinguish empathy from related approaches to understanding others' subjective experience, and I shall elaborate an account of empathy that highlights its potential contribution to moral reflection. Finally, I shall call into question the ability of impartial reason to accommodate empathic insight into others where difference cannot be assimilated to universal moral categories (for an empathy friendly account of moral reflection, see Chapters 6 and 7). The problem of unjust social exclusion will remain intractable, I believe, if we channel moral reflection exclusively into impartial reason.

Before proceeding, however, let me set out one caveat. In the discussion that follows, I shall not attempt to do justice to Kant's complete moral philosophy nor to any neo-Kantian variant. Unquestionably, Kant's moral philosophy and the work of contemporary Kantians are far more complex than the criterion of universalizability. Still, this criterion is arguably the centerpiece of Kant's moral theory, and, in the United States and similar societies, this criterion is pivotal in moral education, in everyday moral thinking, and in public political debate. What concerns me is not whether there is some version of Kantianism that could possibly furnish a fully adequate account of moral reflection, nor whether human beings could be expected to fulfill the ideals of the best possible Kantian theory. Rather, I shall consider the folk strategy of impartial reason—summed up in the quintessentially Kantian question "How would I like to be treated that way?"—as it is applied by ordinary moral deliberators who are not pure Kantians (or, for that matter, pure anything elses). I shall ask whether this strategy supplies an approach to moral reflection that is capable of addressing the problem of difference. When I give examples of impartial reasoning, then, the question to ask is not whether a "true" Kantian would think this way. More to the point is the question of whether ordinary people seeking to apply the test of universal-izability and to approximate the ideal of impartial rationality commonly think along the lines I sketch.

1. Impartial Reason: Recovering Sameness and Redefining the Person

To see the relevance of impartial reason to the dilemma of difference, it is helpful to begin by examining a model of a successful public policy response to difference—Social Security in the United States. The institutionalization of Social Security has not eliminated prejudice against elderly people—employers resist hiring them, and purportedly humorous images of doddering old fools remain in currency. However, this persistent prejudice does not taint Social Security—a transfer payment program in which funds are redistributed from younger wage earners to the elderly. (I leave aside Social Security's less publicized missions, such as providing disability payments and providing income for the minor children of deceased participants in the program.) Why aren't Social Security pensioners grouped together with "welfare mothers" and resented for the same reasons?

It seems to me that three major factors have contributed to the acceptance of Social Security. First, it is not perceived as a transfer payment program. The illusion that Social Security is an insurance program into which workers pay premiums and from which they eventually draw their fair share of dividends has been successfully maintained. Thus, receiving Social Security checks is not likened to taking charity from welfare. Second, Social Security appears to relieve adult children of financial responsibility for their parents. Believing the Social Security taxes they are now paying to be savings for their own eventual pension, wage earners do not see that they remain indirectly responsible for their parents' economic well-being. Yet, it is doubtful that general recognition of the redistributive structure of Social Security would bring the system into disrepute, for, third, old age is a universal problem. Though some people will not reach retirement age, everyone must anticipate this eventuality. Thus, Social Security is perceived as universally beneficial.

Accommodating difference does not perpetuate the stigma of difference when the interests of the "different" coincide with the interests of others and when no "different" group is explicitly targeted to receive special benefits.[1] Some familiar solutions to the dilemma of difference follow this pattern. For example, the United States Supreme Court has framed the issue of maternity leave in terms of the gender-neutral standard of being entitled to have a family and a job (Minow, 1990, 58). Until family relations have been reconceptualized in a way that assigns men equal responsibility for childcare and eldercare, laws conferring the right to take family leave and to return to work without penalty will benefit women primarily (for related discussion of coparenting, see Chapter 6, Section 5). Yet, the gender-neutral language in which these laws are cast prompts people to understand the problem of caring for dependents, like the problem of old age, as a universal one. Moreover, since two incomes have ceased to be a luxury for many United States families, feminist demands for maternity leave may eventually converge with everyone's household needs.

This type of resolution of the dilemma of difference is most perspicuously explicated in terms of impartial reason. For impartial reason, the guiding question is "How would I like to be treated that way?" or, in political terms, "Would you want to live in a society in which everyone had (did not have) that freedom or in which everyone could (could not) claim that benefit?" Answers to this question are presumed to yield answers to the questions, "What do we all have in common?" and "What conduct befits our common humanity?" Justice is achieved through the consistent application of nondiscriminatory categories that capture universal human capacities and basic interests. The aim is to set up a social structure that protects these shared interests while affording all members of society the opportunity to realize their potential. Although people are expected to avail themselves of their rights in ways that suit their particular talents and aspirations, the conceptual infrastructure of impartial reason is homogenizing. What is morally significant about people is what they have in common.

Recall John Rawls's defense of his principles of justice. Rawls urges his readers to leave aside all knowledge of their personal situation and to endorse a conception of justice that maximizes their share of primary social goods (Rawls, 1971, 62, 92–94). Underlying this account of impartial reason is the assumption that people's basic interests are uniform. This is not to say that Rawls denies that people care deeply about their personal projects. On the contrary, it is this very involvement with individual life plans that serves to justify robust individual liberties (Rawls, 1971, 206–208). But notice that what justifies these liberties is the universal human interest in conceiving and carrying out one's own life plan, not each individual's commitment to his or her particular life plan. If people share the same profile of interests, as Rawls claims they do, one lone person performing the deduction from the original position can represent everyone—my conclusions about justice will be duplicated by anyone else (Rawls, 1971, 139). Moral judgment based on impartial reason does not require consulting with people who seem to be different from oneself.

For impartial reason, difference, if it is not superficial and accidental, violates the regnant paradigm of the person. To accommodate difference impartially, then, is to make it vanish morally by assimilating it to established categories or by expanding established categories. By classifying the elderly as workers in a later phase and caregivers as family members, Social Security and Family Leave finesse difference in this way.

But, of course, opening economic and political life to "different" people often conflicts with the interests of a dominant group, and many differences resist absorption into neutral categories. For example, some people suffer from disabilities that will not obligingly disappear, morally or otherwise, and that require extra consideration. Other people—many women see themselves this way—have identities that reflect their experience of segregation and oppression, but that they could not strip away without betraying themselves.

Now, it might be pointed out that impartial reason is equipped to address cases of this kind, as well. The converse of the impartialist dictum, "Treat like cases alike," is "Treat different cases differently." This back-up precept handily disposes of situations that are covered by well-established principles of fairness—parents have rightful authority over their minor children; victims of force or fraud should be compensated; the punishment should fit the crime. However, the dilemma of difference arises only when difference is not generally believed to warrant special moral consideration. When this skepticism prevails, treating "different" people differently calls attention to their historically despised difference and reinforces exclusionary tendencies.

Impartial reason can countenance departures from the moral norm of uniform treatment, but such departures are usually conceived as addressing exceptional predicaments or temporary conditions. The presumption is that, for moral purposes, people are alike and ought to be treated the same way. Consequently, impartial reason is not well adapted to envisaging moral responses to irremediable or cherished differences.

Susan Moller Okin's discussion of the traditional woman reveals how impartial reason's insensitivity to difference can go awry. The housewife and mother who is economically dependent on her husband seldom has equal standing in major family decisions, such as whether to relocate to pursue career opportunities and how income is to be allocated. By the standards of impartial reason, such subordination is demeaning and demands rectification. Okin traces the traditional woman's subservience to her economic dependence and proposes a dual paycheck remedy (Okin, 1989a, 181). The idea is that, since the person who is performing unpaid domestic services is making as valuable a contribution to the family economy as the person who is working for a wage, it is right that the worth of this contribution be officially recognized. This recognition should take the form of a paycheck—the wage worker will receive checks for half of his salary, and the domestic worker will receive checks for half of the wage worker's salary. Through this device, the domestic worker is not only duly compensated for her labor but also freed of the liability of economic dependence. With an income of her own, she gains an equal voice in major family decisions.

Now, it seems obvious to me that this scheme will not bring about the results that Okin seeks.[2] What is the homemaker going to do with her checks? Probably, like me, she will deposit them in the couple's joint checking account. Surely, we cannot legally require couples to maintain separate finances. But, even if we did, the traditional woman's status would hardly be transfigured, for she would remain economically dependent on her spouse. If he leaves her and marries another homemaker with whom he must share his income, she loses a sizable chunk of her income in this three-way split. Should we prohibit divorce and remarriage in single-income families? What is missing, I believe, in Okin's plan is any empathic understanding of the traditional woman. Maybe Okin thinks the traditional woman is just like many academic women—give her professional status and economic rewards, and, in time, she will blossom into a self-assertive agent. But I doubt that this portrait is accurate. The traditional woman believes that her husband is the head of the household and that her proper role is that of helpmeet. A symbolic paycheck will not change her values and consequently will not make her an equal partner in her marriage.

The futility of Okin's proposal is not its worst failing, however. More serious still, it fails to *respect* the traditional woman. No doubt, there are many women who are stuck in the traditional feminine role and who badly want to escape from it or would want to escape if escape were feasible. Impartial reason, as Okin interprets it, holds that basic human interests dictate that no woman fulfilling this role could reasonably feel otherwise (Okin, 1989a, 175). But, if there are women who sincerely and freely embrace this role, and, though I personally wish it were not so, I am confident that there are, it is morally repugnant to visit an alien ideal of marital equality upon them.[3] Impartial reason assumes a single model of personhood. If this model is highly abstract, it will support only the most general prescriptions, but if this model is richly detailed, it will not fit all persons. In the name of justice, then, impartial reason may seek to eradicate differences that are constitutive of people's avowed identities and thus abrogate its own commitment to respect persons.

2. Impartial Reason's Need for Empathy

At this point, partisans of impartial reason might urge that impartial reason would not yield such unsatisfactory results if it were supplemented by empathy. Since what one personally cares about is not a sufficient basis for moral judgment, empathy could be assigned an instrumental role in moral reflection. Empathy not only enables people to discern situations that call for a moral response, but also it is needed to identify morally significant considerations.

The first of these points is straightforward enough. To act morally, one must be able to identify opportunities to do so (Hill, 1987, 137). Spotting such opportunities requires grasping what other people are going through—is she suffering? does he have unmet needs? what would please her? and so forth. Lacking empathically obtained information about the people one encounters, one could pretty reliably respect rights to noninterference. All one has to do is leave people alone.[4] Still, it remains clear that without empathy one could discharge the Kantian duty to help the needy only by delegating responsibility to proxy relief organizations and social service agencies. On the assumption, however, that one would sometimes be remiss in this duty if one did not respond personally—think of a friend undergoing an emotional crisis during bitterly contested child custody proceedings—no one can do without empathy. Lacking empathically obtained information about the people one encounters, one would be morally paralyzed.

Still, it might seem that the task of empathy is complete once one knows what is going on with the people who might be affected by one's conduct. But, as Joel Kupperman argues, that is not so, for impartial reason may fail to reveal all relevant moral considerations. Kupperman asks whether any type of argument should dissuade the members of a dominant social group (he grants that there is no argument that must dissuade them) from engaging in practices that inflict great suffering on members of socially excluded groups.

He discards arguments grounded in the facts of human life since these considerations do not apply to relations between humans and nonhumans, as well as arguments based on contracts that the members of a dominant social group have not agreed to and will not agree to (Kupperman, 1991a, 311). Likewise, he denies that an argument from universalizability can dispose of the problem, for the members of a dominant social group "may fanatically insist that any beings that have the same advantage over [them] that they have over [others] would be justified in inflicting [great suffering] on randomly selected [members of their group]" (Kupperman, 1991a, 313). Alternatively, these individuals could maintain that there are special reasons not to torment them—reasons that do not obtain with respect to the members of socially excluded groups—and one cannot rule out a priori that such special reasons exist (Kupperman, 1991a, 314).

In view of this impasse, Kupperman follows Barbara Herman and concludes that universalizability arguments depend on judgments of moral salience, that is, judgments about which differences are morally significant (Herman, 1985, 418–420; Kupperman, 1991a, 314). But, again, if these judgments are to make sense to the members of a dominant social group, they cannot be derived from needs that they do not share or from contracts into which they have not entered. Impartial reason cannot ground them.

According to Herman, the rules of moral salience "make up the substantive core of the agent's conception of himself as a moral agent" (Herman, 1985, 428–429; also see Herman, 1990, 318–319). Since these rules are culturally transmitted, they are not universal (Herman, 1985, 425). Yet, they are not arbitrary, for they provide interpretations of the Kantian commitment to respect for persons, and they are susceptible to criticism on the grounds that they are inconsistent or that they presuppose errors of fact (Herman, 1985, 428–430). But, as we have seen in Okin's impartialist negation of the traditional woman, projecting one's conception of agency may violate the agency of others who are different from oneself and who cherish their difference.

Here, Kupperman parts company with Herman and denies that judgments of moral salience are confined to articulating a core conception of agency. Expanding the purview of judgments of moral salience, Kupperman claims that these judgments are judgments about what is valuable (Kupperman, 1991a, 314). Furthermore, since Kupperman takes on the vexing problem of intercultural relations and therefore cannot invoke the heritage of a moral community to ground judgments of moral salience, he seeks to furnish a method for arriving at judgments of value and disvalue.

Kupperman locates the source of these judgments in empathy, and he proposes a novel view of the powers of empathy. He rejects Hare's understanding of empathy as imaginatively paralleling an individual's motivations and/or preferences. As Kupperman rightly maintains, one can assimilate others' preferences and motivations and yet be persuaded that they are misguided—empathizing with the lotus eaters' motivations and preferences is compatible with questioning the value of a life devoted to hallucinatory dalliance (Kupperman, 1991a, 316). Thus, the members of a dominant social group who are indifferent to others' suffering or who relish the spectacle of such suffering might be fully cognizant of the pain their victims endure and also of their victims' aversion to this torment. Yet, they might judge that such pain is sometimes a good thing and that this is a case in point (Kupperman, 1991a, 316–317). To outflank this rejoinder, Kupperman contends that empathizing with an individual entails grasping the value or disvalue inherent in that individual's experience (Kupperman, 1991a, 319; also see Blum, 1991, 704–705). Knowledge of value and disvalue in turn constrains impartial reason.

This line of thought is certainly appealing; however, it is not altogether clear how empathy discloses value or how empathy is to address the dilemma of difference. Plainly, empathy is not an infallible guide to value, and the potential for misguided empathically based judgments swells exponentially when incommensurable values and rival ways of life are at stake, as they are where the dilemma of difference arises. Thus, it is necessary to ask when one can trust one's empathically based judgments of value. How are the members of a dominant social group to assure themselves that their conduct toward the members of socially excluded groups creates disvalue? How is Okin to realize that some traditional women's lives embody value?

Posing this kind of question raises suspicions about giving too much credence to unmediated empathic apprehensions of value and disvalue.

Here I propose that we take up another case of gender difference—a case that pinpoints a deficiency of impartial reason with respect to the dilemma of difference. Confusion and anger about gender harassment have become commonplace on United States college campuses. Consider a typical case. A white male professor of engineering who is from a middle-class United States background peppers his lectures with jocular wisecracks about the high frequency with which women fail his course. Some of the women in his classes are mortified by his remarks. Upon realizing that their feelings of humiliation are undermining their academic performance, they ask him to stop joking at their expense.

No argument from impartial reason could by itself persuade the professor that his conduct is morally objectionable. He may honestly affirm that it does not bother him when people who have power over him crack jokes about the frailties of bourgeois white men. Indeed, as a concession to even-handed classroom humor, he might decide to mix in a few barbed remarks putting down his own social group. Moreover, it will not help to tell him that some of the women in his classes are crushed by his remarks and that refraining from such humor follows from the higher order principle forbidding us to harm others—a principle that he presumably does accept. He may reasonably question whether these insecurities are the sort of vulnerabilities that a conscientious moral agent ought to be shielding.[5] Thus, he may dismiss norms of sensitivity and supportiveness as reinforcing needless and undesirable weaknesses.

People cannot act morally without understanding the impact of their conduct on others. One may believe that others should not feel as they do. Nevertheless, one cannot make recognizably moral choices unless one takes people's actual feelings into account. It is one thing to seek by morally acceptable means to change people's feelings; it is another to trample on them with abandon. Furthermore, without empathic familiarity with a wide range of human experience, one is hardly in a position to determine how people ought or ought not to feel. Indeed, without empathic understanding of others, one would be left in the dark as to whether one's actions have proven effective as measured by one's own values and goals. Thus, the engineering professor might choose to empathize with the women students who have protested his conduct and, seeing how miserable and discouraged they have become, decide that he ought to relent. How might he reach this conclusion?

One possibility would be to take Barbara Herman's advice and use impartial reason to filter the information he has obtained empathically. He might, for example, say to himself: "Their position and their psychic make-up makes them vulnerable in ways that our traditional students haven't been. So, I'd be betraying my belief in equal opportunity if I didn't go easy on them." This line of thought involves according moral significance to gender—that is, recognizing a second model of the recipient of justice to explain why identical treatment violates equal opportunity. Unfortunately, recognizing difference in this way leads almost inexorably to further musings: "Isn't it curious that these women mind being treated in a way that I don't mind at all? In effect, they're making demands on me that I don't make on them—seems they need *extra* consideration. Sure starts to look like they're not simply different—looks like maybe they're, well, just a tad inferior." Here, impartial reason provides the professor with grounds for changing his behavior, but it does not change his mind about his students' feelings. As far as he is concerned, these feelings are signs of deficiency. Thus, impartial reason stigmatizes, at the same time as it accommodates, gender difference.

Still, impartial reason might take the professor in another direction. He might argue: "Look, these women are falling apart over nothing, but keeping up the pressure isn't going to toughen them up. So, I'll cut the jokes from my lectures on the condition that they undergo desensitization training and learn to cope with the rough and tumble of everyday masculine humor." This thinking does not require that the professor recognize a second gendered model of the person. Instead, it analogizes the women students to children—people who are immature, but who can be brought up to par. This variant of impartial reason does not stigmatize the students as different, but it does require them to conform to the white male professional model of the person. Difference is condemned and ultimately denied.

In confronting the dilemma of difference, impartial reason allows the deliberator's needs, capacities, and interests to serve as the moral baseline.[6] Supplemental empathy may demonstrate to impartial reasoners that special consideration ought to be granted to people with different needs, capacities, and interests. But since the baseline is set by the deliberator, difference is construed as inferior or temporary—something to pity or change, not something to appreciate. Is there any way to escape the condescension and stigmatization that seem endemic to approaching difference through impartial reason? I shall urge that an impoverished form of empathy exacerbates such purblind moral judgment.

3. The Case for Relying on Empathy in Moral Reflection

Neither shrewdly sizing people up nor sympathetically fusing with people is well adapted to the purposes of moral reflection, and contrasting empathy with these orientations highlights empathy's virtues as a basis for moral reflection. One may size someone up out of idle curiosity or perhaps preliminary to selfishly or cruelly manipulating that person. The detachment from others that enables one to size them up can interfere with the apprehension of moral concerns. Masterful torturers who inflict suffering tailored to each prisoner's distinctive vulnerabilities must be astute observers of human nature. But their insight into their victims does not stem from empathy, for empathizing with another presupposes some degree of concern for that person—a degree of concern that rules out the malign instrumentalism of the torturer. Though it is axiomatic that acrimonious lovers often use knowledge that was originally gained through empathy to torment one another as their relationship falls apart, one cannot empathize with such aims in view.

The presumption of concern for the individual one empathizes with underwrites one usage of the term "empathy" that equates it with sympathy. To sympathize with another is to share that person's feelings. In the words of Milan Kundera, sympathy is "emotional telepathy" (Kundera, 1984, 20).

Paradigmatically, bereavement elicits sympathy—friends and acquaintances share the immediate family's sorrow and join in mourning the death. Yet, some forms of sympathy do not involve empathy. The term "sympathy" is sometimes used to denote feeling sorry for the other. One may not oneself share the mourners' grief, but one may respond compassionately to those who have lost someone they loved. One need not empathize with the deceased's partner to send a sympathy card. Furthermore, sympathy can be incidental to or it can be caused by another's state of mind. One might feel saddened by the death of a great artist or a respected political leader independently of anyone else's feelings. In that case, it is coincidental that one's feelings match those of the deceased's close friends and relatives. One may be in sympathetic accord with others without attending to them and hence without empathizing with them. Alternatively, one may feel saddened by a death because someone else is saddened by it. One is concerned about the bereaved individual, and one is affected by that person's feelings. In that case, one's sympathy is empathetic. Of course, one can mistakenly believe that one's feelings match those of another, and therefore believe that one is sympathizing when one is not. But successful empathetic sympathy presupposes that one is so attuned to another that synchronizing one's feelings with the other's is not problematic.

Outside of occult literature, however, individuals are not fated to feel along with one another, and the willingness to join in another's feelings implies accepting them as appropriate. Thus, empathetic sympathy is often morally significant, and it is not always morally desirable. Misplaced sympathy gives rise to sentimentality and worse. Sympathizing with a bad person aids and abets that person's aims, for sharing another's feelings leads one to act in concert with that person.

Nevertheless, the link between sympathy and self-knowledge suggests a role for empathetic sympathy in moral life. Sympathizing with another person may disclose dimensions of oneself that one had never noticed before—that one is capable of feeling the way such-and-such a person feels or that one is capable of desiring what this person desires (Bartky, n.d.). Of course, the potentialities that one discovers may be potentialities for good or ill. Thus, if sympathy is to contribute to moral reflection, it is crucial that sympathizers judge the value or disvalue of the potentialities that sympathy reveals and decide whether to act on these potentialities. Unfortunately, when one's sharing of another's subjective state is occasioned, as it often is, by intense emotional involvement with that person, one is likely to be carried along by one's sympathy and drawn into the other's projects regardless of the wisdom of doing so. Empathetic sympathy often preempts moral reflection.

A second form of empathy places a little more distance between people than empathetic sympathy, but not as much distance as sizing people up. To empathize with another in this sense is to construct in imagination an experience resembling that of the other person. As Adrian Piper puts it, empathy enables one to "comprehend viscerally the [other's] inner state" without being "vicariously possessed" by it (Piper, 1991, 735–737; for another imagination-based account of empathy, see Wiseman, 1978). Though the vividness of empathic imaginings is often moving, empathizers do not share the subjective states of those with whom they empathize (Goldman, 1992, 29). One can imagine another's grief without grieving oneself.[7] To mark the distinction between sharing another person's feelings and imaginatively reconstructing another person's feelings, and to avoid introducing cumbersome neologisms, I shall use the term "sympathy" for the former and reserve the term "empathy" for the latter.

It is important to recognize that, although one draws on one's stock of emotional experience and one's present emotional responses to empathize with another, empathy is defeated if one simply projects one's own characteristic emotional responses onto the other. Undeniably, one cannot empathize with someone if one has nothing in common with that individual, for otherwise the other's experience would be so alien that one could not get a purchase on imagining it. One needs to know, for example, that the other's subjective experience of humiliation is in some ways like one's own. But one must be prepared to discover that what occasions the other's humiliation is different or that the other experiences humiliation more abjectly since she has greater difficulty putting it behind her. Likewise, one's immediate emotional reactions to another's behavior or reports can provide clues to what the other is going through. Here, the point is not that one's own state of mind duplicates that of the other, but rather that one's typical response patterns may be good indicators of what the other is experiencing. If, for example, one knows that one often experiences a peculiarly disgusted dismay in response to another's humiliation, one may be able to use one's reading of one's own feelings to discern another's unspoken, but incompletely suppressed humiliation. One's emotional life is an important resource in imaginatively reconstructing another's subjective state.

Still, to empathize well, it is in certain respects necessary to hold one's bounteous emotions in check and to mobilize one's powers of attentive receptivity and analytic discernment. Particularly when the other's background or circumstances are very different from one's own, empathy may require protracted observation and painstaking imaginative reconstruction of the minutiae of the other's viewpoint. The metaphor of putting oneself in the other's shoes is misleading, for it is a mistake to assume that the other feels the same way as one would oneself feel in the same circumstances (for related discussion of "boomerang perception," see Spelman, 1988, 12). Indeed, prematurely claiming to empathize with someone can seem infuriatingly presumptuous to the misunderstood, and perhaps silenced, recipient of one's "empathy."

In imaginatively experiencing another's state of mind, one incurs a risk that one will succumb to the other's influence and come to identify with that point of view. Nevertheless, empathy by no means entails sharing the other's point of view or endorsing the other's state of mind. Although we usually reserve our empathic exertions for people whom we like and with whom we hope to maintain relationships, nothing in principle bars one from empathizing with someone for whom one feels no affection. Psychotherapists and social workers do not always like their clients. Indeed, they may find a client's values or conduct repugnant. Presumably, social workers who counsel convicted woman-batterers are repelled by their clients' mentality, yet to do their work well they need to empathize with these men. Plainly, their empathy does not condone woman battery or whatever state of mind gives rise to it. Still, such empathy would not be possible unless these professionals were capable of feeling concern for their clients. Of course, empathic experience of another could subsequently lead one to distance oneself decisively from the other or to seek communion with the other. But neither disinterested curiosity about nor ready immersion in another's subjective life supports empathy.

Unlike shrewdly sizing people up, empathy is grounded in a protomoral fellow feeling for other persons. Yet, unlike sympathy, empathy seeks understanding of others and preserves independent judgment and agency. Nevertheless, I believe that the concern that animates empathy, on the one hand, and the vividness of imaginative reconstructions of other people's viewpoints, on the other, often interact synergistically to offset harmful moral tropisms. If I am not mistaken, empathy with members of socially excluded groups would help to resolve the dilemma of difference by dislodging egocentric categories that either eclipse difference or revile it.

4. Incident-Specific Empathy and Broad Empathy

It is important to recognize that the scope of empathy varies. The most common form of empathy is incident specific—that is, imaginatively experiencing another person's state of mind within a fairly well demarcated time frame and in relative isolation from other aspects of the individual's psychology. Focused in this way, empathy seeks to answer the question, "What are you going through now?" Incident-specific empathy may occur within a context of personal acquaintance, but it need not. Knowing nothing about the lives of any individual Bosnians, one might empathize with the privation and brutality to which they are being subjected. Or one might empathize with a nodding acquaintance on being told that she has recently been diagnosed with breast cancer. Incident-specific empathy with strangers is accomplished by learning as much as one can about them and the situation they face, and then projecting as best one can one's own profile of interests, needs, and the like into that constellation of circumstances.

Since incident-specific empathy with strangers affords little opportunity to exchange information or to verify the understanding one reaches, it is relatively crude and conjectural, and, consequently, it is not likely to greatly enrich one's moral view. It may help one to see that one's principles apply more widely than one had realized—for example, Colin Powell might discover that gay and lesbian soldiers who are discriminated against suffer no less than African-Americans who are discriminated against. Also, incident-specific empathy helps people to recognize occasions for acting on their principles—the engineering professor might see that his jokes are differentially impeding his students' academic progress and denying them equality of opportunity. But incident-specific empathy seldom provides grounds for overhauling one's moral outlook.

Still, empathy can range more widely—that is, one can ask "What is it like to be you?" and one can undertake to empathize with another person's subjectivity as a whole.[8] Broad empathy, as I shall call this second form, has greater potential as an aid to moral reflection, for it involves one in a more extensive and more complex relationship than incident-specific empathy.

First, since the aim of broad empathy is to achieve an understanding of another's psychic constitution and the ways in which the various components of that constitution interrelate, it presupposes intimacy. Since conversation with the other coupled with observing the other's conduct in a variety of situations is ideal, friendship provides a hospitable context for broad empathy. But reading detailed and candid autobiographical materials penned by a stranger (or biographical materials describing a stranger) can substitute for personal contact.

Second, broad empathy engages complex intellectual capacities along with affective ones. To empathize with another's subjectivity is not only to draw on one's past emotional life to conjure up that person's experiences in one's own mind, but it is also to grasp the circumstances of that person's life along with the beliefs, desires, abilities, vulnerabilities, limitations, and traits of character that give rise to these experiences. Broad empathy yields an interpretation of the sources—both the sources in the person's social context and the unique individual sources—of the other's experiences. Since one's empathic familiarity with these sources can be more or less extensive, it is clear that there is a spectrum of degrees of empathy ranging from the most minimal incident-specific empathy with a stranger to the broadest empathy with an intimate. Likewise, it is clear that previously established broad empathic understanding can be called on to empathize more perspicaciously with an individual on particular occasions.

Third, broad empathy is inescapably evaluative. While one can remain neutral about many beliefs and desires, it is clear that abilities are generally desirable, whereas limitations are generally undesirable and that some traits of character are generally desirable, whereas others are generally undesirable. These valuations are encoded in our language. "Intelligence" and "vigor" carry positive connotations; "ignorance" and "clumsiness" carry negative ones. "Cheerful," "openminded," "trusting," "prudent," and "self-respecting" carry positive connotations; "gullible," "bitter," "cynical," "stubborn," and "wary" carry negative ones.[9] Undeniably, states of mind that are generally regarded as positive can be inappropriate, for example, misplaced trust, and states of mind that are generally regarded as negative can be appropriate, for example, warranted anger. But these complications are linguistically marked by qualifiers. Likewise, it is clear that true beliefs and compatible desires are generally desirable and that false beliefs and incompatible desires are generally undesirable. Here, too, there are exceptions. False beliefs sometimes help people survive misfortunes that would otherwise destroy them. Conflicting desires sometimes spark social critique and political activism. Still, affirming that error, illusion, frustration, or ambivalence are on balance good calls for an explanation.

Here, someone might object that formulating empathic interpretations in value-laden terminology allows empathizers to insinuate their own values into their understanding of others. For example, a person whom a trusting empathizer might describe as tolerant might be described as naive by an empathizer who tends to be suspicious of others. In this regard, I would urge that several features of broad empathy provide a corrective to the tendency to project one's own values onto others, a corrective that is not available to incident–specific empathy (but for discussion of how prejudice taints empathy, see Chapter 4). Not only does broad empathy require extensive communication with the other, but also it requires attention to that individual's life as a whole, or at least a good-sized stretch of it taking various aspects of it into account. In addition, broad empathy sets up an interplay between imaginative replication of the other's circumstances and subjective states and analysis of these circumstances and states. Since one cannot imaginatively reconstruct another's life in real time, broad empathy must rely to some extent on the economies of conceptualization and selectively imagine salient dimensions of the other's life. The resulting interplay enables intellection to check flights of fancy while imagination presses intellection to break out of habitual analytical categories. Though these constraints are by no means foolproof, they do guard against crass "empathic" self-cloning.

Through broad empathy with various individuals, then, one grasps the values and disvalues that are *realized* through different collocations of abilities, limitations, traits of character, beliefs, and desires in diverse circumstances. A modest additional imaginative and analytical investment enables one to anticipate many of the values and disvalues that are *realizable* for a particular individual (for a related view, see Stein, 1989, 109). Thus, empathizing broadly with another may raise suspicions about the other's basic decency or worries about the other's future welfare, or, contrariwise, it may enhance one's appreciation of the other and disclose values that are worthy of respect, if not emulation. Grounded in protomoral concern for the other, broad empathy yields protomoral knowledge of the other. Moreover, broad empathy is especially suited to mediate relations between so-called different individuals and members of dominant social groups. Indeed, if I understand them correctly, Maria C. Lugones and Elizabeth V. Spelman call on feminists to engage in this wide-ranging form of empathy as a basis for doing feminist theory that is not culturally imperialistic (Lugones and Spelman, 1986).

Let us now return to the beleaguered women engineering students and their unreconstructed professor, and consider how broad empathy could alleviate their problem. The interaction that grounds broad empathy affords the professor the opportunity to discover that the students are not just pathetic victims and the students the opportunity to discover that the professor is not just a sadistic autocrat. Empathizing with the students might lead the professor to discern capacities worth cultivating. He might find in these women an admirable subtlety and delicacy of sensibility. Indeed, he might compare his own bluff imperturbability unfavorably with their attunement to their surroundings, and he might see how to integrate some of their virtues with his own. Likewise, empathic dialogue would give his students a chance to learn from him. These women might discover that their professor enjoys reserves of strength and resilience that are not reducible to the sort of callousness that they deplore. Perhaps, they would realize that they are clinging to exaggerated norms of feminine fragility that could be abandoned without compromising their compassion. Still, it might not be psychologically possible to combine the students' virtues with those of the professor. Perhaps, the students could not gain the professor's insouciance about being razzed without becoming less responsive to others than they would care to be. Perhaps, the professor could not gain the students' compassion without sacrificing his self-possession in the face of adversity. Whether or not broad empathy spurs change in the parties, it enables people to recognize different, yet desirable collocations of traits, values, goals, and the like.[10]

Now, I want to make it clear that I am not claiming that broad empathy inevitably leads to life-enhancing discoveries of the sort I have envisaged—the students could find out that their professor is tormenting them for the fun of it or because he hates women. Nor, I should add, would the students' discerning some estimable quality in their professor oblige them to withdraw their objections to his behavior. Nevertheless, I want to emphasize that, as a result of broad empathy, people who are institutionally positioned as antagonists may come to respect one another and even to regard one another as exemplars, for through empathy new constellations of needs, desires, beliefs, and values can be forged.

5. Empathy: Handmaiden to Impartial Reason?

If morality is not reducible to consistently imposing one's personality, its insularity or disorders notwithstanding, on others, empathy is indispensable to moral reflection. Yet, the superficiality of incident-specific empathy can lead one to overlook the virtues of people different from oneself and to regard them as deficient when they are not. Broad empathy, by contrast, neither ignores nor abhors difference. Recognizing difference without imperiling the equal moral status of those who are classed as different and without undermining respect for these individuals, broad empathy provides an antidote to the condescension to and stigmatization of difference that is too often associated with impartial reason. Still, it is not clear how the understanding of others obtained through broad empathy fits into impartial reason. Respecting and morally responding to difference entails neither accepting others' wishes uncritically nor granting others whatever they demand. The understanding of the other's perspective that empathy affords gives one insight into the values and disvalues at stake in a given situation, but it does not settle the question of what one ought to do.

To decide whether to undertake a proposed course of action, impartial reason asks "Would I want to be treated like that?"[11] I think it is clear that raising this question and abiding by one's answer to it can curb many despicable impulses and can prompt admirable behavior. But, as we have seen, since people are not all like oneself, posing this question is not a sufficient basis for moral reflection. One must also ask "What is it like to be you?"—a question that is best answered through empathy.

Now, empathizing with others can be construed as a preliminary data-collecting task subsidiary to impartial reason. That is, one might qualify the prime query of impartial reason to read as follows: "Would I want to be treated like that if I were like you?" This formulation captures the dictum that different cases should be treated differently, and it casts empathy in the role of furnishing the information needed to meet the additional knowledge condition. But how is a moral deliberator to interpret this question? What is being asked? Plainly, impartial reason cannot ask merely "How do you want me to treat you?" For "Tell me what you want me to do, and I'll do it" is a recipe for mindless servility, not for moral judgment. Notice, moreover, that this problem cannot be corrected by amending the question to read "Would I want to be treated the way you want me to treat you if I were you?" By hypothesis, what occasions moral reflection is the fact that the way the deliberator would want to be treated conflicts with the way the moral patient wants to be treated. In the case of gender harassment we have been considering, the professor would not want to have his weaknesses "coddled" and thereby reinforced. Also, I take it to be uncontroversial that resolving such conflicts by declaring that everyone wants to be treated nicely or respectfully is an unacceptable evasion since this move would amount to a concession that impartial reason has no systematic way of assessing the morality of responses to difference.[12]

If impartial reason is to morally justify conduct, it must somehow constrain moral judgment. When the moral agent's desires coincide with those of the moral patient, consistency is the constraint to which impartial reason holds moral judgment. Follow principles that you are willing to have others follow in their interaction with you. But consistency cannot get a foothold when the moral patient's needs and desires differ from the moral agent's. Following principles that you are willing to have others follow in their interaction with you will deny and penalize difference. But the principles that individuals who are different from you would want others to follow in interacting with them are inconsistent with the principles that you would want others to follow in their relations with you. Consistency makes sense as a moral constraint only if no nonuniversal categories are deemed morally significant—that is, if for purposes of morality human nature is homogeneous.[13]

It seems to me, then, that impartial reason must ask, "How do my principles apply to you, given your circumstances and subjectivity?" But notice that, on this interpretation, the object of posing the question has shifted. Instead of asking whether one should admit a certain action-guiding principle into the moral pantheon, one is now asking what action an established set of rationally certified principles prescribes in a particular situation.[14] Moreover, this interpretation is not especially attractive since it is rarely obvious what action one's principles commend when difference is at issue. For example, if the professor is committed to defending academic freedom and also to minimizing gratuitous suffering, he may be torn between self-censorship and standing on his free speech rights. Unless impartial reason can demonstrate that defending academic freedom takes precedence over minimizing gratuitous suffering or vice versa, and I doubt that it can, impartial reason will not be of much help to the professor.

At this point, it might be suggested that it is misguided to seek general solutions to problems such as these. The way to circumvent this difficulty is to generate a highly detailed maxim characterizing one's action and to check to see if this maxim can be universalized. In other words, could the professor agree that, in all cases in which students are exceptionally vulnerable as a result of historical oppression of their social group and in which the students request classroom practices designed to minimize the adverse impact of these vulnerabilities, their requests should be honored? Since the professor does not belong to a marginalized social group, this maxim would have no practical application to him, and, since the professor would shun special treatment if he were a member of a marginalized social group, he would not want this maxim applied to him. Nevertheless, he could accept it as a policy to be implemented whenever students do not share his bravado.

At first, particularized universalizability looks like a workable solution for impartial reason, but I think it is much too liable to abuse. Particularized universalizability could fail to weed out some unreasonable demands on the part of members of excluded groups. There are many ideas that are disturbing for some of the members of socially excluded groups to hear but that should not be suppressed. Likewise, particularized universalizability could authorize people in positions of power to engage in harmful forms of paternalism. If deliberators are permitted to specify the class of moral patients so as to exclude themselves and ensure that they will not be subject to the treatment they propose to mete out, they may use this license to justify ostensibly benevolent, yet morally objectionable intrusions in others' lives. The scheme I mentioned earlier (Section 3) to enroll the protesting women engineering students in a desensitization program designed to make them more tolerant of sexist humor would be a case in point. Once impartial reason is severed from the requirement that moral deliberators accept being treated as they propose to treat others, universalizability is at most a necessary condition for the moral justifiability of proposed conduct.

When difference cannot be assimilated to universal categories, the dilemma of difference explodes the logic of impartial reason. Either one reflects without the benefit of empathy, and impartial reason ratifies principles that are oblivious to the reality of individual and social difference, or one incorporates empathically reached understanding of difference into one's thinking, and impartial reason is deposed as an arbiter of the morality of candidate principles. Now, it might seem that this conclusion drives us into the arms of intuitionism or utilitarianism. In Chapters 6 and 7, however, I shall argue that there is another approach to moral reflection—one that does not violate the empathic framework. But before this alternative can be cogently presented, it is necessary to consider an additional obstacle to moral reflection regarding group-based social exclusion—namely, prejudice and its distortion of moral perception and moral judgment.

3

Prejudice and Cultural Imagery

That empathy is necessary to insightful moral reflection and sound moral judgment strikes many people as intuitively obvious. Concurring with this view, some exponents of the major traditions in moral philosophy have sought to insert empathy into their theories (e.g., Hare, 1981; Hill, 1987; Okin, 1989b). It seems to me, however, that these theorists invoke empathy without considering the psychosocial obstacles to empathic understanding and thus without appreciating the complexity of moral reflection.

There is evidence that the world is divided into empathetic islands, for people empathize more readily with people who are like them (Goldman, 1992, 35). Within social groups, empathy is easily aroused and generally provides reliable information about others' subjective states; however, when individuals attempt to reach beyond the boundaries of their social group, empathy often succumbs to parochialism and misrepresents others' subjectivity. Simple ignorance of people different from oneself is seldom the only force powering unjust social exclusion. Typically, ignorance is compounded and misinformation is shielded from correction by a second moral pathology, namely, prejudice. Alarmingly pervasive, prejudice rests in part on unconscious, emotionally entrenched bias that is "innocently" broadcast as common knowledge and enacted in everyday behavior.[1]

I have argued that empathy with the members of socially excluded groups is necessary to resolve the dilemma of difference (for an account of the dilemma of difference, see Chapter 1, Section 1; for the role of empathy with respect to this dilemma, see Chapter 2, Sections 2–4). But when prejudice taints empathy, claiming to empathically understand others perpetuates crude, demeaning, stereotypical thinking about members of target groups. Thus, the deliverances of bigotry are equated with documented fact, and discrimination continues unchecked.

There are two forms that prejudice takes. In the first, prejudice is forthright. Groups of people are singled out as inferior, undesirable, or threatening, and social exclusion is defended on these grounds. In the second, prejudice goes underground. People who profess egalitarian moral and political principles are unconsciously in the grip of prejudices that are expressed in less blatant, yet seriously harmful discriminatory behavior. In either form, prejudice is highly resistant to change. When the "wisdom" of prejudice is taken for truth, people's suspect emotional investment in these attitudes is disguised as a passion for realism and candor. Opponents of prejudice are dismissed as naive, if not traitorous. When the existence of prejudice is denied, those who point to its manifestations are accused of hypersensitivity, if not paranoia. Moreover, these critics may be castigated for insulting honorable people who take refuge in indignation instead of examining their underlying attitudes. The dilemma of difference becomes a fixture on the moral and political landscape.

It seems, then, that empathy's liability to be distorted by prejudice must be counteracted and that confronting and dislodging prejudice should be regarded as one of the principal tasks of moral reflection and argument. Yet, beyond noting that moral deliberators must be sincere and conscientious, classical and contemporary ethical theory has surprisingly little to say about this topic. Indeed, to judge by the articles in ethics journals, many philosophers are so preoccupied with observing canons of clarity and consistency that they overlook two of the central missions of practical argument: (1) critique—demonstrating that moral controversy exists where few had noticed it; and (2) reform—especially, eradicating arbitrary prejudice. If one starts from the dilemma of difference, however, these projects are salient.

Still, it is understandable that philosophers have had little to say about prejudice, for impartial reason and conventional methods of philosophical argument are inadequate to address it. In this chapter, I shall begin by reviewing John Rawls's efforts to contend with prejudice in *A Theory of Justice,* and I shall argue that one can achieve reflective equilibrium without overcoming one's prejudices. Taking a cue from Julia Kristeva, I shall then offer an account of the immunity of prejudice to impartial reason as well as the pervasiveness of prejudice. Prejudice is encoded in culturally entrenched figurations of "different" social groups, and through this device prejudice is easily transmitted and perpetuated. Indeed, such figurations remove prejudice from the domain of simple individual vice and transform it into the menace that I call "culturally normative prejudice." Since these figurations cannot be debunked by pointing out their contradictory nature or by presenting disconfirming data about the actual lives of socially excluded groups, culturally normative prejudice is not accessible to standard philosophical tactics. In sum, the problem of group-based social exclusion exhibits the centrality of figurative discourse to moral perception and moral reflection, while also demonstrating the need for emancipatory counterfiguration of socially excluded groups.

1. Impartial Reason and Prejudice

Proponents of impartial reason acknowledge that prejudice can cloud moral judgment, and they hold that we must counteract these pernicious influences by subjecting them to the scrutiny of impartial reason. Some seem to regard universalizability as a powerful antidote to prejudice (Herman, 1983, 247). However, John Rawls's account of reflective equilibrium supplies a more complex and sophisticated treatment of the role of impartial reason in counteracting prejudice.

One achieves reflective equilibrium by deriving a set of principles from a conception of the original position and then by bringing one's principles into conformity with one's considered convictions. Impartial reason is implicated in Rawls's account of moral reflection at three points. First, the veil of ignorance in the original position, which denies deliberators knowledge of their social and economic status, their talents, and their conceptions of the good, enforces impartiality (Rawls, 1971, 137). The parties to the original position must deduce principles of justice without knowledge that would enable them to skew the principles in favor of themselves. Second, considered convictions are those judgments that most reliably reveal a person's sense of justice; they are judgments that are not affected by distorting conditions, such as haste, fear, or conflict of interest (Rawls, 1971, 47). In other words, they are moral judgments that meet traditional standards of impartiality and rationality. Yet, Rawls acknowledges that intuitions that are confidently affirmed after calm and careful reflection can nevertheless prove to be misguided. Thus, third, Rawls thinks that people may be moved to modify their considered convictions to coincide with the principles they obtain in the original position (Rawls, 1971, 48). Again, impartial reason constrains untutored moral judgment.

Still, since Rawls also recognizes that people can err in deducing principles from the original position, he does not maintain that considered convictions that conflict with those principles should always yield. One must decide whether to modify one's principles or adjust one's considered convictions in order to bring them into alignment. Unfortunately, Rawls gives no criteria or procedure for deciding between these options. He appears to think that once we have derived a set of principles from the original position and checked our intuitions for disqualifying factors, we have no further moral recourse (Rawls, 1971, 51). Thus, when principles fail to mesh with considered convictions, it is often arbitrary whether one alters one's principles to suit one's considered convictions or transforms one's considered convictions to fit one's principles (Rawls, 1971, 20).

This view has led to the charge that reflective equilibrium allows us to doctor our principles to suit our prejudices. If we are allowed to resurrect unconscious prejudices under the guise of considered convictions, it is plain that impartial reason cannot extirpate them. It seems, then, that the exercise of reflective equilibrium may serve merely to rationalize and reinforce people's preconceptions, odious though they may be.

Rawls's repertory of moral concepts and reasoning skills allows people to enlarge the purview of their principles, to qualify their principles with exceptions, or to arrange their values hierarchically. But it is sometimes baffling whether an adjustment in moral conceptualization is called for or which sort of adjustment is in order. Consider the problem of gender and the resources that impartial reason brings to bear on it. With the benefit of hindsight, the contradiction between universal human rights and the disenfranchisement of women seems indisputable. Yet, I imagine that, in the nineteenth century, many people found the thought of women voters as preposterous as many people now find the thought of men caring for children. (The inherent hilarity of men's supposed bemusement and clumsiness around young children provides the comic premise for two recent, box-office hits, *Three Men and a Baby* and *Kindergarten Cop*.) What might rattle a person's considered conviction that women do not belong in politics and enable a person to judge that the principle of universal suffrage should be extended to women?

It goes without saying that the publicity surrounding the suffrage movement helped to disengage people from their ingrained habits of thought regarding gender. Moreover, once the Nineteenth Amendment to the United States Constitution was ratified, most people gradually became inured to the practices it authorized. But, while it is undeniable that social and political developments influence people's moral beliefs, what is at issue is moral reflection and justification. Thus, the question is how we are to test the considered convictions we bring to bear on issues concerning gender. Rawls's theory offers three possible approaches—an argument from the formal constraint of universality, an argument from maximin, and an argument from the difference principle.

Since Rawls maintains that the formal constraint of universality rules out classification according to special biological characteristics (Rawls, 1971, 132), the considered conviction that voting is unseemly for women might be rejected on the grounds that it violates universality. But it seems improbable that people who sincerely believed in the propriety of women's confinement to the domestic sphere would have been dissuaded from opposing women's suffrage on purely formal grounds; it seems more likely that they would have questioned this application of the requirement of universality. On an issue of this moment, a substantive argument is surely needed. Thus, one might expect Rawls to dispose of classification by sex by invoking maximin. Not knowing whether they will turn out to be female or male, the argument would go, the parties to the original position would protect their interests by rejecting discriminatory classification by sex and endorsing equal rights for women and men.[2] The weakness of this argument is that it, too, fails to address the antisuffragist's conviction that women and men are different and will not find satisfaction in identical roles.

Apparently, Rawls finds these lines of argument no more persuasive than I have claimed the opponent of women's suffrage would, for he does not unequivocally reject sex-based inequalities.[3] Discussing the problem of identifying relevant social positions for purposes of implementing the difference principle, he suggests that fixed, nonvoluntary characteristics, such as sex, race, and culture, might demarcate social positions that this principle should take into account. Though he contends that multiplying relevant social positions in this way is ill-advised, he allows that there may be institutionalized sex inequalities provided that the difference principle certifies them—that is, they must redound to the benefit of the disadvantaged, namely, women (Rawls, 1971, 99). Unfortunately, where controversy is alive, but tradition is strong, this criterion is not sufficient to pick out reliable considered convictions.

During the suffrage debate, both sides fielded arguments conforming to the approach Rawls recommends (Kraditor, 1965). Proponents of women's suffrage urged that women needed a voice in government for the same reasons as men—so that their status as rational subjects would be respected and so that their wisdom would infuse public policy. Opponents of the suffrage initiative argued that the fair sex with its precious and distinctive virtues was best served by being sheltered from the vulgarity and hurly-burly of politics. Women remain divided on the issue of protectionism to this day. While some welcome the opportunity to join the fray of public life, others relish the cosseting of the traditional feminine role.[4] Similarly, before gaining the vote, some women regarded their disenfranchisement as a crippling limitation, but many others, along with the legions of men who scorned women's suffrage, regarded equal rights as a calamity from which women would never recover. It seems, then, that deliberations about how to apply the difference principle to women's voting rights would have proved inconclusive.

Moreover, it is doubtful that people's considered convictions would have settled the matter in favor of equal rights. Many of those inclined to see benefits for women in unequal rights believed, and believed adamantly, that politicking and voting were irredeemably unbecoming to women. Likewise, I suspect that many of the early proponents of women's full political participation initially shared this considered conviction and had to struggle with themselves to overcome it. As Rawls would put it, they faced an inconsistency between their principles and their considered convictions. Why should they resolve the inconsistency by eschewing their considered convictions about femininity? Those suffragists whose considered convictions did not clash with their principles had aberrant considered convictions. Why not cede these new-fangled ideas about women's rights and acquiesce in the tried and true status quo?

Considered convictions could not be the final check on principles, for some considered convictions are nothing more than unconsciously entrenched prejudices. Accepted principles could not be adduced to decide which route to take, for the scope of these very precepts was at issue.[5] Reflective equilibrium may leave prejudice untouched.

2. A Kantian Account of Prejudice

One reason for Rawls's failure to come to grips with prejudice is that he never develops a systematic account of it. Lacking any clear idea of the problem prejudice poses, he neglects it. In contrast, Adrian M. S. Piper furnishes a Kantian theory of prejudice. In her rationistic view, xenophobia is "a moral vice of a purely intellectual kind" (Piper, 1990, 304).

Piper treats discrimination as a species of xenophobia, and she distinguishes first-order discrimination from higher-order discrimination. Xenophobia is fear of strangers "who do not conform to one's preconceptions about how persons ought to look or behave" (Piper, 1992–93, 189). First-order discrimination is conscious bigotry—contempt for and dismissal of persons simply because they bear a "primary disvalued attribute," such as membership in a socially excluded group (Piper, 1990, 286–287, 289). In contrast, higher-order discrimination is nonconscious prejudice. For the higher-order discriminator, "a primary disvalued attribute in turn confers disvalue respectively on further [seemingly unrelated] attributes" of an individual (Piper, 1990, 289). Traits or capacities that a higher-order discriminator generally considers desirable are deemed undesirable and denigrated when an individual who has them belongs to a socially excluded group (Piper, 1990, 289–91).

What sets higher-order discriminators apart from first-order discriminators is that the former do not acknowledge their antipathy to primary disvalued attributes (Piper, 1990, 297). Since they deny that gender, race, class, sexual orientation, ethnicity, and the like are legitimate bases for judgment, they focus on other attributes and lodge their reasons for dismissing members of certain social groups in these secondary attributes. Whereas an assertive male manager is regarded as a business asset, an assertive female manager is passed over for promotion. The higher-order discriminator maintains that women should receive equal treatment in employment yet inexplicably finds assertive women terribly disagreeable and undeserving of advancement. Though fictional, Darryl Pinckney's depiction of a high school teacher's inability to credit the intelligence of an African-American does not lack verisimilitude:

> Scene 1. The English teacher who believes the harrassment of
> having a large family has taught him all he needs to know about

being understanding calls out the scores on the Dickens multiple choice test. He holds back the new student's test paper for an after-class conference. "I want you to be honest with me. I can't help you if you don't let me know when the material is too hard for you. Now be honest with me. Did you cheat?" The hands of the surprised Negro student—"I was so conscious of having passed through scenes of which they could have no knowledge"— fly to cheeks that Clearasil hasn't helped. (Pinckney, 1992, 87)

As Piper puts it, an attribute, "in the way it is borne" by the member of the socially excluded group, is thought to have negative value (Piper, 1990, 295; for related discussion of "reflexive aversive responses," see Young, 1990, 142).

Piper cites "pseudorational" mechanisms to account for first- and higher-order discrimination. First-order discrimination relies on rationalization and dissociation (Piper, 1990, 296). By magnifying the properties of the members of a group that disqualify them as persons, the first-order discriminator rationalizes a moral view that denies the full personhood of these individuals. Through dissociation, whole groups of people are tarred with terms of opprobrium, such as "sub-human" or "perverted," and hence excluded from the class of full-fledged persons. Higher-order discrimination, too, is grounded in rationalization and dissociation. But, to protect the moral subject's self-ascribed innocence, higher-order discrimination adds denial to this pseudorational repertoire (Piper, 1990, 296). Higher-order discriminators deny that their thinking is contaminated by blanket contempt for the members of any group. They view themselves as judging people on their individual merits, yet they unerringly underrate the personal qualities, the talents, and the credentials of the members of certain social groups.

According to Piper, higher-order discrimination results from "superveniently self-subverting" rationality (Piper, 1990, 305). In fact, higher-order discriminators wield a defective moral theory that denies the status of personhood to whole groups of persons. But these same people have an overarching commitment to an inclusive moral theory that recognizes all persons as equals and that requires that all persons be accorded full moral consideration. This commitment and the need to believe themselves to be living up to it leads higher-order discriminators to deny that they embrace a moral theory that arbitrarily limits the scope of the class of moral patients. The result is compound pseudorationality. The higher-order discriminator's denial of his or her devaluation of a group and discrimination against that group is a pseudorational application of an inclusive moral theory to his or her pseudorationalized exclusionary moral theory (Piper, 1990, 305).

These contradictory commitments are enshrined in stereotypes. An "honorific stereotype" is a set of valued attributes that is taken to be definitive of personhood (Piper, 1992–93, 217). A "derogatory stereo-type" is any set of attributes other than the honorific stereotype (Piper, 1992–93, 218). As honorific self-stereotyping is interdependent with derogatory stereotyping of others, so reciprocally higher-order discrimination—that is, giving automatic preferment to one's own kind—is interdependent with higher–order discrimination against others (Piper, 1992–93, 190; 1990, 293). Self-flattery and elitism are inextricable from unconscious prejudice.

Now, it might be objected that pseudorationality is not rational at all and therefore that higher-order discrimination is not a purely intellectual vice. Here, I think Piper would make two replies. On the one hand, she claims that xenophobia (and thus higher-order dis-crimination) is "a paradigm case of resistance to the intrusion of anomalous data into an internally coherent conceptual scheme—a threat to the unity of the self defined by it" (Piper, 1992–93, 189). Such resistance is rational, for it is a form of self-preservation. Although this strategy of self-preservation relies on thought processes that distort reality, the pseudorational contrivance that sustains xenophobia and higher-order discrimination serves a rational end.

On the other hand, Piper acknowledges that higher-order discrimi-nation is linked to emotional needs. Higher-order discriminators have a "personal investment" both in the restricted moral theory they put into practice and also in the inclusive theory they consciously avow (Piper, 1990, 296, 298; also see Piper, 1992–93, 217). To give up contempt for an excluded social group and recognize these individu-als as equals would be a blow to one's self-esteem, for contempt shields feelings of personal inferiority (Piper, 1990, 300, 304). Furthermore, to admit one's failure to live up to one's professed morality would be a blow to one's self-esteem, for one would stand exposed as an unjust and despicable person (Piper, 1990, 298–299). Thus, pseudorational defenses are mobilized to secure the higher-order discriminator's self-esteem, and the higher-order discriminator would be deeply disturbed if this system of defenses were to unravel.

According to Piper, it is possible to have mistaken beliefs about other social groups without being a xenophobe. What marks the

xenophobe is his or her "personal investment" in denigrating others—
that is, the emotional needs that contempt and discrimination satisfy.
Pseudorationality is not self-perpetuating. It resists correction in the
face of contrary evidence when it satisfies urgent emotional needs.

Higher-order discriminators consciously endorse an inclusive and
egalitarian moral theory that explicitly condemns the practices authorized by the pseudorationalized moral theory they unwittingly live by.
In light of this tension and in light of the wide availability of evidence
disconfirming rationalized and dissociated beliefs, one would expect
the higher-order discriminator's position to be unstable. But it is not.
To protect their self-esteem and our fear of apparent difference,
higher-order discriminators devalue whole social groups and deprive
members of these groups of opportunities and benefits, all the while
proclaiming their commitment to equal rights and their freedom from
prejudice. Higher-order discriminators convert anxieties about their
own worthiness and security into unacknowledged animus toward
others, and this self-protective animus provides an inexhaustible well-
spring that sustains pseudorationality. The higher-order discriminator's acrobatic act succeeds because it satisfies compelling, albeit
shameful, emotional needs. Plainly, the higher-order discriminator's
intellectual failings are inseparable from his or her emotional vulnerabilities. Though Piper stresses the "cognitive errors" involved in
higher-order discrimination, she recognizes an emotional component,
and she recognizes that this emotional component is indispensable to
the most pernicious forms of prejudice.

3. Culturally Normative Prejudice

Piper argues that xenophobia is not biologically programmed and
that higher-order discrimination is a consequence of empirical conditioning (Piper, 1992–93, 191, 221–225). Yet, she seems to regard
stereotypes as arising from individual cognitive dysfunction (Piper,
1992–93, 212–216). Moreover, she characterizes higher-order discrimination as a "personal problem" (Piper, 1990, 309). Undeniably, there
is a sense in which it is a personal problem. Higher-order discriminators are injuring others in order to satisfy their own emotional needs,
and they are responsible for the wrongs they inflict. Yet, it would be
a flabbergasting coincidence if so many people independently hit
upon the same defense for their self-esteem. Indeed, it is no accident.
I shall urge that an account of the figurative encoding and transmission of prejudice is needed to explain both the prevalence of preju-

dice and also its intractability. The cognitive errors that Piper analyzes are mightily seconded by potent cultural imagery.

If people are xenophiles by nature, as Piper claims, the empirical conditioning that turns vast numbers of people into xenophobes must be extraordinarily efficient (Piper, 1992–93, 225). People from isolated homogeneous communities are taken in. But it also casts its spell on people who are in a position to know better—many urban dwellers who have encountered members of different social groups all their lives are prejudiced. Likewise, sexist stereotypes remain in force despite extensive, daily interaction between women and men in many communities. Moreover, this conditioning must operate very subtly since for the most part it goes unnoticed. First-order discriminators regard their prejudices as empirical generalizations confirmed by their own experience, and higher-order discriminators are altogether unaware of their prejudices. Where do restricted, provincial ideas of personhood come from? Why do they have such a powerful grip on people's thinking and action? By hypothesizing that cultures define the identities of socially excluded groups through vivid figurations that turn up in widely disseminated stories and pictures, we can explain the efficacy of the conditioning that inculcates prejudice.

Consider the case of the gender issues first raised by the women's suffrage movement and still under discussion today (see Section 1 above). What are generally taken to be the facts about gender within a given culture are encoded in captivating systems of imagery: in individual figures of speech, e.g., women as babes, dolls, foxes, or chicks, and also in myths and cautionary tales populated by protagonists who represent ideals of womanhood, e.g., the beatific mother, or who express prevalent attitudes toward womanhood, e.g., the sinister witch. Complex behavioral and psychological imperatives are condensed into memorable, emotionally compelling figurations, and sexism becomes a culturally normative prejudice.

Many children are in fact exposed to forthrightly bigoted statements and villifying epithets—if not in the loving context of family life, then very likely while at play with friends. Still, introducing culturally entrenched, prejudicial figurations of socially excluded groups explains how higher-order discriminators can shun such doctrines and yet be prejudiced. Imagery is seductive, and it is often absorbed subliminally. Thus, people can be inducted into culturally normative prejudice—their attitudes and behavior shaped—without explicit instruction. Parents need never take their children aside and level with them about their conviction that this or that social group is inferior or dangerous. Culturally entrenched figurations are passed on without obliging anyone to formulate, accept, or reject repugnant negative propositions about any group's standing or self-congratulatory positive propositions about one's own. It is no wonder, then, that higher-order discriminators have no idea they are prejudiced. They may never have taken bigoted utterances the least bit seriously, and they need never have had a malicious impulse to harm someone just because of that person's group membership. Yet, prejudicial figurations structure their imagination and therefore their moral choices.

Figurations of socially excluded groups function as a kind of shorthand in which group norms are crystallized and through which these norms are embedded in the "geology of desire" [I borrow Barbara Herman's phrase (1991, 787)]. Or perhaps it would be more perspicuous to say that these figurations *fossilize* these norms, for they integrate the norms into the corpus of common sense and render them impervious to criticism (de Beauvoir, 1989, Chapter 9; Kittay, 1988; Rooney, 1991).[6] A danger of figurative language, warns William Carlos Williams, is that it can make up minds like beds.

Encoded in this way, prejudice is adaptable yet firm. Imagery is open to interpretation, and this elasticity enables it to stretch to cover new situations and to authorize discrimination on new grounds. As Piper observes, disvaluation expands to ensure exclusion wherever the opportunity for exclusion presents itself (Piper, 1990, 290). If a black person's having rhythm is devalued, then this person's being a good dancer will be devalued, too (Piper, 1990, 290). Still, culturally entrenched figurations of socially excluded groups are narrowly prescriptive; imagery sets limits on interpretation. People who violate a culturally entrenched figuration, however demeaning it may be, provoke resentment and antagonism. A black whose dancing displays classical styling is despised as much as a black who expressively improvises (Piper, 1990, 190). A member of a socially excluded group cannot earn respect by conforming to the dominant group's self-figuration.[7]

Culturally entrenched figurations of socially excluded groups define norms, and people do not take kindly to violations of these norms. Piper explains this emotional investment in terms of individual psychopathology—enforcing stereotypes protects the self-esteem of discriminators. I believe, however, that the figurative encoding of social identities suggests a further explanation of this emotional power.

Let us return to the case of gender. Phyllis Rooney inventories some of the ways in which gender has come to function as a "root metaphor, one that has become so deeply embedded in our thought that we no longer recognize it as such" (Rooney, 1991, 87, 91–95). Gender constructs the relationship between people and nature—man is to dominate mother nature (Lloyd, 1993, 10–17). It constructs the nature of reason and its relation to passion and appetite—masculine reason is altogether distinct from feminine passion and appetite, and the former must control the latter. Eva Feder Kittay shows how men have appropriated women and their reproductive function to represent their own capacities and accomplishments, for example, Plato describes Socrates as a midwife to philosophical ideas (Kittay, 1988, 72–77). Moreover, Nancy Stephan argues that nineteenth-century figurations of race echo figurations of gender: "Lower races represented the 'female' type of the human species, and females the 'lower race' of gender" (Stephan quoted in Rooney, 1991, 89; for related discussion of "somatophobia," see Spelman, 1988, 126–127). Sander Gilman's work complements Stephan's and documents the intertwining of race and gender in the nineteenth-century construction of female sexuality (Gilman, 1985, 76–108). Kimberle Williams Crenshaw adds contemporary examples of how race and ethnicity intersect with gender to create images of Latina, African-American, and native American women that epitomize wickedness and degradation in popular movies and video games (Crenshaw, 1993, 118–120; also see M. Walker, n.d.b). Racialized and ethnicized images of gender personify the forces of evil and thus construct morality.

Through figurative linkages, gender, race, ethnicity, sexual orientation, class, and the like become fundamental organizing principles that structure a culture's world view. No doubt, violations of stereotypically defined norms threaten some individuals' self-esteem. But much more is at stake. What is at stake in the perpetuation of culturally entrenched figurations of socially excluded groups is nothing less than a society's understanding of the human species and its place in the universe. No wonder, then, that challenges to these figurations raise the alarm and meet vigorous opposition. Notice, too, that defenders of such imagery can innocently aver that they have no desire to oppress anyone and that their only interest is in preserving a great cultural tradition.[8] Even people who are victimized by these very figurations have reason to hesitate to overturn them. Insofar as members of socially excluded groups share the dominant culture's world view, their world view hangs in the balance, as well. Rooney contends that we need to "remythologiz[e] voice and agency and [to] remythologiz[e] reason, emotion, intuition, and nature" (Rooney, 1991, 96). Her proposal is as intimidating as it is exhilarating.

The philosopher's artifice of construing stereotypes as lists of pre-scribed or forbidden attributes and behaviors is misleading. Figura-tions of social groups convey complex ideas in an easily assimilable and nearly indelible form. Their vibrant immediacy facilitates their transmission and retention. Their constrained flexibility ensures their applicability in a wide range of circumstances, and this adaptability ensures their survival despite momentous social and economic change. Likewise, the linkages between disparate conceptual and experiential domains that figurative language effects ensures that, once entrenched, figurations of social groups will galvanize emo-tional commitment and resist critique.

Now, it might be thought that all that is needed to root out preju-dice is to point out discrepancies between cultural figurations of a widely despised and historically excluded group and the facts about group members' actual characteristics and potentialities. However, it is not possible to refute a figuration with counterexamples or statis-tics. Sometimes propositions derived from a figuration can be rebutted in this way. Maggie Thatcher's conduct as British Prime Minister seems to bely the claim that all women are passive, yet she might be regarded instead as the "exception that proves the rule." Since no finite set of propositions exhausts the expressive content of a figuration—that is, since imagery supports multiple interpretations that can be elaborated indefinitely—this kind of criticism always leaves an expressive residue untouched and the figuration intact.

This problem is compounded in several respects. First, cultures never rely on a single figuration of a social group. They furnish an array of images, and it is not uncommon for some of these images to conflict with others. Women are figured both as madonnas and as whores. As a result, these figurations present a baffling and elusive tar-get. Refuting one figuration may be taken as proof of the other, and vice versa. Second, many of these figurations oscillate between essen-tialist claims about the nature of group members and normative claims about how these individuals should conduct themselves. A woman who has no propensity for motherhood shows nothing about women's essential nature. She *should* want to have children, for maternity is her destiny as a woman. That she is not maternally inclined shows that she is not a "real" woman. Once it is accepted that individuals can defy their essential nature, no counterexample can defeat claims, however incredible they may be, about such essential natures.

Worse still, empirically grounded arguments attacking proposi-tional paraphrases of these figurations fail to make contact with their emotional underpinnings. As John Stuart Mill remarks, "So long as an opinion is strongly rooted in the feelings, it gains rather than loses in stability by having a preponderating weight of argument against it . . . [W]hen it rests solely on feeling, the worse it fares in argumentative contest, the more persuaded its adherents are that their feelings must have some deeper ground, which the arguments do not reach" (Mill, 1986, 7). It comes as no surprise, then, that dry recitations of countervailing facts seldom convert dyed in the wool sexists and other bigots to less benighted views. Culturally normative prejudice seems immune to criticism.

4. Dissident Speech: Figuration as Critique

By recasting the problem of prejudice in psychoanalytic terms, Julia Kristeva establishes a framework that suggests an alternative to conventional philosophical criticisms of prejudice. Her psychoanalytic framework likens culturally entrenched figurations of socially excluded groups to the neurotic's symptomatic tropes and hence likens the solution to the problem of culturally normative prejudice to the therapeutic figurations of psychoanalytic clinical practice. For Kristeva, the cure for the social pathology is the talking cure writ large. Only by substituting novel, emancipatory figurations for repressive, culturally entrenched ones can prejudice be uprooted.

According to Kristeva, political and economic arrangements dictate patterns of repression—children are customarily brought up to deny some of their experience, while institutions withhold outlets for certain types of desire.[9] Repression walls off certain needs and renders them inaccessible to consciousness except in disguised forms. On the one hand, repression channels behavior in ways that make social cooperation possible. But, on the other hand, it gives rise to compulsions that limit people's possibilities for fulfillment and to animus toward others that sometimes erupts abusively. In moral reflection, these compulsions can surface in the form of complicity in one's own oppression, and these animosities can surface in the form of staunch support for the oppression of others.

Bigoted preconceptions can infect well-intentioned attempts to empathize with others, and, as I have argued, impartial reason is not a reliable antidote for the corruption of emotionally entrenched prejudice. Since neither impartial reason nor empathy is secure until the effects of social repression have been addressed, Kristeva turns inward and directs our attention to the need for intrapersonal insight. Since repressed needs are deeply disturbing and potentially dangerous, she recommends the medium of figurative language to decode and subdue them.

In *Strangers to Ourselves,* Kristeva explicates the psychological dynamic underlying the phenomenon of xenophobia:

> [T]hat which *is* strangely uncanny would be that which *was* (the past tense is important) familiar and, under certain conditions (which ones?) emerges. A first step was taken that removed the uncanny strangeness from the outside, where fright anchored it, to locate it inside, not inside the familiar considered as one's own and proper, but the familiar potentially tainted with strangeness and referred (beyond its imaginative origin) to an improper past. The other is my ('own and proper') unconscious. (Kristeva, 1991, 183)

Here, the reference of the term "other" is double: (1) it is that part of one's infantile experience that one is obliged to repudiate and repress in order to demarcate psychic and corporeal boundaries, and (2) it is the foreigner to one's social group who demands admission to one's society but who refuses to assimilate. One hates foreigners, according to Kristeva, because they remind one of the unassimilable material that must remain expelled from one's conscious subjectivity if one's sense of identity is to remain intact and also of the permeability of the borders between conscious and unconscious life and therefore the fragility of one's precious sense of identity (for a Kantian account of the way in which xenophobia protects the unity of the self, see Piper, 1992–93). A baleful defense mechanism, prejudice converts anguish about the "stranger within" into attacks on the members of "strange" social groups. Repressed desires are transformed into virulent hate.

To counteract culturally normative prejudice, Kristeva recommends a "cosmopolitanism of a new sort that . . . might work for a mankind whose solidarity is founded on the consciousness of its unconscious" (Kristeva, 1991, 192). Following Kristeva, Iris Young advocates becoming "more comfortable with the heterogeneity within ourselves" (Young, 1990, 153).[10] But, needless to say, one cannot just decide to accept that one is not the master in one's own house, to echo Freud's classic turn of phrase. Not only is a substantial degree of unity necessary if one is to function successfully in society, but also one cannot easily abdicate coherent subjectivity and enjoy heterogeneity, for the defenses that protect coherent subjectivity are deeply ingrained. Still, that vague, but gnawing discontent often precipitates innovative and fruitful moral reflection suggests that such reflection is often rooted in nonconscious materials and that it would be a mistake to dismiss Kristeva's approach.

On Kristeva's view, everyday disruptions of identity and intentionality signal the intrusion of nonconscious materials into conscious life and constitute an implicit critique of the repression society enforces as well as the social norms that presuppose this repression. It is the task of social dissidents to confront these intrusions and to offset their deleterious moral ramifications. Calling upon dissidents to "give voice to each individual form of the unconscious, to every desire and need," Kristeva attributes a vital progressive potential to nonconscious materials (Kristeva, 1986, 295–296). Tapping the unconscious not only enhances self-understanding but also sparks moral and political regeneration, for it is possible to uncover and come to terms with repressed material, and doing so neutralizes its harmful effects.

Of course, Kristeva denies that nonconscious materials can simply be released from repression. If these materials are to serve as moral resources, their sexual determinants, especially the cruel and violent ones, must be dissolved, usually, in her view, through psychoanalysis (Kristeva, 1980, 145–146). Thus, Kristeva characterizes psychoanalytic therapy and the exploration of transference love that takes place there as a journey toward an "ethics of respect for the irreconcilable" (Kristeva, 1991, 182). The aim is not to relinquish coherent subjectivity altogether, but rather to become a "questionable subject-in-process"—a subject capable of alternating between the indispensable illusion of unified, agentic subjectivity, on the one hand, and attending to the outcroppings of nonconscious material that bedevil conscious life, on the other (Kristeva, 1980, 135–137; 1987a, 380; 1987b, 9). For Kristeva, the normalization of decentered subjectivity is the key to overcoming xenophobia.

According to Kristeva, psychoanalytic interpretation facilitates coming to terms with nonconscious materials by fashioning new metaphors for them (Kristeva, 1987a, 10, 276). For this reason, psychoanalysis numbers among the "aesthetic practices"—practices through which nonconscious materials are figuratively articulated (Kristeva, 1986, 210; 1991, 189–190). Although psychoanalytic refigurations seek to free analysands from the stultifying meanings that have become annexed to their experiences, nonconscious materials and the tropes that give expression to them still resonate with desires that must remain unfathomable for a coherent subject. Psycho-analysis never domesticates the unconscious. What aesthetic practices can accomplish is to articulate these nonconscious materials in a form amenable to pleasurable contemplation. Sustaining the "questionable subject-in-process" in this way, aesthetic practices defuse threats to the individual that become the pretext for prejudice when they are deflected onto others.

Elsewhere, Kristeva identifies aesthetic practices with cultural dissidence, and she counts rebels, psychoanalysts, writers, exiles, and, surprisingly, women as dissidents (Kristeva, 1986, 295–298, 300; for related discussion, see Meyers, 1992, 144–151 and Chapter 5, Section 1). Freeing the imagination and mobilizing its powers of representation, these outsiders "demystify" the established social order and envisage alternative social forms (Kristeva, 1986, 210–211). To stress the role of aesthetic practices in critical moral reflection and to do so in terms that are in keeping with Kristeva's account, I shall call the activity of giving benign figurative expression to nonconscious materials that would otherwise distort moral judgment *dissident speech*.[11] Kristeva's more picturesque appellation is "heretical ethics" or "herethics" (Kristeva, 1986, 185).

As we have seen, the legacy of contempt for and hatred of "different" social groups does not vanish when people become consciously committed to principles of equality and fairness. This legacy survives in higher-order discrimination and in reflexive aversive responses to members of socially excluded groups (Piper, 1990; Young, 1990, 142). In addition, it is encoded in imagery that outlasts the political doctrines that the imagery originally served. The liberalization of explicit political beliefs notwithstanding, this figurative detritus continues to structure perceptions and expectations and hence moral judgment. Dissident speech prompts people to discard inveterate ways of framing issues by introducing counterimagery designed to rid moral reflection of the vestiges of prejudice.

The artist, Alexis Smith, sums up the way in which figuration can feed on itself and stimulate its audience:

> Once you start working with an image or a metaphor, you have it in your mind, and then you just keep seeing other things it could mean. Then you are not only punning or playing against the different meanings that the object could have, but you're playing against the different meanings that you've assigned it in the past—a dialogue within the work. (Smith, 1991, 12)

Though one must be cautious about romanticizing figurative language, it seems clear that among its virtues is the capacity to rupture familiar cognitive and emotional templates. Dissident speech capitalizes on this virtue. Whereas culturally entrenched figurations of socially excluded groups lock perception and feeling into reflexive, standardized patterns, dissident speech refigures gender, race, sexual orientation, class, ethnicity, and the like. In so doing, it displays properties of people that have gone unremarked, and it projects possible constellations of their relationships that have not heretofore been appreciated. In short, dissident speech stymies routinized thinking and bestirs improvisational thinking—receptive, generous attention to oneself or others; playful, yet probing imagination; acute, yet synthetic interpretation.

If I am right that cultures encode their defining, though often unacknowledged, values and norms in figurative systems that galvanize emotional commitment and reinforce established social practices and attitudes, all of our considered convictions are formed under suspect conditions.[12] Thus, moral reflection is incomplete, and possibly seriously warped, until the power of nonconscious materials is brought to heel through dissident speech. Moreover, since resolving the dilemma of difference requires empathizing with "different" others, and since prejudicial figurations confound empathy, advocates of justice for socially excluded groups cannot fully achieve their objectives unless they successfully contest this imagery. Dislodging culturally normative prejudice requires "seeing" the members of a socially excluded group in a new light, and transforming moral perception requires resymbolizing these social groups and social relations between historically dominant and subordinate groups. Not only would fresh figurations help to restructure moral perception, but they would also prevent the figurative vacuum left by the delegitimation of the traditional imagery from being filled by a resurgence of that selfsame imagery. But what do emancipatory counterfigurations look like, and where do they come from?

Endorsing the idea of "social therapy," Iris Young calls for creating public forums and accessible media in which this "therapy" can be conducted, and she points to consciousness-raising as an egalitarian practice that anticipates the sort of setting needed to develop and assess novel social interpretations (Young, 1990, 153).[13] Young's proposals for politicizing and democratizing cultural interpretation are attractive, and, in Chapter 5, I shall situate dissident speech in the context of feminist politics. I would add, however, that it is important not to neglect Kristeva's suggestions about the rhetoric of interpretation. Figurative narrative—a rhetorical mode that psychoanalysts have used evocatively and incisively—suggests a model worth adapting for purposes of exposing and debunking retrograde cultural imagery and for generating alternative emancipatory imagery. I shall pursue this theme in Chapter 4.

4

Psychoanalytic Feminism and Dissident Speech

Psychoanalysis has long had an ugly reputation amongst feminists, and this reputation is richly deserved, for Freud's account of femininity is condescending and narrow-minded. He privileges masculine sexuality—a girl's sexuality is masculine until she discovers that her clitoris is much smaller than a penis, contracts penis envy, and evolves a secondary feminine sexuality. He belittles women's anatomy—they are castrated. He besmirches women's character and intellect—they are jealous, narcissistic, less exacting in matters of morality, and less creative than men. Freud's psychoanalytic figurations of gender codify and seek to ratify cultural conventions and expectations regarding maternity and female domesticity. This history has forged a lasting bond between psychoanalysis and traditional feminine norms, and it has made psychoanalysis complicit in the subordination of women, for Freud supplied some of the most damaging and pervasive imagery working in Western culture to sustain unconscious prejudice against women along with woefully consistent, repressive treatment of women.

It is hardly surprising, then, that many feminists are wary of psychoanalysis. Yet, some have not dismissed psychoanalytic theory as a soon-to-be-extinct patriarchal dinosaur. Acknowledging that classic psychoanalytic tropes tap into a deep layer of prejudice about gender while worrying that these tropes help to perpetuate retrograde understandings of and attitudes toward women, psychoanalytic feminists have nonetheless sought to capitalize on and to augment the emancipatory potential of psychoanalytic rhetoric. Indeed, the power and ubiquity of gender imagery have combined with the adaptability of psychoanalysis to combating retrograde imagery to spark a feminist renaissance in psychoanalytic theory. Psychoanalytic feminism represents a sustained and variegated attempt to deploy the rhetoric of grandiose metaphor and mythic narration that Freud pioneered to address the problem of gender, and this literature provides many vivid examples of the uses of figurative discourse for purposes of dislodging prejudice regarding gender. In the hands of psychoanalytic feminists, I submit, the psychoanalytic interpretive apparatus becomes a form of dissident speech.

Before turning to feminist appropriations of psychoanalysis, I shall review Freud's account of femininity in some detail, for it is among the key figurations of gender in Western culture. This discussion will underscore the ways in which Freud's psychoanalytic rhetoric serves fundamental normative ends and secures a prejudicial view of women. Still, I believe that some psychoanalytic feminists have successfully modified Freud's rhetoric to redress the relations of domination and subordination between men and women that he used it to reinforce. Here I shall survey four representative strategies: (1) Jessica Benjamin highlights the pathos of a polarized, eroticized conception of gender; (2) Nancy Chodorow revalues traditional feminine qualities; (3) Julia Kristeva disrupts established gender images; (4) Luce Irigaray reconstructs femininity by emphasizing neglected dimensions of women's experience.

1. Freud's Figuration of Femininity

In Freud's various discussions of femininity, there is some confusion as to just what he takes his subject to be. In an early essay, Freud distinguishes three senses of the femininity-masculinity dichotomy (Freud, 1990, 136). Femininity and masculinity are sometimes identified with passivity and activity, respectively. But there are also biological and sociological senses of the terms. The biological sense concerns the individual's physiological role in reproduction, whereas the sociological sense consists of generalizations based on observations of the character traits of "actually existing masculine and feminine individuals" (Freud, 1990, 136). Now, this last definition is circular. One cannot decide whom to include in one's data base of feminine or masculine individuals unless one already commands criteria of femininity and masculinity. Thus, Freud declares the first of the meanings to be the "essential one and the most serviceable in psychoanalysis" (Freud, 1990, 136). But he also holds that there are no purely feminine or masculine individuals—real people always mix characteristics from both of the gender categories (Freud, 1990, 136, 311, 314).

Freud's remarks are a queer blend of tedious repetition of conventional views about gender and sensible acknowledgment that the people we know elude these stereotypes. What, then, are we to make of the subject matter of an essay entitled "Femininity"? Is Freud writing about an "ideal" passive type? Or is he writing about the development of women?

At the outset, he rejects the equation of femininity with passivity on the grounds that there are plenty of examples of active females in the animal world and that human mothers actively nurture their children (Freud, 1966, 579; also see Freud, 1990, 320, 334). Still, Freud does not abandon this line of thought. On the contrary, he asserts that the "suppression of women's aggressiveness is prescribed for them constitutionally [biologically] and imposed on them socially" (Freud, 1966, 580). Insofar as a woman's personality reflects her "sexual function"—her biological destiny to reproduce the species—she will be passive (Freud, 1966, 579–580, 583). After all, a woman who has been raped can contribute as much to the survival of the species as a woman who has consented to intercourse (Freud, 1966, 595). The feminine woman, in sum, is one who is best suited for her biological role in the reproduction of the species, and passivity best suits women to breed. Still, a woman "may be a human being in other respects as well" (Freud, 1966, 599). But, to the extent that women exhibit activity, they are masculine. Gender need not invariably match sex.

Despite the care Freud takes to demarcate his subject and to disavow pretensions to be providing a comprehensive account of female psychology, he immediately drifts into an unqualified description of the "sexual development of women" (Freud, 1966, 581). Although he notes in passing that this developmental process can get sidetracked —a woman can become frigid or lesbian—divergence from the path he outlines blocks the emergence of a "normal woman," "normal femininity," the "normal female attitude" (Freud, 1966, 581, 590; 1990, 327). By "normal," Freud does not mean merely "typical." Rather, he identifies the normal with the ideal (Freud, 1990, 313). Accordingly, it is hard to avoid the conclusion that Freud's normative thrust explains his scant attention to the tensions within and the complexity of actual feminine personalities. His liberal protestations about the normality of homosexuality and the evidence of his senses that women are by no means essentially passive notwithstanding, Freud embarks on an account of the heterosexual childbearer and implies that it is the best course for women's development to take.

Following this course is, alas, especially difficult for women (Freud, 1966, 581). Girls, like boys, first bond with their mothers, but women must redirect their emotional and erotic attachments and learn to love men (Freud, 1966, 582–583). Also, a girl's first experience of masturbation, like that of a boy, is phallic, for clitoral sexuality is phallic according to Freud (Freud, 1966, 582). But women must relinquish this barren masculine pleasure and replace it with a fertile, passive, vaginal sexuality (Freud, 1966, 582). To become normal women—women who want to marry men and who want to give birth to children—girls must reverse their earliest and strongest inclinations.

Freud's account of the preliminaries to girls' heterosexual reorientation is instructive since it affords a glimpse into Freud's view of mothers and of relations between mothers and daughters. The pre-Oedipal period of attachment to the mother prepares the girl to reject her mother and turn to her father. An initial idyll of mother-infant fusion quickly gives way to a period of frustration and strife. Freud maintains that the primary relationship between the mother and the child is inherently ambivalent (Freud, 1966, 588). Part of the trouble is that babies are insatiable. Since they can never get enough milk and love, they will always end up feeling deprived (Freud, 1966, 586, 587; 1990, 328). Though the cause of this felt deprivation is in the child, it is the mother who is blamed for it. Furthermore, the mother-child relationship is so intense that disappointments are inevitable and grounds for hostility are bound to accumulate (Freud, 1990, 331). But the mother's role in caring for the child is also a source of resentment. Mothers arouse phallic pleasure in the process of bathing and caring for children, yet they forbid their children's autoerotic experiments (Freud, 1990, 329; 1966, 587). They issue a come-hither but cancel it with an admonitory slap.

At the earliest stages of their children's development, then, Freud casts women in a baneful role. They withhold gratification; they seduce only to discipline. In short, they tyrannize. Gentle attentiveness and glad altruism are nowhere to be found in Freud's account. The child loves its mother because she satisfies its needs, not for the quality of the relationship she creates with the child. Although Freud comments that the complaints that his patients retrospectively lodge against their mothers must be exaggerated, he himself accentuates the negative in describing mother-child relations (Freud, 1966, 586). For Freud, a structural character flaw is built into women's biological function—mothers cannot help but be perceived as and, in some respects, be tyrants, and their victims are the most vulnerable and helpless population, namely, young children. That feminists must take exception to this one-sided image of motherhood is obvious. Nevertheless, it is central to Freud's account, for it establishes an atmosphere of hostility toward the mother that is needed for the Oedipus complex to have its effect on girls.

Surely, anyone would welcome an opportunity to escape from the maternal oppression of the pre-Oedipal period—that is, one might expect girls to become heterosexual and boys to become gay. But, of course, that is not Freud's scenario—only girls are driven away from their mothers. Strangely enough, Freud simply assumes a masculine heterosexual outcome. He assumes that boys will remain attached to mother substitutes, i.e., women, but that a girl's defection from her mother needs explaining (Freud, 1966, 588). However, since mothers repel children of both sexes, the more plausible assumption would have been that boys' continued erotic allegiance to women needs explaining. Indeed, in one of his essays, Freud seems to concede this point in maintaining that boys find an outlet for their hostility toward their mothers by deflecting it onto their rival Oedipal fathers (Freud, 1990, 332). However, Freud's account of gender would have been altogether different if he had been baffled by boys' pliant sexual fidelity to women, despite their tyrannical mothers, rather than by girls' seemingly well-motivated sexual rebellion against them. If the girl's resentment of her mother were sufficient to account for her heterosexual defection, there would be no reason to belabor the "anatomical distinction between the sexes." But Freud's unisex story branches into dual gender tracks as a result of the girl's discovery that her sex organ does not measure up to her brother's.

On Freud's account, the inferiority of girls' genitals provides the chief impetus for their heterosexual, reproductive shift. The girl sees a penis, compares it with her own tiny organ, and recognizes the significance of this difference (Freud, 1966, 589). To her lasting humiliation, she grasps that she has been short-changed—she is "mutilated" (Freud, 1990, 309). She responds by developing a feminine castration complex. She does not fear castration; she knows she is castrated.

Despising her own anatomy, she falls prey to penis envy (Freud, 1966, 589). Henceforth the dominant theme of the woman's psychic life will be the management of this inevitable and crushing psychic blow—the "narcissistic wound" of the castration complex—and the envy of men to which it gives rise.

Of course, a girl cannot have the penis she wishes for, but she can cope with her deficiency by realigning herself emotionally and sexually. She can reject her mother (Freud, 1966, 590–591). Not only is her mother castrated and, as such, contemptible, but also her mother is responsible for endowing her with a defective sex organ (Freud, 1990, 311). Building on sizable reserves of pre-Oedipal resentment, girls come to hate their mothers at the Oedipal stage (Freud, 1966, 585). In addition, with the assistance of "passive instinctual impulses," the girl can attach herself to someone who has a penis—namely, her father (Freud, 1966, 582–583, 592, 594). If, however, the girl is to become a fit sexual partner for a man, her erotic focus must change. Feminine vaginal sexuality must supersede her masculine clitoral sexuality. The castration complex provides the pretext for this shift, as well. No longer able to enjoy masturbating with her despised "phallic" genitals, she renounces this pleasure (Freud, 1966, 590; 1990, 312).

At this juncture, the girl has attained heterosexuality, but she has yet to attain femininity proper. Until her penis envy is sublimated in the wish to have her father's child, until she embraces the reproductive consequences of vaginal sexuality, an excess of pre-Oedipal masculinity remains (Freud, 1966, 592). Ultimately, a woman can obtain feminine gratification only by having a baby to replace the penis she is missing (Freud, 1966, 592; 1990, 312). Ideally, her baby will be a boy, for giving birth to a male child brings with it the added satisfaction of producing a penis (Freud, 1966, 592). Thus, remarks Freud, the vestiges of penis envy never entirely disappear from women's psychic economy (Freud, 1966, 592–593). Women's "enigmatic" bisexuality is never decisively overcome (Freud, 1966, 595; also see Young-Bruehl, 1990, 12–41).

There is little that could appeal to feminists in this account. A prime target of feminist criticism has been Freud's attribution of penis envy to women. Luce Irigaray argues that a phobia—specificially, Freud's own castration anxiety, his fear of losing his penis—lies behind this view (Irigaray, 1985a, 27, 47, 51, 79). Simone de Beauvoir, Betty Friedan, Kate Millett, and Shulamith Firestone take issue with Freud's biological essentialism and argue that it is not the male sex organ that girls envy, but rather male power and privilege (de Beauvoir, 1989, 276–278, 286–287; Friedan, 1974, 108; Millett, 1969, 187; Firestone, 1970, 60). Moreover, Millett doubts Freud's affirmation that the significance of not having a penis is self-evident. There is no reason, she contends, why girls would not see the penis as an excrescence as opposed to a treasured possession (Millett, 1969, 181). In view of children's pleasurable experience of suckling, it is more likely that boys would envy women's breasts (Millett, 1969, 183). In a similar vein, Eva Kittay follows Karen Horney and counters Freud's penis envy thesis with the claim that he overlooks boys' suffering from womb envy—they wish they had women's marvelous capacity to give life (Kittay, 1984, 94). For Kittay, boys, too, discover that they are lacking, but they compensate for this perceived deficiency by subordinating women. More generally, Freud's account deprives women of any intrinsic worth and dignity. Mothers are caricatured as hateful despots who are loved only as long as their daughters are under the illusion that they have phalluses (Freud, 1966, 591). Daughters devote themselves to a lifelong quest for a male sex organ—a quest that leaves them morally and intellectually stunted, though fulfilled as women.

The decisive force in a woman's life, penis envy shapes her character—she will become vain, capricious, and jealous—and it also shapes her aims in life—she will want to have a baby, preferably a boy, to compensate for her missing organ (Freud, 1966, 589, 592, 593, 596). On the question of feminine character, penis envy is a rather ham-fisted term of art that figuratively summarizes the undesirable qualities traditionally assembled under the feminine stereotype. Freud evokes an array of purportedly feminine foibles by ascribing the mean, yet pitiable vice of envy to women, and he alludes to women's alleged irremediable inferiority to men in the suggestion that what is envied is male anatomy. As for the aim of motherhood, it is arrived at through a process of reconciliation and substitution. Whereas the boy's castration complex, which develops when he discovers that women do not have penises, represents his fear of loss and issues in his determination to prevent this loss, the girl's castration complex, which develops when she discovers her lack, represents the onset of disillusionment and irreversible disappointment (Freud, 1966, 588–589, 593). The girl relinquishes any personal aspirations she may have had and submits to her maternal fate. Thus, Freud's notion of the castration complex, in its masculine and feminine variants, symbolizes activity and passivity, respectively. The forces Freud sees driving the process of feminine and masculine development are themselves figurations of gender.

Freud's phallocentric psychology condemns women to self-hate and self-denial. He expatiates at length on the topic of women's (and men's) disdain for the clitoris, and he has more to say on the subject of the commonness of frigidity than he has to say about women's "mature" sexual desire (Freud, 1966, 596).[1] Indeed, he seems content with the thought that male aggression obviates the need to account for female eroticism and identifies a distinctively feminine form of masochism that magically transforms the miseries he assigns to women into pleasures (Freud, 1990, 285–286). Suppressing their own erotic needs, women adjust their sexuality to suit the taste of men and pare down their life plans to accommodate the Darwinian imperative of the survival of the species. Childbearing and childrearing are women's destiny; giving birth to and caring for boys are women's deepest satisfaction. Thus, Freud's figuration of femininity amounts to a potent rationalization of the sexual division of labor and the subordination of women.

2. The Refiguration of Gender in Psychoanalytic Feminist Dissident Speech

Challenging images of women in mainstream culture has long been a staple of empirical feminist scholarship. Historians, sociologists, and psychologists have questioned the accuracy of prevalent conceptions of gender by documenting the lives of women. In the 1970s, however, feminist theorists tried a different tactic. They introduced a counterimage, namely, androgyny. One formulation of androgyny sought to unite traditionally feminine and masculine virtues in a single human ideal; another formulation sought to free personality traits from their conventional gender associations and to authorize people to cross gender lines (Trebilcot, 1982). Both sought to furnish an image that would enable people to conceive of themselves and to perceive others without reverting to traditional gender norms.

The image of androgyny soon came under fire in feminist circles for its insensitivity to the complexities of the gender issue—its perpetuation of gender polarities in the very attempt to transcend them and its naive assumption that a genuine human ideal could be cobbled together from traditionally feminine and masculine qualities

(Beardsley, 1982). Moreover, apart from its influence on some clothing and hairstyle fashions, this image has had little impact on the cavalcade of gender stereotypes pouring from the media. Neither has it enjoyed much popular appeal or made significant inroads into people's values and choices. If my undergraduate students are at all typical, women, many of whom are electing occupations that are conventionally associated with masculinity, still want to be perceived as feminine. Despite their career goals, they are not self-described androgynes. Also, as the proliferation of expensive, sometimes dangerous reproductive technology and the upward spiral of the cosmetic surgery industry attest, women's consuming interest in becoming mothers and in keeping a youthful, if not stunningly beautiful, appearance has not abated. It is doubtful, then, that this image has contributed much to women's emancipation, and, for this reason, many feminists have discarded it.

Feminist experience with the trope of androgyny is instructive. Not only did this image prove amenable to critical scrutiny, but also it helped to spark a fruitful and continuing discussion of the nature and meaning of gender—a discussion that has not forsaken the strategy of fighting images with images. The labeling of the restrooms at the Dia Foundation (an exhibition space for installation art on West 22nd Street in New York City) is very much in the spirit of this new rhetoric. The graphic style of the signs on the two adjacent doors is familiar block lettering, but, instead of "Women" and "Men," the signs read "Us" and "Them"—a compelling political point, put as succinctly as possible. With growing frustration over the slow pace of progress in achieving feminist goals has come an escalation of the intensity and long-range aims of feminist image insurgency. Deploying increasingly powerful and sometimes exotic figurative strategies in their own work, Judith Butler, Kathryn Morgan, and Drucilla Cornell are among those who urge feminists to move dissident speech regarding gender to the top of their agenda.

Judith Butler argues that feminists must expand their conception of the political so as to accord imagery its proper role in political resistance. For Butler, gender is a "corporeal style" constituted by a regimen of repeated acts and gestures (Butler, 1990, 136, 139–140). This repetition both secures the "illusion of an abiding gendered self" and legitimates gender (Butler, 1990, 140). But since gender rests on performance, it is vulnerable to guerilla theater, and Butler maintains that this theatrical tradition is already well established, albeit largely underground. Specifically, she contends that female impersonators assume "parodic identities" that lampoon the notion of a true gender identity and expose the imitative structure of gender itself (Butler, 1990, 137). These "dissonant and denaturalized performance[s]" dramatize the contingency of ties between anatomical sex, gender identity, and gender performance (Butler, 1990, 137, 146). Recasting Butler's theory as a work of dissident speech, Jennie Livingston's 1991 portrait of the lives of drag queens and the practice of voguing, *Paris Is Burning*, makes a persuasive cinematic case against rigid gender categories (for Butler's comments on this film and qualification of her claim that drag is subversive, see Butler, 1993, 121–140, 231, 237).

Embellishing Butler's line of thought, Kathryn Morgan invites us to contemplate the possibility of countercosmetic products and countercosmetic surgery (Morgan, 1991, 46–47). Consider, for instance, undergoing plastic surgery in order to have wrinkles carved into your face. Morgan's exposition is sly, for she lays out her countercosmetic vision with a straight face. Never letting on that she is engaged in anything but genuine persuasion, she acknowledges with an air of disappointment that women are not likely to hasten to hospitals to have this disfiguring surgery performed. Confined though it may be to the page and the imagination, Morgan's satirical imagery undoubtedly makes many readers' skin crawl.[2] It transgresses against standards of attractiveness that few people can pretend to have transcended, and it makes the gratuitous and therefore grotesque physical violation that is involved in all cosmetic surgery inescapable and palpable.

Drucilla Cornell focuses on a double bind women face as a corollary to the dilemma of difference: either they collaborate in their own oppression by embracing traditional norms of femininity or else they betray their womanhood by embracing traditional masculine norms. On Cornell's view, feminist theorists must resort to heterodox rhetorical methods if this dilemma is to be finessed. To write as women and also as feminists, Cornell argues, women must adopt Luce Irigaray's strategy of mimesis (Cornell, 1991, 147). They must "circle within the metaphors of the feminine"—that is, they must affirm traditional feminine imagery in order to work through it and rework it (Cornell, 1991, 146–147). By refusing to accept myth as reality while also refusing to deny the power of myth, "feminist visionar[ies]" loosen the hold that traditional imagery has over women and invite readers to "dream from the standpoint of the mythical figures who could redeem the feminine" (Cornell, 1991, 179). For Cornell, figurative narrative is an indispensable ally in the battle to voice women's subjectivity, for to renounce traditional imagery is to lose its capacity to kindle women's imaginations and thus to forfeit its potential as a point of departure for conceiving variant or opposing imagery.

The views of Butler, Morgan, and Cornell reflect a recognition on the part of feminists of just how deeply ingrained traditional views of gender are and how hard it is to overcome these repressive norms. Moreover, their work suggests the wide variety of forms that dissident speech can take. I want to stress, however, that I cannot begin to canvass fully the work feminists have done to refigure gender. Still, to clarify what feminist dissident speech is, it is necessary to provide some examples, and any selection is bound to be somewhat arbitrary. Since Freud's gender imagery has been extraordinarily influential, and since the rhetoric of psychoanalysis is especially well adapted to the purposes of dissident speech, I shall illustrate dissident speech by presenting figurations of gender from the work of Jessica Benjamin, Nancy Chodorow, Julia Kristeva, and Luce Irigaray.

Dissident speech need not be embedded in psychoanalysis, but one reason to show that dissident speech can be embedded in psychoanalysis is that doing so helps to make sense of the power of psychoanalytic feminism, despite warranted skepticism regarding its tenability as an approach to developmental psychology (see Chapter 1, Section 3A). In offering narratives of childhood development framed as mythic dramas, psychoanalytic feminists in effect announce to their audience, "Here is a story of your life—either a story which should trouble you if you identify with it or one with which you should be pleased to identify."[3] Thus, psychoanalysis provides a particularly compelling framework for dissident speech.

A. Jessica Benjamin: Rational Violence

Jessica Benjamin rejects Freud's claim that women are characteristically masochistic, and she also denies that men are characteristically sadistic. Still, femininity and masculinity are associated with masochism and sadism, respectively, and the imagery of sadomasochism constitutes in no small measure the imagery of gender in Western culture (Benjamin, 1988, 74). Among Benjamin's central projects, then, is her examination of this sinister erotic undercurrent of gender—the interpersonal dynamic of sadomasochism. Narrated psychoanalytically as arising from a failure of parent-child interaction and therefore as a problem of derailed childhood development, Benjamin's account of sadomasochism laments the tenacity and destructiveness of the "rational violence" she discerns at the core of gender.

Infants, according to Benjamin, have a dual need to be cared for and protected, on the one hand, and to have their choices and acts recognized as issuing from an independent agent, on the other (for further discussion of Benjamin's developmental theory, see Chapter 6, Sections 1 and 2). Paradoxically, they are dependent on others, not only for the satisfaction of their physical needs, but also for their sense of their own autonomy. On Benjamin's view, the caregiver's response to the baby's early aggressive forays is critical to the emergence of distinct identity (Benjamin, 1985, 60). The child's psychic future hinges on whether the caregiver recognizes these acts by respecting them as stemming from the child's own desires or instead withholds recognition by ignoring or retreating from the child or by repressing the acts.

Nurturing a child's sense of self requires maintaining a delicate balance. If the caregiver imposes no constraints and permits the child to mistreat him or her, the child will know how to gain a sense of self only by negating others and will not emotionally register other people as deserving consideration—in short, such a child will be "sadistic" (Benjamin, 1988, 70). If the caregiver punishes the child too harshly or simply absents himself or herself from the child, the child will feel negated and, longing for someone to discover its identity and affirm its agency, will become "masochistic" (Benjamin, 1988, 72). But if the conduct of the caregiver simultaneously expresses both that individual's own sense of independent selfhood and also that individual's recognition of the selfhood of the child, identity formation will escape the traps of defensive domination or passivity, and the child will grow up to be capable of interpersonal reciprocity.

Unfortunately, patriarchal societies assign childcare exclusively to women and deny women's subjectivity (Benjamin, 1988, 82). Moreover, they privatize and denigrate childcare while confining women to this role (Benjamin, 1985, 64). The upshot is that women's self-esteem comes to depend on their vicarious experience of their children's accomplishments, and "[t]his breeds . . . an instrumental attitude in the heart of the nurturing relationship" (Benjamin, 1985, 64). When mothers are deprived of their own subjectivity and self-chosen work, their children inherit either a psychology of domination and fierce differentiation from others or a psychology of submission and helpless continuity with others. In societies in which mothers have exclusive responsibility for childcare, boys are seen as needing to break the bond with their mothers to achieve masculine identity, but the feminine identity to which girls are supposed to aspire is seen as continuous with maternal bonding. Thus, these polarized psychic dispositions become attached to prevailing conceptions of gender, though not to biological sex. There are dominant females, and they are deemed masculine; likewise, there are submissive males, and they are deemed feminine.

To crystallize this view of gender, Benjamin embarks on an examination of the sadomasochistic psychic relations depicted in the infamous pornographic novel, *The Story of O*. The novel opens as O (this initial is all the name the author gives her) is taken to Roissy castle where a secret confraternity of men keep women as sexual slaves. During O's stay at Roissy castle, René and his surrogates subject O—always with her consent—to increasingly painful and demeaning treatment. When O, now a willing slave of "love," and René return to Paris, René first asks and receives O's permission to share her with his older and revered stepbrother, Sir Stephen. Soon after, he gives O to Sir Stephen. More psychologically acute and far more ruthless than René, Sir Stephen divines O's resistances and attacks them with a regimen of abuse. Throughout, O is asked whether she consents to her treatment, and, though no one ever threatens her, she never refuses. Not only does O betray a woman whom she adores and with whom she is having an affair, but also she fearfully, yet gladly undergoes genital mutilation. The novel ends ambiguously. When Sir Stephen decides to leave O, it is not clear whether O is abandoned at Roissy castle or takes her own life.

It might seem strange that in sketching the plot of *The Story of O* I have not used such seemingly apt terms as "captive," "inmate," and "victim" to characterize O's condition. I have avoided this kind of language deliberately, for I am taking care not to suggest that O has been abducted against her will or that she yearns to be released from the precincts of the castle or to be freed from Sir Stephen's service. As Benjamin stresses, O's willing compliance is necessary to the sadomasochistic relationship. In egalitarian reciprocal relationships, each individual has a double role—acting on the need to assert oneself by negating the other while also fulfilling the responsibility to recognize the other as an independent subject and agent. However, sadomasochistic relationships divide this need and this responsibility between the sadist and the masochist—the sadist only negates; the masochist only recognizes.

O's volition, though she invariably wants whatever René or Sir Stephen wants her to want, must remain intact. Without O's choice to submit, the desires of these men would go unrecognized (Benjamin, 1985, 52). In *The Story of O,* the infantile aggressive impulse that seeks to delimit the self by eliciting a limiting, yet nonpunitive response is represented as pure, brute negation—the desire to subjugate O. But here the dilemma underlying sadism becomes apparent. The demands of dominance steadily escalate. If O has been dominated in one way, her lover must find some new and worse degradation to visit upon her. Otherwise, his dominance will lapse. It follows that O must ultimately be destroyed and that Sir Stephen must lose the person he relies on to recognize him. O's psychological position is equally perilous. O seeks to find herself through submission (Benjamin, 1985, 57). Rather than discovering desires of her own and demanding to be recognized as a subject who has those desires, she settles for being recognized as the object of her lover's desire (Benjamin, 1985, 56). Self-abasing as she is, O becomes unable to recognize Sir Stephen, and, debased as he has made her, Sir Stephen does not recognize O.

It would seem, then, that no one's most fundamental needs are satisfied in sadomasochism. The logic of sadism is ultimately self-defeating, unless the sadist's need for the other's recognition can be eliminated. According to Benjamin, it can be eliminated, and in a way that secures the position of the masochist who, recall, is empty of desire and therefore needs the other to fill that lack. The sadomasochistic relationship is tenable, on Benjamin's view, through "rational violence" (Benjamin, 1985, 61–62). Rational violence is the control that sadists exercise, that is, the limits sadists set and observe in catering to the sexual proclivities of masochists. The sadist's exquisite mastery over his death-dealing powers makes masochism "safe," indeed, pleasurable, for O and also inspires her "love" (Benjamin, 1988, 64). Moreover, from the standpoint of the sadist's needs, this mastery substitutes for the masochist's recognition. In exerting control over their violence, René and Sir Stephen demarcate their own psychic boundaries independently of O (Benjamin, 1985, 53–54, 62). This vaulting individualism is the source of the sadist's satisfaction. Without rational violence, relations of domination and submission would collapse.

Now, gender has historically been premised on the dominance of men and the submission of women and on the feasibility of heterosexual eroticism within that asymmetric framework. Though Benjamin does not identify heterosexuality with sadomasochism, she does not confine rational violence to sadomasochism. The organization of her 1985 essay suggests the connection between rational violence and gender. Here, sections commenting on the problematics of gender identity under a practice of exclusively female nurturing bracket her analysis of sadomasochism. The expression "rational violence" figures most prominently in her explication of sadomasochism, and it is that context that confers a determinate meaning on this initially baffling oxymoron. Nevertheless, her developmental psychology extrapolates that figure of speech to the broader issue of gender (Benjamin, 1985, 63–66; 1988, 82).

In outline, her account concurs with Nancy Chodorow's well-known views (see Section 2B below). In the traditional nuclear family with the mother at home caring for the children and the father away from home earning a living, the boy's rite of passage is a solitary journey in which he spurns the mother and identifies with abstract, remote masculine norms, whereas the girl's acquisition of a feminine identity could hardly be described as a rite of passage since it takes place imperceptibly and in close communion with the mother. The boy's break with the mother gives rise to sharp ego boundaries, and the girl's unbroken bond with the mother leaves her with permeable ego boundaries. Masculine hyper- and autodifferentiation and feminine underdifferentiation parallel the psychologies of sadism and masochism, as Benjamin portrays them. *The Story of O* is thus presented as isolating and exaggerating key elements of masculinity and femininity.

The rational violence that sustains O's relationship to René and Sir Stephen is the tragic core of gender, as we have inherited it. Moreover, if gender is a system of rational violence, society is a system of "solitary confinement" (Benjamin, 1988, 83). People can be dazzled by their own splendid individuality or by that of someone else. Having a life of one's own while being connected to others is ruled out (Benjamin, 1988, 82).

What makes "rational violence" a powerful figuration of gender is that it can be interpreted in straightforward terms that link it quite directly to phenomena associated with gender, yet Benjamin's oxymoron ultimately resists attempts to domesticate it. We are accustomed to the idea of rational force—force used to achieve legitimate and superordinate ends that would otherwise elude us. But the juxtaposition of "rationality" and "violence" produces a collision of incompatibles—a paradox that never completely dissolves.

"Rational violence" conjures up a cultural tradition in which violence perpetrated against women is not seen as abrogating reason. The Enlightenment maintained that reason prohibited violence against men and their property. Yet, until the late nineteenth century in the United States, a husband who beat his wife did nothing unlawful unless he used a rod thicker than his thumb. Belief in the compatibility of reason with violence against women has not entirely disappeared. In some circles, grabbing women's buttocks and pawing their breasts at professional social events is considered appropriate behavior (*New York Times*, June 14, 1992, Section 1, p. 1). Also, surveys show that many young men regard forcing a woman to have sex as unobjectionable if they have spent a lot of money on entertaining her (*New York Times*, August 29, 1989, Section C, p. 1). Violence is rational (or, at any rate, rationalized). Likewise, Benjamin gives the phrase "rational violence" a coherent technical meaning within her psychoanalytic account of sadomasochism—that is, the sadist's deliberate and subtle calibration of the pain inflicted on the masochist to suit the masochist's needs. Here, violence is neither contrary to reason in the sense of "out of control" nor contrary to reason in the sense of "disproportionate."

These ways of reconciling rationality with violence notwithstanding, it is impossible, finally, to see rationality and violence as genuinely compatible. Moreover, by introducing the concept of rational violence in the context of an analysis of the dark, convoluted logic of the Roissy dungeon and by associating gender with Sir Stephen's and O's consuming dementia, Benjamin intensifies the unsettling quality of her trope. Since rationality and violence are fundamentally antithetical, linking them to each other and then linking the pair to gender raises deep suspicions about gender.

Compare the statement, "Gender norms have been and continue to be detrimental to women, and they are not very good for men either," with the statement, "Gender is a system of rational violence." The former entirely misses the poignancy and the implacability of the harmfulness of gender, but Benjamin's oxymoron is compelling. Its form is apt. As femininity and masculinity are conventionally understood to be polar opposites, so an oxymoron brings together opposing concepts. Moreover, conjoining rationality with violence creates a compact, yet volatile trope that at once suggests both the intimacy in which women and men commonly live and the abiding discontents, sometimes torments, of many heterosexual relationships. In addition, the expression "rational violence" evokes cruelty and devastating injury at the same time as it implies effective adaptation and therefore sustainability. Thus, "rational violence" depicts gender as causing grievous harm that is so well concealed that it seems not to call for any remedy. Still, since "rational violence" is an irreducible and outrageous contradiction in terms, using this trope to represent gender holds out the hope that this needless contortion of human lives and relationships will be noticed and condemned and that change will ensue.

B. Nancy Chodorow: A Revalued Mother

Nancy Chodorow has done groundbreaking work reexamining and recasting motherhood from a feminist point of view. Like Benjamin, Chodorow enlists psychoanalysis to pursue her inquiry. Unlike Benjamin, however, Chodorow never condenses her line of thought into a signature figure of speech. Her rhetorical methods are more diffuse and more conventionally argumentative. Her ostensible aim is to get psychoanalytic theory right—to make it accurately represent the facts of psychic development (Chodorow, 1978, 40, 53; 1980, 5). Many skeptics, feminists and nonfeminists alike, consider this aim misguided (see Chapter 1, Section 3A). Still, it is clear that Chodorow's reconceiving and revaluing of motherhood warrant serious study. In what follows, I shall draw out the themes and turns of phrase that have made Chodorow a leading light among feminists who are engaged in resisting contempt for traditional feminine qualities and activities. Although I think that Chodorow's efforts to explain how women's desire to mother is reproduced lead her to reproduce a polarized view of gender in many passages of her work and that this side of her thought supplies ammunition to her critics (see Meyers, 1992, 138–141), I would urge that where the project of revaluing mothering comes to the fore she presents a more balanced and more attractive view of gender.

The title of Chodorow's first and most influential book, *The Reproduction of Mothering,* anticipates a major shift away from orthodox maternal imagery. Chodorow calls our attention to the activity of mothering, not to the status of motherhood. In verbalizing the more commonly nominal "mother," Chodorow begins to erode the passivity that Freud and others attribute to women's procreative role. Early in the text, Chodorow makes this reorientation explicit. She writes of mothering as something women typically want to do, as something they generally get gratification from doing, and as something they by and large succeed at doing (Chodorow, 1978, 7). These claims are obviously true. But to acknowledge their truth is to overturn some widespread, fundamental, and cherished assumptions about women and maternity. Chodorow is denying that women mother simply because they lack economic opportunities or other avenues of fulfillment; she is denying that mothering is tedious, unrewarding drudgery; she is denying that children always have grounds for reproaching their mothers. Mothering is no less compatible with human dignity than other projects people devote themselves to. Indeed, mothers make an indispensable social contribution that draws on valuable, though often misunderstood and maligned, feminine qualities.

Chodorow uses psychoanalysis to make a three-pronged case for revaluing motherhood in this way. Her reconstruction of the psychoanalytic developmental tale reconceptualizes motherhood, valorizes feminine capacities, and defends coparenting.

One of the most striking features of Chodorow's developmental story is the emphasis she places on the pre-Oedipal period, a period that Freud neglected. For Freud, nothing much happens in the pre-Oedipal phase since the emergence of sexual orientation and the emergence of gender identity are indissoluble and take place at the Oedipal stage. In contrast, Chodorow contends that the personality traits that constitute gender identity—for example, feminine nurturance and masculine independence—do not arise as a result of the Oedipus complex, but rather stem from the child's earlier relationship to the primary caregiver (Chodorow, 1978, 150–151). For Chodorow, the accomplishments of the pre-Oedipal period lay the foundation for the later establishment of sexual orientation in the Oedipal period. Whereas the father is the key figure and the consolidation of sexual orientation is the key issue in the Oedipal period, the mother is the key figure and the initiation into gender identity is the key issue in the pre-Oedipal period. Thus, to claim that psychoanalytic research should concentrate on the pre-Oedipal period is both to claim that the mother's importance has been vastly underestimated and also to call for a major theoretical revision to correct this error.

Chodorow's contribution to this revision is extensive and rich, but I shall give only a few salient details here. Setting aside Freud's claim that children are originally bisexual, Chodorow maintains that they are originally matrisexual—that their love fastens on the person who cares for them (Chodorow, 1978, 164). Likewise, denying that the sequencing of erogenous zones from oral through genital is biologically programmed, she attributes this progression to the primary caregiver's cues coupled with the child's need to sustain its relationship to this person (Chodorow, 1978, 48, 65). Libido follows a route indicated by mothers, not blind organic directives. Also, Chodorow rejects the view that the child's attachment to the mother rests primarily on elemental need fulfillment. Rather, it is the quality of the interaction between the mother and the child that emotionally bonds them (Chodorow, 1978, 72). As Chodorow presents it, then, the pre-Oedipal period is a time during which core features of the child's identity are taking shape and in which the mother is the center of the child's world. Moreover, the mother does not merely serve as an animate physical prop. Her interpersonal capacities are critical to the child's welfare.

The interpersonal capacities that enable mothers to care for children are central to Chodorow's account of femininity. Freud's shaming inventory of feminine traits—vanity, envy, moral inconstancy, and so forth—is supplanted by a positive characterization of femininity. For Chodorow, women have a "richer, ongoing inner world" and a "complex layering of affective ties;" they are "connected to the world;" they are "attune[d] to [others'] needs" (Chodorow, 1978, 169, 179, 198). Apart from wanting to mother, Chodorow's woman bears little resemblance to Freud's. To have a feminine identity is to be psychologically complex and responsive to other people. Gone is the woman trapped in her desolation and bitterness over her inferior genitals and consequently doomed to exhibit a host of petty vices. In her place, we find Chodorow's diagnosis of the pathology underlying the traditional negative construction of femininity that Freud retails.

Men's devaluation of women, claims Chodorow, is a defense that protects masculine identity (Chodorow, 1978, 182, 185). In the father-absent family with the mother in charge of childcare, boys can attain a masculine gender identity only through positional, as opposed to personal, identification (Chodorow, 1978, 175). They must reject the gender-inappropriate mothers to whom they have been attached and conform to a role and a set of standards that are transmitted by media images and by rules that peers pass along and hector one another into complying with. They have no loving and accessible masculine adult whose conduct and values they internalize. As a result, masculine identity is relatively superficial and precarious, and the possibility of backsliding into feminine identification poses a lingering threat. Despising the feminine in order to distance themselves from it, men buttress their masculine identity.

In Chodorow's telling, there is no courageous young hero mastering his impulses, overcoming his castration complex, and taking his place in the exalted and honorable society of men. We find instead a forlorn and lonely child deprived of emotional succor (Chodorow, 1978, 174). For Chodorow, people are social beings from the beginning, and they need human connection (Chodorow, 1978, 63). Thus, the self-reliant, self-assertive individualism that masculine norms prescribe exacts a terrible loss from boys and men. In contrast, girls are never obliged to break their connection with their mothers. Distinct identity is not only compatible with, but also is sustained by an intense relationship. Girls' affiliative needs are never suppressed, and feminine identity is expressed in the fulfillment of these needs. To a large extent, then, women's sense of self reflects relationships to other people. A collapsed or collapsing relationship ruptures individual identity, as well. Since people who are interpersonally defined are sensitive to others' needs and want to meet these needs, they are especially well equipped to care for children. The maternal self is a "self in relationship" (Chodorow, 1978, 73, 76–77, 169, 209).

As this string of citations suggests, the "self in relationship" is the mother's principal leitmotif in Chodorow's psychoanalytic narrative. Additionally, Chodorow peppers her text with assorted variants: "relational potential" (1978, 53, 166), "relational capacities" (1978, 51, 173, 200), "relational needs" (1978, 170, 199), "relational history" (1978, 200), the "relational sphere" (1978, 170), and so forth. In one respect, it is not the least bit surprising that relationship is a recurring theme in Chodorow's book. Since she is working in the object relations tradition, one expects her to focus on human relationships. Nevertheless, I would urge that there is more at stake here than Chodorow's commitment to a psychoanalytic school. In adopting the tenets of object relations theory, Chodorow adopts a discourse that accentuates the importance of human relationships and that demonstrates the value of these ties. Being inextricably connected to others is not a weakness or a drawback. It is an inescapable precondition for individuation and a source of lifelong satisfaction. When Chodorow rhetorically links motherhood to this value, then, she is subtly but firmly associating mothering with a pivotal and enduring human good.

While insisting on the importance of the mother-child relationship and underscoring the value of the self in relationship, Chodorow resists the temptation to inflate the mother's virtues and power. The alternative to denigrating mothering is not venerating it as a cure for all of our troubles. Chodorow affirms that women succeed at mothering. But the successful mother is not the "perfect" mother—the tireless mother who is always available to her child, whose empathic understanding of her child's needs never falters, and who happily subordinates her needs to her child's. These expectations do not stem from the exigencies of adequate primary care, but rather from "unprocessed, infantile fantasies about mothers" (Chodorow and Contratto, 1982, 63; also see Chodorow, 1978, 82; 1980, 7–8). Moreover, since no one could live up to this ideal, mothers will be blamed for most of the world's woes as long as this maternal mythology remains in currency. Injecting a salutary note of realism into her theorizing about maternity, Chodorow characterizes successful mothering as "good-enough mothering" and identifies "good-enough mothering" with raising a nonpsychotic child (Chodorow, 1978, 33, 85). Mothering need not be, nor should it be, a thankless task. Once the aims and methods of mothering are demystified, it is evident that most women who mother do it successfully.

So far, I have emphasized the ways in which Chodorow valorizes mothering, but it is important to recognize that she is aware of the risks associated with the feminine qualities that enable women to mother well. Nurturance and overidentification can elide. Though there is nothing inherently wrong with feminine qualities, Chodorow argues, certain institutional contexts can turn them into liabilities (Chodorow, 1978, 205).

For Chodorow, the institutional villain is exclusively female primary parenting in the nuclear family. This family structure enforces excessive continuity between mothers and their daughters, which jeopardizes women's autonomy, and it drives boys away from their primary caregivers, which perpetuates sexist attitudes among men (Chodorow, 1978, 212–213). Symbolically, femininity comes to represent dependency and nondifferentiation, while masculinity comes to represent freedom and independence (Chodorow, 1978, 121). On Chodorow's view, the only way out of this quagmire is to reorganize childcare, that is, to distribute childcare responsibilities equally between fathers and mothers (Chodorow, 1978, 215, 217–218).[4]

According to Chodorow, there is no insurmountable psychological obstacle to this redistribution (for related discussion, see Chapter 6,

Section 5). Men who have received good-enough care have at their disposal the basic resources needed to parent, though typically they have suppressed these capacities in order to establish masculine gender identity (Chodorow, 1978, 87–88). Also, some fathers who are not primary caregivers realize that they are missing out on much of the excitement and pleasure of having children and would welcome the opportunity to be more involved (Chodorow, 1978, 213). Furthermore, the interests of children argue for shared parenting. If fathers are to avoid passing relational impairments on to their sons, they need to participate fully in childcare (Chodorow, 1978, 196, 199). Both for their own sake and for the sake of future generations of men—not to mention women—fathers need to join in parenting. Mothering, concludes Chodorow, is a value for fathers, as well as for mothers.

Chodorow reshapes gender concepts by integrating them in a reformulated psychoanalytic narrative. In recasting the story of childhood development from a psychoanalytic feminist perspective, she furnishes a countericonography for Freud's mythic figures—the Oedipal father, the phallic mother, etc. But her countericonography is conceived in an altogether different register. Instead of a pantheon of awe-inspiring parental protagonists, Chodorow presents a medley of humanizing leitmotifs—the self in relationship and its variants. Similarly, instead of the dramatic spectacle of the castration complex and its resolution, Chodorow describes some patterns of family interaction and the meanings attaching to them. Taking exception to Freud's theory as she proceeds and periodically noting the adverse social consequences of embracing the gender status quo, Chodorow patiently and incrementally builds up a positive image of maternity that is profoundly at odds with the diametric views of motherhood that have dominated Western culture. Chodorow jettisons both the saccharine glorification of the self-sacrificing mother and the contemptuous dismissal of the degraded biological vessel that reproduces the species but stands outside of culture. Her alternative celebrates the loving attention that "good-enough" mothers bestow on their children as a paradigm of human connection. In so doing, she redeems maternity without resorting to falsifying idealization.

C. Julia Kristeva: The Degendered Father of Prehistory

Julia Kristeva is best known among U.S. feminists for her essays on motherhood and feminist politics, "Stabat Mater" and "Women's Time" (Kristeva, 1986; 1987a; for related discussion, see Chapter 5,

Section 1). However, in an essay that does not explicitly address feminist issues, "Freud and Love: Treatment and Its Discontents," she elaborates a basic psychoanalytic doctrine along lines that feminists should find congenial. Broadly, Kristeva's topic is the question of how a distinct ego begins to form, that is, how the process of coming to see oneself as a separate individual is initiated. In the course of examining Freud's views on this question, she confronts and subverts key elements of prevailing gender stereotypes, and she reassesses the metatheoretical status of the gendered figures who people the psychoanalytic narrative.

She starts from Freud's assumption that infants are cognitively and emotionally fused with their mothers and his hypothesis that a male figure must obtrude itself into the mother-child dyad in order to give the child a distinct object to identify with and therefore a means of feeling separate from the mother (Kristeva, 1987a, 26). For Freud, Kristeva notes, the figure who occasions the child's first movement out of the maternal orbit and who serves as the object of primary identification is the "father in individual prehistory" (Kristeva, 1987a, 26). But, Kristeva tartly remarks, this is a "strange father if there ever was one," since Freud holds that the infant has no awareness of sexual difference at this stage (Kristeva, 1987a, 26). She then offers an alternative characterization of this figure—this Imaginary Father. The object of primary identification is none other than "both parents," and, as such, it is not consistently gendered (Kristeva, 1987a, 26). Thus, Kristeva assigns this powerful figure a gender-neutral, yet awesome tag—the "Third Party" (Kristeva, 1987a, 33–34).

Still, if the object of primary identification is a parental unit, it remains to be asked what it is about this figure that provides the impetus for differentiation. Kristeva takes up the question from three points of view, and her comments about good mothering compass all of them. She stresses the importance of having a caregiver who distinguishes herself from her child by loving someone besides her child and by talking to someone else about her child (Kristeva, 1987a, 34). First, then, the Third Party is someone whom the mother desires—someone else, no definite person, maybe the father, but certainly "not I" (Kristeva, 1987a, 41). Likewise, the Third Party is someone whom the mother discusses. Identifying with the Third Party under these guises gives the infant the possibility of becoming distinct as an object of someone's desire and as the subject of others' conversation. But then Kristeva shifts away from this idea of an unknown Third Party in the shadows and focuses on the maternal figure herself. The Third Party is also the "maternal desire for the Phallus" or the "coagulation of the mother and her desire" (Kristeva, 1987a, 40–41). To be a subject, it is not enough to be someone who can be desired; one must be someone who can desire. Finally, Kristeva emphasizes that, in speaking about her child, the mother represents language. To be a subject, it is not enough to be someone who can be discussed; one must be someone who can speak—a "subject of enunciation" (Kristeva, 1987a, 26).

Evidently, the maternal figure can represent desiring and speaking as well as the paternal figure can, and the paternal figure can represent being desired as well as the maternal figure can. Still, Kristeva does not eschew formulating the object of primary identification as a parental unit—the "father-mother conglomerate," as she now calls it (Kristeva, 1987a, 40). Indeed, it is in virtue of being "endowed with the sexual attributes of both parents" that this figure exerts its irresistible attraction (Kristeva, 1987a, 33). Nor does she dismiss the Imaginary Father, though she does deny that this paternal figure is identical to the fearsome, law-giving, punishment-inflicting father of the Oedipal period (Kristeva, 1987a, 30–31, 41, 46). Quite the contrary, the father of individual prehistory is a glowingly loving figure that embodies a seldom acknowledged masculine modality. Her Imaginary Father is reminiscent, not of Michelangelo's virile David or his stern Moses, but rather of the statues of magnetic, yet gracious and smiling male figures that have survived from archaic Greek and Etruscan art.

Feminine, masculine, and parental images are layered and interwoven in Kristeva's exposition. One variant is never decisively rejected in favor of another; no variant is ever decisively affirmed to the exclusion of another. What does Kristeva accomplish?

From a feminist viewpoint, Kristeva's representation of the object of primary identification as simultaneously masculine, bigendered, reverse gendered, and nongendered scrambles standard gender symbolism in three important ways. First, it undercuts the myth of the archaic mother—a mother with whom the infant is fused in a conflict-free relationship, but whose tremendous power is frightening. If the mother is a desiring being, she wants something beyond herself and must be incomplete. Thus, the totalizing figure of the self-sufficient Phallic mother does not exhaust the personae of the maternal figure in the pre-Oedipal period (also see Kristeva, 1986, 204–205). Second, it supplies an image of the mother as an independent source of desire—as someone who has a desire for another and whose desire the child needs in order to achieve a separate identity. The maternal figure ceases to be a doting barrier to individuation; it becomes a self-defining and other-defining agent. Finally, the paternal figure is stripped of the role of the liberator coming from afar and arriving in the nick of time; instead, it assumes the mien of the loving father who beams with tenderness and pride.

In addition, Kristeva severs gendered psychoanalytic imagery from real mothers and fathers. She writes of the "imaginary mother" and the "imaginary father," of the maternal and paternal "figures," and of the maternal and paternal "positions" and "functions" (Kristeva, 1987a, 22, 29, 33, 41, 46). It would be a mistake, then, to read Kristeva as generalizing about the roles that actual mothers and fathers play in their children's development or as recommending that appropriately sexed parents enact the gendered imagery she sets forth. In fact, she allows that the developmental process need not be played out entirely within the family; social agencies might serve as alternative sites of developmental movement (Kristeva, 1987a, 46; also see Kristeva, 1988, 139–140). But if Kristeva is not writing a script for parents to follow, what is her project? She is defending the therapeutic strategy of assuming both the "maternal" and the "paternal" functions vis-à-vis the analysand and of interpreting clinical discourse from the standpoint of the first awakening of the capacity to love (Kristeva, 1987a, 28–29). Thus, Kristeva extricates mothers and fathers from the confines of gender norms at the same time as she destabilizes the norms themselves.

D. Luce Irigaray: Two Lips and Women's Desire

Gender, as we know it, is a system of inequality in which masculinity is regarded as superior to femininity. In Simone de Beauvoir's terse summation, "He is the Subject, he is the Absolute — she is the Other" (de Beauvoir, 1989, xxviii). In classical psychoanalysis, the preeminence of the masculine is evidenced by the derivative status of women's desire (see Section 1 above). Generations of psychoanalytic feminists have protested that this exceedingly narrow view of feminine eroticism is merely a projection of masculine eroticism (most recently, Irigaray, 1985a, 22, 31–32, 54, 103). It reveals a great deal more about what Freud wants women to want than it does about

2. Feminist Refigurations of Gender / 87

women's pleasure, and it denies sexual difference by reducing women's sexual economy to an insipid reflection of men's.

Many psychoanalytic feminists have sought to accord women's desire equal standing and to fill the vacuum left by Freud's negation of women's desire. Jessica Benjamin rejects Freud's genital figuration of desire and sketches a spatial interpretation of women's eroticism (Benjamin, 1988, 124–130). Julia Kristeva complains of Freud's obtuseness about motherhood and offers a poetic evocation of her own satisfactions and anxieties in giving birth to and caring for her baby (Kristeva, 1987a, 234–263). In this section, however, I shall concentrate on Luce Irigaray's widely discussed image of two lips. Irigaray's image is both a striking extension of and a concerted rebellion against the classical psychoanalytic view of women's desire and relations between women, for it follows Freud in invoking genital imagery yet discards Freud's legacy of biologism and misogyny.

In "This Sex Which Is Not One" and "When Our Lips Speak Together," Irigaray explores the implications of taking the anatomy of lips as a controlling image for women's psychic economy. Women have two lips in two senses—two pairs of lips, the mouth and the vulva, with each pair consisting of two lips. Irigaray takes advantage of the first of these ambiguities to interweave linguistic issues and sexual issues. Since lips are organs of speech and emotional expression as well as sex organs, they represent human intercourse in the broadest sense. Moreover, playing on the relationships between the two lips that make up each pair of lips and between these constitutive lips and the pairs of lips they constitute, her commentaries on touching and counting articulate a utopian vision of relations among women.

Lips baffle counting, for, as Irigaray remarks, they are "neither one nor two" (Irigaray, 1985b, 24, 26, 207, 218). One pair of lips consists of two distinct but inseparable lips. Any counting principle that captures the composite misses the components, and vice versa. Still, they are all lips. Since lips defy individuation by enumeration, Irigaray uses this trope to represent the confounding inexhaustibility she attributes to women's sexuality and to women's speech.

Irigaray denies that women's sexuality must have a single focus—either vaginal or clitoral, as Freud supposed, but not both. On the contrary, she asserts that the sites of women's erotic pleasure are manifold, for virtually the entire female body is erotically attuned (Irigaray, 1985b, 28). Plainly, then, Irigaray's image of two lips is not a prescription for a preferred feminine sexual modality (Irigaray,

1991, 97). Rather, it symbolizes the inapplicability of such prescriptions to women's sexuality—that is, a refusal of such prescriptions.

Likewise, Irigaray insists that women's speech is a pluralistic conversation among many subjects voicing many points of view (Irigaray, 1985b, 209). Though she claims that women urgently need to engage in a collective project of self-definition, she holds that this discussion cannot proceed by linear argument and must never settle on a definitive truth (Irigaray, 1985b, 29, 208, 214–218). As lips cannot be counted coherently, so conversations among women should not be accountable to masculine standards of consistency and conclusiveness. They should range freely, picking up serendipitous leads and dropping false starts, and they should remain permanently unfinished.

Again, lips resist counting since no single scheme of individuation suits them. Thus, they provide an apt image not only for states of affairs and processes that confound demands for unity, clarity, and closure, but also for a form of relationship that does not presuppose sharp distinctions between persons. Irigaray's treatment of touching draws out the implications of the image of women's two lips with regard to interpersonal relationships.

Lips, Irigaray often reminds us, constantly and unavoidably touch one another (Irigaray, 1985b, 24, 26, 206, 208, 209, 211). Neither held apart nor pressed together, they touch. Whereas the masculine sexual economy privileges sight, the feminine sexual economy privileges touch (Irigaray, 1985b, 26). Moreover, in contrast to the lone male sex organ, the lips of the vulva touch inevitably and innocently (Irigaray, 1985b, 24, 211). This unobtrusive, unwilled feminine auto-eroticism cannot be forbidden. Thus, the trope of two lips touching is antithetical to relationships founded on rules, shame, and control (Irigaray, 1985b, 217). But what is the alternative to castration anxiety and the reign of the superego?

Consider further the touching of two lips. Though different, two lips that touch are inseparable and the same. They are different lips, but they are parts of a single pair of lips. Also, they are different lips, but they are both lips. Irigaray takes the touching of lips as a metaphor both for mother-daughter individuation and also for relations between women.

Traditional psychoanalytic theory echoes Hegel and assumes the need to define oneself against a different other who is seen as a threat and therefore comes to be feared and hated. For the boy, the mother serves as the other. But, if the mother is the exclusive caregiver, no different other is available to the girl, and, consequently, she has trouble individuating. Irigaray invokes the image of two lips touching to exorcise the demon of the master-slave dialectic and to vitalize the mother-daughter relationship. If the other is within—one of a pair of lips—and if the other is like the self—another lip—the tension needed to establish coherent subjectivity is set up, but the hostility toward the other and the defensive desire to subjugate the other are eliminated (Irigaray, 1985b, 30–31; also see 1991, 50). For Irigaray, the lips represent the mother-daughter dyad as well as the daughter's primordial psychic striation.[5] But these contiguities are not rendered as inert geometry. The touching of the lips as they open and close animates the image. Thus, the two lips touching symbolize the daughter's receptivity to differentiation (despite her antipathy to separation) and also the gentle dynamic of mother-daughter differentiation that complements the daughter's predisposition (also see Irigaray's vision of a mother and daughter playing a gentle game of catch with images of one another, Irigaray, 1981, 61–62; and her call for maternal genealogies 1985a, 76; 1993a, 15–22).

Extending her image to relations among women generally, Irigaray revisions reciprocity. When two lips come together, it is impossible to tell which is touching and which is being touched (Irigaray, 1985b, 26). Symmetrically situated, there is no agent or patient—"I/you touch you/me" (Irigaray, 1985b, 209). Moreover, that two lips, two things of the same kind, are touching implies an identity between that which touches and that which is touched (Irigaray, 1985b, 206). If this identity obtains, one's intimate is so close—so like oneself—that one cannot treat her as an object or as something to possess (Irigaray, 1985b, 31). If other women cannot be commodified in this way, relationships between women cannot intelligibly be modeled on market transactions. No one can make a gift of herself, no one can incur emotional debts, and no one can get the better of anyone else (Irigaray, 1985b, 206). Domination and subordination are ruled out (Irigaray, 1985b, 209). Still, exchange remains (Irigaray, 1985b, 213). But exchange is not conceived on the model of trade. Exchange is conceived on the model of lips touching. Countering the traditional portrayal of women as jealous of one another and competing to attract men, Irigaray proposes an image of mutual responsiveness between women who are simultaneously moving and being moved.

Much more could be said about the themes Irigaray elaborates through the image of two lips. Also, many commentators have located her work in the history of psychoanalytic theory and have offered provocative metatheoretical interpretations of her imagery. However, I shall not attempt to recapitulate this extensive literature here (for a survey of this literature and for Margaret Whitford's own illuminating interpretation, see Whitford, 1991, 171–182). In view of my present purposes, I shall limit myself to sketching a defense of Irigaray's overall theoretical strategy.

Despite Irigaray's professed feminism, it would be easy to read her as a fundamentally unreconstructed disciple of Freud. On this view, Irigaray, like Freud, seeks to legislate feminine sexuality and feminine psychology on the basis of female anatomy. Yet, since Irigaray explicitly disavows this position, no charitable reading of her work can saddle her with it (Irigaray, 1991, 97). In this connection, Margaret Whitford's account of Irigaray's project furnishes an invaluable corrective to essentialist readings.

Whitford maintains that the paradigm for Irigaray's theoretical program is the psychoanalytic clinical intervention (Whitford, 1991, 31, 35–36). As the analyst presents figurative interpretations of the analysand's speech with the aim of propelling the analysand out of stultifying patterns of thought and action, so Irigaray's essays interpret cultural materials in ways designed to disrupt entrenched beliefs and practices and to intimate a more humane and more just social order. Viewed this way, Irigaray is not advancing definitive theses about women. Rather, she is participating in the process of social therapy that Iris Young advocates (Young, 1990, 153). As a feminist, she is concerned with gender, and her contributions center on the ways in which gender is culturally encoded—specifically, on the denial of women's subjectivity (Whitford, 1991, 43, 49). But Irigaray does not confine herself to critiquing existing gender norms. She seeks to figuratively anticipate the form women's subjectivity and relationships might assume in a postpatriarchal future.

If this is correct, it is a mistake to interpret Irigaray's trope of two lips as postulating or mandating the true form of women's sexuality and the true nature of women's relationships. On the contrary, it is offered in a provisional spirit. It provides an alternative to prevailing figurations of women's sexuality and women's relationships, and, as Irigaray's texts demonstrate, it is a trope that repays exploration. However, it is not offered as a canonical gynocentric image to supplant phallocentric ones, nor is it offered as a depiction of the suppressed truth of women's lives today. It is one psychoanalytic feminist's contribution to a collective and, presumably, never-ending conversation in which women aspire together to reconstruct femininity on their own terms.

3. The Positivist Worry about Dissident Speech

The mythic chronicles of the emergence of gendered subjectivity that psychoanalytic feminists proffer draw readers into narratives composed of what Laura Mulvey has termed "reverie-generating images" (Mulvey, 1989, 133–134).[6] By different means, Benjamin, Chodorow, Kristeva, and Irigaray seek to release their readers' imaginations from the confines of orthodox gender concepts and to arouse speculation about alternative understandings of women, men, and their relations. Benjamin's oxymoron, "rational violence," represents gender as a sinister clash that sharply contrasts with familiar images of male-female complementarity. Chodorow's leitmotif, "the self in relationship," gently, but tenaciously pries one away from the standard androcentric individualist paradigm of identity. In juxtaposing fantasy and irreality with masculinity and authority, Kristeva's figure, "the imaginary father," disappoints one's settled expectations about gender and obliges one to reconsider the meaning of paternity. As one ponders Irigaray's metonym, "women's two lips," from different angles, intriguing interpretations of femininity rapidly multiply, and these interpretations afford opportunities to chart fresh approaches to human relations.

The project of recounting the human life story in emblematic, emotionally charged terms imbues psychoanalytic feminist narratives with the gravity and scope of myth, and the exoticism of these counterfigurations intrudes on and upsets ingrained thought patterns. Yet, none of these tropes is overly prescriptive. Suggestive, yet open-ended, they invite readers to indulge their fantasies and to entertain novel possibilities that may at first seem farfetched.

But the very features of psychoanalytic feminism that free the imagination and prompt fresh thinking about gender raise questions about the epistemological status of dissident speech. It is undeniable that not all established cultural imagery is invidious; some is worth preserving. Moreover, it is plain that figurative narrative can be abused. Hitler traded in iconic figures woven into a mythic narrative, as did Social Darwinism. Consequently, those who place a premium on addressing moral controversies in straightforward, unambiguous terms may accuse psychoanalytic feminists and other advocates of feminist dissident speech of muddying otherwise lucid debate by relying on figurative language and other literary devices to advance their views.

From this standpoint, dissident speech is open to two major objections: (1) that it leads to no firm conclusion and leaves important moral questions unsettled and (2) that it is relativistic. With regard to the first objection, I have argued that standard methods of argument have little, if any, impact on culturally normative prejudice (see Chapter 3, Section 3). Thus, the indefiniteness of dissident speech is not a vice; its ambiguities enable it to effectively disrupt accustomed patterns of thought and feeling regarding marginalized social groups. Inadvertently bigoted clarity is no virtue. Still, it might be objected that there is no way of assessing the relative merits of the alternative figurations that dissident speech generates. *Chacun à son gout.* Moral judgment collapses into the allures of rhetoric. This is a more troubling objection. Thus, it is necessary to ask whether there is anything suspect about the appeal of psychoanalytic feminist discourse or, in other words, whether emancipatory uses of figurative language can be distinguished from repressive ones. I shall take up this question in Chapter 5.

5

Dissident Speech: Figuration and the Politicization of Moral Perception

Kathryn Pyne Addelson understands impasses between backers of established cultural values and norms and opponents of these conventions as revolutionary moments, and she likens moral revolution to the paradigm shifts that Thomas Kuhn invoked to explain scientific revolutions. Moral revolutionaries, such as the proponents of women's suffrage, can call for change, but they cannot justify the changes they advocate because the vision of social relations they are advancing is incommensurable with accepted principles and accepted interpretations of those principles (Addelson, 1991, 21–24). For Addelson, then, moral revolutionaries must create values by recreating themselves (Addelson, 1991, 29–31). They must conceive anew what it is to be a person, and their judgments of value and their choices must be filtered through that conception.

Addelson is right not to underestimate the profundity and the difficulty of transforming moral perception. To transform moral perception of socially excluded groups, nothing less than the reconstitution of the social identity of these groups is required. I think, however, that her view of moral justification is unduly narrow. Apparently, Addelson subscribes to what Margaret Walker calls the "theoretical-juridical model" of moral theory (M. Walker, 1992, 28). Stressing codification and application of general principles, this model certifies a proposition as morally justified if it can be deduced from an accepted action-guiding principle or set of principles in conjunction with noncontroversial interpretations of relevant facts. Although this model of moral justification is widely accepted, it plainly is not a model that can accommodate justification in the context of radical moral innovation. Yet, it is never more important to be able to defend one's views—both to reassure oneself of the wisdom of one's opposition and also to convince others—than when one is seeking to overturn culturally normative prejudice. Indeed, Addelson herself speaks of the role of human need in shaping facts and the role of reconstituted facts in shaping moral theory (Addelson, 1991, 26). In this chapter, I shall pursue this line of thought in order to develop an account of the justification of dissident speech.

Julia Kristeva offers a maternal account of dissident speakers, and Martha Nussbaum offers an account of the role of imagery in moral judgment that draws on Henry James's depiction of a father-daughter relationship in *The Golden Bowl*. Although I find their views flawed in some respects, they provide a useful point of departure, for both of them recognize that emotional ties serve as catalysts for dissident speech, and both of them recognize the need for a basis for deciding whether a novel figuration should replace an established one. I argue, however, that their accounts are too apolitical and that dissident speech is inseparable from politics in two respects. First, with respect to the production and justification of dissident speech, I maintain that socially excluded groups must band together to refigure their respective social identities and to judge whether the quality of social relations improves when conducted through a novel figuration. Intimations of unrecognized and unmet interpersonal and material needs prompt critical moral reflection. Whether a novel figuration is emancipatory depends on whether it facilitates the recognition and satisfaction of such needs for the members of socially excluded groups. Second, with respect to the dissemination of emancipatory counterfigurations, I urge that dissident speech cannot succeed alone. Without complementary social and economic gains, dissident speech is unlikely to capture the popular imagination. But, without dissident speech, social and economic gains are unlikely to dislodge prejudice. Thus, dissident speech must be integrated in a comprehensive political struggle.

If my account of dissident speech is correct, it raises provocative questions about the nature and practice of philosophy itself—that is, what counts as philosophical inquiry. If the dilemma of difference falls within the purview of normative moral philosophy, and if dissident speech is necessary to address the dilemma of difference, it is incumbent on us to rethink what should be classified as pre- or extraphilosophical. Figurations, it seems, are more central to philosophy than is generally supposed, and doing philosophy is a more social and democratic activity than is generally supposed.

1. Women as Dissidents: Kristeva's View

There are a number of ways in which the project of dissident speech could go awry. Dissident speech could be tied too tightly to psychoanalytic interpretive schemas or to psychoanalytic therapy. Thus, I want to emphasize that one need not embrace a psychoanalytic theory of gender—that is, one need not relinquish one's skepticism about penis envy or the Oedipus complex—to appreciate the role of repressed desire in motivating social dissent and the potential of dissident speech to enrich moral reflection. Almost from the inception of psychoanalysis, its adherents have been generating variants, and these variants are perennially and often stridently contested. In calling attention to the way in which nonconscious materials subvert moral reflection, I am not endorsing any of these interpretive systems. Nor, for that matter, am I advocating universal psychoanalytic therapy or pop autoanalysis. A privatized and elitist conception of dissidence must be resisted.

Aiming to circumvent these very problems, Julia Kristeva gives an account of women as dissidents. For Kristeva, mothers epitomize the "questionable subject-in-process"—a subject that is responsive to the encroachments of heterogeneous unconscious material into conscious life and hence a subject that lacks a fixed or unitary identity and that regards coherent subjectivity as a provisional illusion (Kristeva, 1980, 135–137; 1987a, 380; 1987b, 9). Describing the confusion of identities she associates with pregnancy as an "institutionalized form of psychosis" and the responsibilities and emotions that accompany maternity as a "bridge between singularity and ethics," Kristeva regards mothers paradoxically as "the guarantee and a threat to its [society's] stability" (Kristeva, 1986, 297; also see 1980, 146).[1] The threat to social stability stems from the fusion experiences some mothers report in tandem with the experience of gradual separation from the developing child, for these processes decenter the self (Kristeva, 1986, 167–168, 173, 179). In such cases, the indissoluble attachment the mother feels for her child throws the bounds of her identity into doubt, and this destabilization makes her receptive to long-sub-merged memories of her own childhood connection to her mother (Kristeva, 1986, 172). According to Kristeva, the destabilization brought on by maternity constitutes a challenge to the unified rational subject and to standard cultural images of gender that conjoin femininity with submissiveness. Thus, in her view, mothers are dissidents, and they are in a position to pose a profound challenge to the political and economic status quo (Kristeva, 1986, 156, 206).

At this point, it is important to consider the dimension of maternity that Kristeva counts on to secure social stability. It is a psychoanalytic axiom that the potentially convulsive process of releasing unconscious materials from repression must be mediated and contained. In the case of the mother, her very love for her child and her concern for its welfare constitute a built-in barrier against the wild propensities of the unconscious and therefore a bulwark against extremism. The mother's preservative orientation secures her commitment to society (Kristeva, 1986, 185). Since the destabilizations of motherhood motivate social criticism, but since the responsibilities of maternity counteract the hostile potentialities of its destabilizations, mothers and women who want to be mothers can be relied on to be provocative, but not crazed dissidents.

By alternating between the exigencies of politics and the replenishing reservoir of the unconscious, Kristeva holds, women can avoid the trap of losing themselves in somebody else's values and institutions or of retreating into bitter reverse sexism and separatism. Unfortunately, Kristeva's account of oppositional capacities generates distinctive problems that snare her in a resuscitation of the cultural stereotype of women as self-sacrificial mothers (for related discussion of Kristeva's views, see Gallop, 1982, 115–131; Rose, 1986, 158–160; Stanton, 1986, 160–161, 171; Nye, 1987, 674–681; Fraser, 1992, 187–188). For Kristeva, the anarchic forces of the unconscious endow people with an inexhaustible store of oppositional potential. Moreover, neither established cultural values nor rational procedures can validate opposition since such values and procedures uphold the status quo. Thus, to prevent social criticism from devolving into opposition for the sake of opposition, Kristeva needs a way of differentiating between legitimate demands and mad clamor. To demarcate the class of legitimate demands, Kristeva introduces the mother's devotion to her child and resistance to any change that might jeopardize her child's future. Because of their inherent conservatism, mothers can be trusted to confine their initiatives to reasonable proportions.

Kristeva heralds the "demassification" of gender difference through the discovery of each woman's "singularity" (Kristeva, 1986, 295). In this connection, she advocates attending to the "multiplicity of female expressions and preoccupations" and "listen[ing], more carefully than ever, to what mothers are saying today" (Kristeva, 1986, 193, 179). For Kristeva, women's speech must be deciphered without regard for orthodox interpretations of gender. Ultimately, she claims, gender difference is nothing but the intersections among these individual revelations (Kristeva, 1986, 193).

Despite her call for the demassification of gender difference, Kristeva's account of women as dissidents *re*massifies difference by invoking a shopworn, but unrealistic image of motherhood. Women's singularity dissolves into a stipulative theory of the feminine. The "real *fundamental difference* between the two sexes" (Kristeva, 1986, 193) proves to be none other than sentimentalized motherhood. It would seem, then, that singularity is reduced to pathology—a distinctive feminine unconscious is just one that has been driven from the track of normal development that leads to sublimation through maternity. If Kristeva's view does not imply that only mothers or maternally inclined women are qualified to press their political demands, thereby establishing a hierarchy among women in which mothers outrank the rest, it implies that all women are intrinsically mothers or maternally inclined, regardless of their professed desires. The former claim reinstates Freud's vision of mature femininity in the guise of reverse elitism; the latter imposes an essentialist account of femininity that Freud would not quarrel with. Yet, Kristeva herself expressly repudiates both reverse sexism and essentialism (Kristeva, 1986, 161, 202–204).

Now, it might be urged that Kristeva is not committed to the claim that being a mother or wanting to be one is necessary in order to access the unconscious while limiting the demands one makes on the basis of that experience. If this is so, Kristeva might be read as proposing motherhood, not as a condition that must be met, but as a paradigm for the type of constrained commerce with the unconscious that she is recommending. Admittedly, Kristeva holds that there are other ways to explore the unconscious and to defuse its explosive power—psychoanalytic therapy is prime among them. Nevertheless, it seems to me that her psychoanalytic approach dictates a more literal reading of her position.

Not only does Kristeva explicitly advocate inquiring into the unconscious desires of mothers and giving motherly women a voice in ethical thought, but also the peculiar problem of distinguishing warranted social criticism from psychotic babbling or totalitarian diatribe that her view poses cannot be solved by a maternal paradigm, as opposed to mothers. Kristeva undertakes to explain how one can criticize patriarchal norms without altogether losing one's moorings. Mainstream psychoanalysis assigns the superego the task of certifying acceptable conduct and condemning unacceptable conduct. But, since the superego is the repository of socially transmitted values and standards, it enforces socially sanctioned repression. Thus, Kristeva needs a functional equivalent for Freud's superego that will not merely echo patriarchal values, and, as the feminine counterpart of the superego, she nominates the nonviolent, caring dispositions of mothers. But, just as it is people who actually have a well-developed superego who can be trusted to exercise control over their behavior, so it is people who have actually developed the dispositions of maternal solicitude who can safely contest social conventions. Neither a superego *paradigm* nor a maternal *paradigm* will prevent people from running amuck. To tame the sinister, turbulent forces of destruction that she ascribes to the unconscious, Kristeva revives the sentimental ideal of beatific maternal devotion.

Plainly, feminists should resist Kristeva's account of women's dissident speech. Still, I think feminists should not reject dissident speech, nor should they reject all of the features of Kristeva's account. Her coupling of retrograde imagery of women with a privatized, apolitical approach warrants feminist suspicion. Nevertheless, her account has two significant virtues: (1) she grounds dissident speech in loving connection to another, and (2) she detaches dissident speech from aesthetic and moral conventions. I shall return to these themes in the discussion that follows.

2. Love, Beauty, and Obligation: Nussbaum's Account of Moral Figuration

In the context of a discussion of Henry James's depiction of Maggie's separation from her father, Adam, in *The Golden Bowl*,

Martha Nussbaum outlines a view of moral reflection in which figuration plays a pivotal role. Picking up the story at the point where it has become clear that Maggie's love for and intimacy with her father, Adam, obstructs her flourishing as an adult woman, Nussbaum maintains that it is only when Adam and Maggie refigure one another and their relationship that they are able to give one another up. Adam comes to see his daughter as a "creature floating and shining in a warm summer sea, some element of dazzling sapphire and silver, a creature cradled upon depths, buoyant among dangers, in which fear or folly or sinking otherwise than in play was impossible" (Nussbaum, 1990, 150–151). Maggie comes to see her father as a "great and deep and high little man" (Nussbaum, 1990, 152–153). Seeing Maggie as capable and independent, Adam trusts her to go her own way. Seeing Adam as retaining his dignity despite his limitations, Maggie can guiltlessly turn her attention to her marriage. Moreover, in sharing an image of the changes taking place in their lives—their "crossing the bar" and their "having to beat against the wind" to reach the open sea—they come to inhabit the same moral world (Nussbaum, 1990, 153). There is a convergence of moral perception.

Nussbaum stresses two points about the role of imagery in moral reflection. First, the imagery through which Maggie and Adam make their moral choices is right and beautiful imagery (Nussbaum, 1990, 152; on the importance of aesthetic qualities in psychoanalytic clinical interpretation, see Spence, 1982, 268–270). It is apt, and its beauty testifies to the fineness of their moral sensibilities. Second, their act of mutual renunciation—renunciation without abandonment or betrayal—is accomplished through imagery (Nussbaum, 1990, 151). In refiguring one another and themselves together, they find their morally best course, and they do what they need to do. Action is inseparable from perception, and perception is inseparable from figuration. For Nussbaum, not only is conceiving new imagery often necessary to recognizing the best course of action, but also finding the right imagery through which to see another person is a morally valuable achievement in itself.

But what is the source of this imagery? According to Nussbaum, love is the emotional crucible in which Maggie and Adam are able to revision one another (Nussbaum, 1990, 157, 160). Their love for one another moves them to create new imagery, and the images they create are loving images. Yet, Nussbaum denies that emotion is their sole guide. Their figurative improvisation is constrained by "standing obligations"—parental and filial duties (Nussbaum, 1990, 155–156). For Nussbaum, "perception without responsibility is dangerously free-floating, even as duty without perception is blunt and blind" (Nussbaum, 1990, 155). The right imagery cannot do violence to fundamental values and principles.

Nussbaum's account is ground-breaking and helpful, but I doubt that it can be transferred whole to the problem of unjust social exclusion and culturally normative prejudice. First, it would be naive to count on the prejudiced to love the socially excluded or, for that matter, to exhibit what Nussbaum calls "civic love"—that is, love for one's country—in a way that neutralizes their fear and hatred of the targets of their prejudice. Indeed, it would be unduly optimistic to assume that the members of socially excluded groups are able to identify with one another in a loving way, for pervasive negative imagery discourages such mutual identification. Second, Nussbaum's requirement that novel imagery be beautiful and also compatible with standing obligations could easily strengthen reactionary positions. Therefore, with the special problems associated with the dilemma of difference in mind, I shall suggest some modifications of Nussbaum's views.

3. Politicizing Love: Solidarity and Dissident Speech

Nussbaum and Kristeva posit love as the emotional background for political, as well as moral, reflection (Nussbaum, 1990, 207, 210; Kristeva, 1986, 185). While I think they are right to highlight the role of emotional connection in moral reflection, I shall urge that a distinctively political form of love, namely, solidarity, is indispensable to addressing culturally normative prejudice and the dilemma of difference.

"[H]erethics," declares Kristeva, "is undeath, love" (Kristeva, 1986, 185; for further discussion of "herethics," see Chapter 3, Section 4). It is "one open system [subject] connected to another" with the result that each subject is emancipated from the grip of repression and renewed through this "destabilizing-stabilizing" emotional bond (Kristeva, 1987a, 15, 274–275). Kristeva observes: "If it lives, your psyche is in love. If it is not in love, it is dead" (Kristeva, 1987a, 15). Psychoanalysis regards love relationships as the condition for perpetual rejuvenation and therefore as the model of optimal psychic functioning (Kristeva, 1987a, 14). In psychoanalysis, transference love collaborates with free association to rouse "desire-noise"—the residue of one's earliest, now repressed drives and identifications (Kristeva, 1987a, 15). Desire-noise can be articulated through, but can also challenge "memory-consciousness"—the conscious, too often calcified systematization of one's experience (Kristeva, 1987a, 15–16). Within the structure of psychoanalytic interaction, this encounter between conscious understandings and unconscious forces yields fresh metaphorical articulations and provides an ongoing occasion for interpretation and reinterpretation of these metaphors (Kristeva, 1987a, 276; 1987b, 7). This process activates the individual's creative powers, especially imagination, and initiates a "true process of self-organization" (Kristeva, 1987a, 14, 15–16, 276, 381). The aim is not to grasp a truth, but to "provoke a rebirth"—to release the individual from emptiness, stagnation, and isolation (Kristeva, 1987a, 381). In dissident speech (or "herethics"), the insights of psychoanalytic theory are transposed to the political sphere (Kristeva, 1986, 210–211). Love combines forces with imagination to refigure the experience of women and thus to attack culturally normative prejudice regarding women.

If one is describing the ideal moral subject, Nussbaum's and Kristeva's views about love seem reasonable. However, concerned as I am to consider the far from perfect moral subjects that most of us actually are, I believe it is necessary to provide a less exigent account of the emotional sources of dissident speech. Where there is unconscious prejudice, either there is no love to inform dissident speech, or love is so warped and the individual so deceived about his or her true feelings that emotion poses a formidable obstacle to insightful moral reflection (for an account of culturally normative prejudice, see Chapter 3, Section 3). Furthermore, it is important to bear in mind that the effects of negative cultural imagery are not confined to the prejudices of members of the dominant group. Since members of socially excluded groups also internalize prevalent cultural imagery and the attitudes the imagery expresses, their ability to love one another may be impaired, as well.

Unlike Kristeva and Nussbaum, Maria Lugones politicizes her discussion of love by locating it in the context of relations between women whose social situations differ and who are divided from one another as a result of these differences. Moreover, Lugones sees love, not as an emotional given that socially excluded groups can tap, but rather as a political achievement. Reflecting on how she grew up believing that loving her mother was compatible with exploiting her,

Lugones recoils: "[L]ove cannot be what I was taught. Love has to be rethought, made anew" (Lugones, 1987, 7). Across generations, across races, and across cultures, women should "learn to love each other by learning to travel to each other's 'worlds'" (Lugones, 1987, 4). When one travels to another's "world," one sees the other through her eyes, and one sees oneself as one is seen by her (Lugones, 1987, 8, 17). In other words, one becomes capable of broad empathy with that person (for an account of broad empathy, see Chapter 2, Section 4).

I am in basic agreement with Lugones' view. I believe, however, that she overlooks an important dimension of "world"-travelling. What is missing from Lugones' account is the role of figuration in blocking or facilitating identification and empathy, that is, an account of dissident speech. Still, her joyful, anti-agonistic conception of playfulness and her focus on the ways in which identities are constructed suggest that she might be receptive to the imaginative uses of language involved in dissident speech (Lugones, 1987, 15–17). Also, while Lugones writes perceptively about travelling to others' "worlds," she does not consider the obstacles to identifying with the excluded group to which one is socially assigned and the difficulty of forming a "world" that members of that group can share. I shall begin by placing the question of love and dissident speech in this context and then go on to the problem of intergenerational, interracial, intercultural, and other ties.

Among feminists and minority activists, the idea of colonized consciousness is a familiar one, as is the idea that alternative communities of discourse are needed in which members of these groups can undertake the process of self-perception and self-definition. Here I can mention just a few influential feminist examples. Nancy Fraser describes the role of "'oppositional' needs-talk" in the "crystallization of new social identities on the part of subordinated persons and groups," and she outlines the conditions that tend to support the emergence of a feminist activist social identity as opposed to a social identity as a passive recipient of state services (Fraser, 1989, 303). Discussing women's self-defeating pursuit of impossible ideals of beauty and consequent alienation from their bodies, Sandra Bartky maintains that it is necessary for women to "create a new witness"— a revolutionary feminist community that redefines beauty for itself and that creates the social conditions necessary for a "non-repressive narcissism" (Bartky, 1990, 43). Near the end of her examination of the history of the Marion cult and its hold on women's psyches, Julia

Kristeva observes that in Western culture today maternity lacks a discourse, and she stresses the need to listen to mothers and to refigure their experience (Kristeva, 1986, 184–185).

An underlying theme in each of these theories is the need for women to overcome alienation from self and self-contempt in order to overcome the demoralization, self-effacement, and frustration of aspirations to which they lead. In Nussbaum's, Kristeva's, and Lugones' terms, women need to achieve self-love. Not love for oneself as an individual, but rather love for other women and love for oneself as a woman. Here, it is important to stress that, in contrast to Kristeva (see Section 1), neither Nussbaum nor Lugones sentimentalizes consciousness-raising. In speaking of love, they are certainly not endorsing saccharine, fawning, indiscriminate acceptance of others, nor do they believe that intense, exclusionary passion supports political thought. When they refer to love in the context of politics, it is clear that they are talking about a steady, compassionate response to other people that is positively correlated with a disposition to act in support of their interests. Although I agree with this characterization, to avoid misunderstanding and to underscore the political nature of dissident speech, I shall speak of *solidarity* rather than love.

Introducing the term "solidarity" to characterize the emotional orientation needed for dissident speech brings out several important asymmetries between addressing the dilemma of difference and moral reflection regarding a beloved intimate. Loving intimates can trust one another to create morally tenable images. However, since the starting point of dissident speech is always a moment in a long history of multiple, cross-cutting systems of domination and subordination, the members of socially excluded groups cannot trust people from other groups to supply imagery for them. There is a presumption that the imagery supplied by the dominant culture transmits culturally normative prejudice and reinforces relations of domination and subordination. Moreover, in view of the insidious influence of this imagery, there is reason to suspect that individuals with significantly different backgrounds—including individuals from other excluded groups—do not feel the unqualified and lively concern for one another that is a precondition for generating emancipatory imagery (but for discussion of "tak[ing] responsibility for [one's] identity" as a way of mitigating these social divisions, see Harding, 1991, 279–290). Although it is undeniable that solidarity is possible across groups, it would be very risky for socially excluded groups to delegate the task of dissident speech to others. Each socially excluded group must speak for itself.

Julia Kristeva conceives of solidarity as based on a universal consciousness of the inescapability of unconscious experience (Kristeva, 1991, 192; also see Chapter 3, Section 4). Understood as an ultimate, long-range goal of dissident speech, Kristeva's ideal is fine. However, in the interim, prejudice, colonized consciousness, and competing interests make it necessary to adopt a more fragmented view of solidarity (for discussion of women's diversity and solidarity, see hooks, 1984, 57–58, 63–64). Initially, solidarity must be achieved within socially excluded groups. Eventually, the scope of solidarity might be expanded to solidarity among socially excluded groups and, finally, to solidarity with all people. At present, however, universal solidarity is not a realistic goal, and prematurely attempting to achieve it would probably be counterproductive for some, if not all, socially excluded groups.

Some additional asymmetries between love and solidarity help to explain why progress regarding the dilemma of difference is so halting and vulnerable to reversal. Whereas love often seems to spring spontaneously from the chance chemistry between two people, solidarity is always hard-won. Of course, love may not survive severe economic hardship or other misfortune. But solidarity can never be taken for granted, and it is sure to dissipate unless it is backed up by political organization and collective action.

Publicity about injustices occasionally kindles and focuses anger, and this anger may inspire a solidarity-building mass response. Recall, for example, Anita Hill's testimony about the sexual harassment Clarence Thomas subjected her to and the outpouring of rage and sympathy her courage elicited. But notice that, without feminist organizations to coordinate letter-writing and petition campaigns, feminist academic institutions to hold conferences about sexual harassment where Anita Hill could be honored, and feminist attorneys to pursue sexual harassment complaints in the courts, militant opposition to sexual harassment might not have materialized, and the opportunity to consolidate solidarity among women might well have been squandered.

Another asymmetry between love and solidarity is that although most individuals give and receive love, relatively few members of socially excluded groups experience solidarity with one another (or, for that matter, with members of other socially excluded groups) in a sustained way. There is ample reason for fragmentation within socially excluded groups. Economic incentives promote assimilation to dominant norms, while widely propagated negative imagery discourages identification with fellow members of a socially excluded group. Moreover, many individuals are torn between competing loyalties—a lesbian African-American might identify primarily with lesbians, with African-Americans, with lesbian African-Americans, or with women. Dissident speech regarding difference can begin only in medias res, but res are always stacked against solidarity and therefore against dissident speech.

At this point, a key contribution of intellectuals and artists to political movements comes into view. Sometimes activists dismiss intellectuals and artists as frivolous, self-indulgent, and irrelevant. Yet, it seems to me that, when intellectuals and artists stand in solidarity with members of a socially excluded group, their work may be dedicated to proposing counterfigurations of that group. Unlike most members of socially excluded groups, intellectuals and artists often occupy social positions that afford them the leisure and the freedom to devote themselves to creating novel figurations (for examples of such work, see Chapter 4, Section 2). Although dissident speech can also originate in consciousness-raising sessions and other grassroots political activity, it is important to recognize that intellectuals and artists can play a vital role in promoting the development of solidarity and group identity within a socially excluded group (but for an argument that these figurations must ultimately be assessed democratically, see Section 5 below).

It is not the case, then, that dissident speech can never get going. Fortunately, solidarity is not an all or nothing matter. It is built incrementally as opportunities present themselves, and dissident speech can be constructed out of whatever solidarity exists. Indeed, solidarity and dissident speech are mutually reinforcing. Solidarity fosters the creation and dissemination of emancipatory imagery, emancipatory imagery expands and strengthens solidarity, and so on. In committing themselves to one another and articulating shared figurations, the members of a socially excluded group constitute an evolving collective identity for themselves. In short, dissident speakers are questionable, *collective* subjects-in-process.

It would be hard to overestimate the moral significance of the emergence of self-ascribed collective identities for socially excluded groups. In itself, this is a moral achievement, for it wrests control over how one is figured and hence how one views oneself away from hostile forces. Moreover, it is a means to a number of important ends. A self-generated identity can be counterposed to the one the dominant culture seeks to impose and used to confront members of other social groups. It can serve as a basis for defining group needs and for advancing group interests through official channels. It can serve as a basis for identifying affinities with other groups, for forming coalitions, and for making common cause—that is, as a basis for solidarity among social groups.

4. Polyvocal Dissident Speech: Counterfiguration without Homogenization

If this picture of the political setting of dissident speech is correct, one would expect highly various figurations to proliferate both within self-demarcated groups and also among them: within distinct groups, because finding apt imagery is a process of trial and error, because the experience of the members of the group is heterogeneous, and because social and economic developments may warrant changes in the imagery that members of the group endorse, and among these groups, because the social and economic system differentially positions them. The dissident speech of different groups may sometimes converge. Indeed, different groups might occasionally benefit by appropriating imagery from the dissident speech of others. However, these convergences may or may not turn out to be lasting. Thus, it would be a mistake for women as a group to seek a single perfect counterfiguration of women. Not only would this approach deny differences among women, but also adopting such an image would freeze women's self-understanding and block emancipatory refiguration. The process of group self-definition through dissident speech is best seen as an ongoing conversation among many and varied proposed figurations.

It is useful to put Catharine MacKinnon's controversial work in this context. MacKinnon is famous, of course, for not pulling her rhetorical punches. According to MacKinnon, our social world is organized so that men fuck and women get fucked (MacKinnon, 1989, 124). Some feminists have sharply criticized MacKinnon for consigning women to the status of helpless victims and blocking all routes to women's emancipation (Cornell, 1991, 141). From one perspective, this criticism is clearly warranted. If read literally, MacKinnon's work is easily dismissed as extravagant, perhaps irresponsible, hyperbole. But, if MacKinnon is read more sympathetically—that is, if her work is read as an extended trope—it becomes clear that her fierce, jarring sexual imagery makes emotional sense of abstract, remote statistics regarding sexual violence and exposes the violent reality behind apparently benign, culturally entrenched gender imagery.

By figuring men as fuckers and women as fuckees, MacKinnon personalizes the data on sexual assault. She thereby counters the common, but misguided assumptions that rape is committed by deviants whom one does not know and that rape victims are women who put themselves in compromising positions. By exploding the confining, hypocritical imagery of women as revered mothers and the cartoon imagery of fuzzy feminine animals (women figured as chicks and foxes), and by figuring all men as capable of sexual violence and all women as vulnerable to sexual violence, she politicizes the issue of sexual violence. Seen in this light, her work can be recognized as an original and in some respects compelling contribution to the debate over justice and gender.

Still, it would be a mistake simply to embrace MacKinnon's figurations as the sole alternatives to culturally entrenched ones. It is important that women's victimization be acknowledged and figuratively expressed, but figurations of women should proliferate. The dominant culture does not rely on a single figuration of women (see Chapter 3, Section 3). Why should feminists? No single figuration can express the diversity of women's experience and the complexity of women's social position. By acknowledging that feminism needs a multiplicity of figurations, moreover, we can move beyond a discourse of fractious contention—your view is wrong! your counterfiguration is repressive!—and move toward a discourse of enrichment and inclusion. Since solidarity does not presuppose homogeneity, we must all remember that our views and our preferred counterfigurations are partial.

Apart from the virtues I have already noted, the proliferation of self-generated figurations of socially excluded groups has the advantage of underscoring the contestability of all cultural figurations and thus politicizes them. This is important, for dissident speech is not addressed only to the members of one's own group. It is also addressed to members of other excluded groups and to members of the dominant group.

Dissident speech reframes moral perception in order to dislodge prejudice. As a first step, the members of socially excluded groups must find imagery that frees them from the self-doubt, self-contempt, and self-limitation that compounds institutionalized oppression. But, if this imagery is to be effective with respect to the larger goal of dissident speech, it must, in Margaret Walker's words, "hijack the imaginary"—that is, it must supplant the controlling system of imagery that sustains unconscious prejudice and keeps it concealed. Given the diversity of the individuals who are sexist and the countless ways in which sexism is manifested, it would be very surprising if a single counterfiguration worked to neutralize sexism. Given the fact that racism, classism, homophobia, and ethnocentrism are often conjoined with sexism, it would be astounding if a single counterfiguration proved effective against all of these permutations. Indeed, the imagery that contributes most to the internal dynamics of an excluded group may not be imagery that members of other groups can readily assimilate. Thus, dissident speech is best developed along mutiple tracks designed to address diverse audiences.

5. Trying on the Trope:
Dissident Speech and Emancipatory Moral Perception

The line of thought I have developed so far raises questions about Nussbaum's criteria for morally illuminating imagery—namely, beauty and compatibility with standing obligations. Certainly, none of the psychoanalytic feminist tropes that I rehearsed in Chapter 4 qualifies as conventionally beautiful in the way that Adam's image of his daughter as a sleek creature swimming in a jewel blue sea does. Indeed, I must confess that upon first coming across psychoanalytic feminist dissident speech, I found much of it disconcerting and a little repellant. From the standpoint of traditional aesthetic values, I suppose, Kristeva's trope of the imaginary father (Chapter 4, Section 2C) is least deviant. But neither Irigaray's metonym of women's two lips (Chapter 4, Section 2D) nor Benjamin's oxymoron of rational violence (Chapter 4, Section 2A) appeals to its readers by conjuring up exquisite images or delightful associations. And Chodorow's leitmotif of the self in relationship (Chapter 4, Section 2B) is hardly notable for its linguistic charms. Yet, I find these tropes rich, and I hope I have convinced the reader that it is rewarding to reflect on them. Moreover, although none of these counterfigurations has escaped feminist criticism, I think it is demonstrable that each of them has contributed to the discussions that are shaping feminist consciousness.

Kristeva adverts to modern art and avant-garde literature to characterize the aesthetics of dissident speech, and Lugones characterizes the playful "world"-traveller as a person who is creative and open to surprise and who holds no rules sacred (Kristeva, 1980, 140–144; 1987a, 253; Lugones, 1987, 16 17). Their views suit the purposes of feminism better than Nussbaum's call for beautiful imagery. Since part of what dissident speech about gender needs to do is to expose the evils of gender-based domination for what they are, it is to be expected that some of this new imagery will seem rather grotesque. Also, since dissident speech about gender needs to supplant entrenched images of feminine beauty as passive loveliness and objectified desirability, it is to be expected that much of this new imagery will violate these conventions and consequently will not immediately strike its audience as beautiful. Feminist dissident speech cannot be bound by established standards of beauty, for reconceiving beauty is central to the feminist project.

Likewise, it is doubtful that feminist dissident speech should be constrained by "standing obligations." Nussbaum's position in this regard is not altogether clear. On the one hand, her discussion of the parental and filial obligations that are fulfilled through Adam's and Maggie's imagery suggests that she has quite specific precepts in mind. On the other hand, in her commentary on Hyacinth Robinson's politics in *The Princess Casamassima,* Nussbaum allows that the violent overthrow of established authority, such as the French revolution, can be justified (Nussbaum, 1990, 215). One way to reconcile these two claims would be to formulate standing obligations at a higher level of abstraction—that is, novel imagery must not violate the obligation to give fair consideration to each person. However, since it is far from clear what counts as fair consideration of despots or other oppressors, and since there is sharp disagreement over whether the French revolutionaries met this standard, this strategy seems to render Nussbaum's constraint otiose. Compliance with specific obligations often leaves the dilemma of difference unresolved and perpetuates domination and subordination, but very general obligations provide insufficient guidance.

In view of the aims of dissident speech, it seems ill-advised to bind dissident speech to established aesthetic or moral standards. Realizations of established aesthetic values and implementations of established obligations that are recognizable as such are conditioned by culturally entrenched figurations—the very figurations that dissident speech seeks to overthrow. Yet, there must be some way to tell when dissident speech is morally tenable and emancipatory and therefore when novel imagery deserves one's allegiance.

Dissident speech is subject to evaluation at two levels. It can be examined in the abstract, in the manner of literary criticism. Is a novel figuration apt? Is it revealing? Is it moving? Why does it succeed or fail? The voluminous critical literature debating the relative merits of the work of different psychoanalytic feminists can be seen as a preliminary screening process for the counterfigurations these theorists set forth (critical collections include Brennan, 1989; Feldstein and Root, 1989; Fraser and Bartky, 1992). To isolate and set aside weak proposals, imaginatively anticipating and critically assessing the probable consequences of adopting a novel figuration may suffice. When an alternative figuration is promising, however, it is necessary to "try on the trope"—that is, one must provisionally adopt it, let it order one's experience, and see what the results are (for discussion of moral experience and its role in moral reflection, see Held, 1989, 272; 1993, Chapter 2).

Here, it is helpful to consider an everyday problem that is exacerbated by cultural figurations of gender—heterosexuality and acquaintance rape. To the extent that masculinity is conceptualized through the image of the aggressive, heroic warrior and the image of the sexually voracious stud, men are discouraged from paying attention to women's sexual choices. Moreover, to the extent that femininity is conceptualized through the images of the fox, the madonna, and the whore, men's inattention to women's sexual choices is rationalized. Foxes are sleek, cunning predators that are hunted commercially for their pelts and by equestrians for the pleasure of the chase and the kill. A foe and a worthy one at that, the fox will outwit the hunter unless he is skilled and uses superior traps or hounds. Thus, men who sexually assault women need not see themselves as cowards picking on defenseless victims, and they can excuse their reliance on force as necessitated by the wiles of their prey. These attitudes are reinforced by the oscillating madonna/whore figuration. Women are figured as sexually insatiable and promiscuous, while at the same time they are figured as so pure that they are embarrassed to avow their sexual desires. Again, men's inattention to women's stated desires seems warranted, for women "really want it" even though they are ashamed to admit it and have to pretend they are chaste.

One consequence of these figurations of gender is men's dysempathic perception of women and the collapse of the easy interpersonal coordination that empathic understanding brings. Too many men are unduly confident that they know what women want, and they end up raping their partners. The date rape prevention policy at Antioch College that requires sexual partners to negotiate intimacy—that is, verbally ask for and explicitly receive permission for everything from caresses and kisses to intercourse at each stage of a sexual encounter—has been the butt of widespread editorial humor and has elicited loud laments over the demise of romance and spontaneity. Unfortunately, romance and spontaneity in the context of a man's dysempathizing with his female partner nullify her autonomy and destroy her pleasure. They transform the delights of seduction into the crime of rape.

No one can be happy with Antioch's protocol, for plodding back and forth between issuing requests and being granted or denied permission is likely to dampen ardor. Indeed, it is precisely because such elaborate protective mandates are both necessary and distasteful that we desperately need dissident speech regarding gender. We need counterfigurations that enhance empathic understanding between women and men and that thereby obviate the need for constantly checking the veracity of one's beliefs about one's sexual partner, not to mention one's business associates and one's friends.

To test a counterfiguration experientially, then, is to determine whether empathic insight is facilitated and interpersonal coordination is improved when people's perception is structured by it. Does a novel figuration help to reduce occluded perception of and wasteful anxiety about the members of a socially excluded group? Does it support the expansion of well-placed trust and mutually beneficial collaboration? In short, do people live better when they are perceived and perceive others through the lens of this figuration as opposed to an established one? To respond to these questions in the affirmative is, I would urge, to justify accepting a counterfiguration. To respond in the negative is to disqualify a proposed figuration.

Of course, the meaning of reconfigured perception and the nature of the results are not self-evident. As Joan W. Scott claims, "Experience is at once always already an interpretation *and* is in need of interpretation" (Scott, 1992, 37). If experience with a novel figuration seems to be going well (or seems disappointing), it is important to consider why. To what extent, for example, is the success of Chodorow's image of femininity as a "self in relationship" due to its serviceability as a refuge for women who are ambivalent about equality and as a weapon for reactionaries who oppose justice for women? To what extent has this image succeeded in securing the respect that traditional feminine qualities and activities deserve? And why hasn't Benjamin's disturbing image of gender as "rational violence" caught on quite as well? Is it because this image misrepresents gender or because it represents gender all too accurately? Or, perhaps, because *The Reproduction of Mothering* was published 10 years before *The Bonds of Love* and saturated the market for feminist object relations theory?

Although experience cannot be regarded as a brute reality that directly and conclusively decides the moral admissibility or the political efficacy of a trope, and although consensus about how to interpret experience with a trope is difficult to attain, it is undeniable that experience can jolt people out of familiar patterns of thought. Finding oneself "so thoroughly dominated that [one] has no sense of [one's] own will or has a sense of having serious difficulties in performing actions that are willed by [one]self and no difficulty in performing actions that are willed by others" justifies "disown[ing] a 'world'" and the figurations that partially constitute it (Lugones, 1987, 12–13). Finding oneself at a loss and groping for words to express one's experience as a member of a socially excluded group prompts dissident speech. Finding one's experience more intelligible and one's life more fulfilling under the aegis of a novel figuration or set of novel figurations gives one reason to adopt it.

As I suggested in Section 3, dissident speakers are best conceived as collective subjects-in-process. Thus, there is no reason to suppose that a system of ideal figurations can be created, nor that a figurative encoding of emancipation can be finalized. In advocating dissident speech, then, I am not urging socially excluded groups to articulate eternal truths about themselves, truths that the dominant culture has suppressed. Rather, I am urging the members of these groups to take political control over the production of experience insofar as salient, group-defining figurations structure experience.

The positivist objection to admitting dissident speech to moral reflection (see Chapter 4, Section 3) is premised on an exceedingly simplistic aesthetics. The merits of a figuration are by no means immune to critical discussion. Nor are they inaccessible to experiential testing. Still, some theorists may regard dissident speech as an unwelcome complication of moral reflection, for dissident speech undeniably opens a vast, new frontier of moral and political debate. Yet, the alternative to viewing dissident speech as integral to moral reflection is unconscionable. To exclude dissident speech from moral reflection would be to give prejudicial cultural figurations of marginalized social groups a free rein. In view of the suffering that culturally normative prejudice inflicts on the members of these groups and the potential for moral insight that dissident speech opens up, an adequate account of moral reflection must countenance dissident speech.

6. Hijacking the Imaginary: The Complementarity of Cultural and Material Politics

Dissident speech must address more than one audience if it is to achieve its political aims. It must address the members of a socially excluded group who are striving for solidarity. It must address other members of the group who do not consciously identify with it. It must address members of other socially excluded groups. It must address members of the dominant group. These audiences are not neatly demarcated. An individual's polyvalent identity—gender, class, race, sexual orientation, ethnicity, and so forth—may align him or her with dominant positions in some respects and with subordinate positions in others. For this reason, I have urged that it would be self-defeating for a socially excluded group to speak with a single voice in a single register (see Section 4). Counterfigurations must be tailored to diverse audiences.

But eloquent counterimagery is no guarantee of social change. If the mass media ignore the figurations that socially excluded groups conceive for themselves, it will not matter how politically sophisticated, linguistically ingenious, or morally insinuating this counterimagery is. Hardly anyone will be exposed to it, and it will not gain currency. But even supposing that the mass media could be won over and that dissident speech was widely disseminated, it is not clear that this counterimagery would automatically supplant culturally entrenched imagery and eliminate prejudice.

Bombarding people with counterfigurations may have little impact on nonconscious predispositions. People compartmentalize entertainment and reality—what one sees on a television show or reads in a novel is labeled fiction and deemed to have no bearing on social relations. Murphy Brown may be funny and wonderful. But real-life single mothers remain "irresponsible welfare leeches" in the popular imagination. Deep-seated cognitive and emotional structures are not easily dislodged.

Max Black's account of how metaphors catch on indicates the dimensions of the problem:

> [A] metaphor works if there is a "system of associated common-places" (about the secondary domain) shared among writer and readers, where "the important thing for the metaphor's effective-ness is not that the commonplaces shall be true, but that they should be readily and freely evoked." (Black quoted in Rooney, 1991, 95)

In other words, when stereotypical thinking permeates common sense, counterfigurations will have nothing to latch onto and will probably die aborning. Since stereotypical thinking about gender, race, class, sexual orientation, and ethnicity does permeate common sense, the prospects for dissident speech look bleak.

Although there is no reason for women and minorities to be sanguine about the pace of progress in subverting repressive imagery, I believe that dissident speech can be effective if it is incorporated into a multipronged, concerted feminist program. Dissident speech must work hand-in-hand with social science. Social scientists can document the vast discrepancies between "what everybody knows" and the actual lives of the members of socially excluded groups, and this information can be publicized through television and print journalism. Meanwhile, the concrete economic and political advances of socially excluded groups put pressure on stereotypes. As members of socially excluded groups enter previously closed occupations and gain positions of power and prestige, the conflict between common sense "truths" and everyday experience becomes harder to deny. The object is to stir up and, whenever possible, to aggravate cognitive dissonance. The confusion and uncertainty that result from cognitive dissonance give dissident speech an entrée. Moreover, to the extent that new commonplaces about socially excluded groups take shape and gain a foothold in common sense, dissident speech can intervene and attach salutary, new imagery to them.

The goals of dissident speech with respect to fighting prejudice are best conceived as phased. From one point of view, the goal is limited to counteracting xenophobia—that is, defusing fear and hatred and securing tolerance and respect for others' basic rights. From another viewpoint, the goal is the more ambitious one of promoting xeno-

philia—that is, creating a climate of receptivity to people from different backgrounds and ensuring appreciation for difference. These
goals should not be pursued sequentially. At any one time, there are
some people who should be addressed from the first standpoint and
other people who should be addressed from the second. Still, since
ingrained prejudice is rarely, if ever, overcome in one fell swoop, it is
important to keep in mind that slight improvements are not failures.

Dissident speech is no panacea. It can succeed only as part of a
comprehensive political struggle, for concrete social and economic
gains are needed to support the popularization of emancipatory figurations. Still, dissident speech must not be treated as a luxury and left
off the political agenda of socially excluded groups. If it is, the influence of prejudicial figurations over moral judgment will go unde-
tected, and moral perception will remain anchored in this entrenched
cultural imagery. By furnishing emancipatory figurations of socially
excluded groups, dissident speech attacks culturally normative prejudice and helps to consolidate these groups' social and economic gains.

7. Postscript: Liberating Philosophy from Narrow Professionalism

It is not worth expending very much energy on questions about the
boundaries of academic disciplines. Nevertheless, it does seem worth
noting that my discussion of dissident speech connects philosophy to
other fields and stretches philosophy. If dissident speech is part of
philosophy, then literature, art, psychoanalysis, and cultural theory
are in some respects philosophical, and philosophers who produce
dissident speech are not interjecting nonphilosophical elements into
their work. Likewise, my account of dissident speech suggests a more
democratic view of philosophy, for, as I have urged, the process of
critically examining novel figurations requires that they be tested in
experience. Thus, political actors are in some respects philosophers,
and philosophers who engage in political activity are doing work that
in some respects contributes to their philosophy.

Philosophers have long considered the articulation, the critical
assessment, and the reformulation of fundamental, often unstated
assumptions central to their discipline. Since these assumptions are
built into the premises of arguments and to some extent determine
which arguments seem plausible and which do not, philosophers cannot perform the task of evaluating arguments unless they address
these assumptions. What my account of culturally normative preju-

dice reveals is that many fundamental assumptions about social groups are encoded in figurations and that these figurations organize many people's thinking about these groups. However, since these figurations are not reducible to propositions, it may seem that the critique of culturally entrenched figurations, the production of counterfigurations, and the evaluation of counterfigurations lie beyond the bounds of philosophy.

To endorse this conclusion would be to rewrite the history of philosophy. Although logical positivism sought to expel figurative language from philosophical discourse, philosophers have not traditionally excluded figurations from the scope of their discipline. I believe that philosophers should reclaim and celebrate this centuries-old tradition.

Consider the image of the social contract. Reframing political relations in terms of the image of the social contract is generally considered to be among the major accomplishments of early modern philosophy, and social contract theory remains a vigorous branch of moral and political philosophy today. Although a few philosophers have taken this figuration literally and (to my mind, misguidedly) maintained that a legitimate government is one that has obtained the actual consent of each citizen, most philosophers regard the social contract as an illuminating figuration of the values of impartiality, fairness, and mutual respect. If this is so, generating figurations, exploring their implications, and assessing their merits are hardly alien to philosophy.[2] Evidently, the enterprise of philosophy overlaps with literature, art, and psychoanalysis. Indeed, it seems clear that philosophers could sometimes enrich their work by appropriating figurations from these and other cultural sources, and it would surely be arbitrary to disavow appropriated figurations as nonphilosophical simply because their authors did not claim to be philosophers or because their authors lack credentials as professional philosophers.

What philosophers may find more objectionable is the suggestion that philosophy is in some respects inextricable from politics. My account of dissident speech roots moral reflection in solidarity among the members of socially excluded groups and directs moral reflection to the goal of articulating a self-ascribed, collective identity for these groups. If dissident speech is a form of philosophizing, then philosophizing is, in part, a social activity shaped by political exigencies.

It is evident that moral and political philosophy feeds on its social context. Philosophical theories often systematize and articulate social and political trends. John Rawls's theory of justice is a case in point. His reformulation of rights-based liberalism—giving liberty priority, while providing economic guarantees through redistributive taxation—mirrors the hybrid doctrine endorsed by contemporary United States politicians who are labeled liberals. Likewise, the intuitions about the desirability (or undesirability) of social practices, policies, and outcomes to which philosophers frequently advert are plainly conditioned by their social background. Part of the reason philosophers continue to do social contract theory is that this figuration has gained currency in Western political discourse and frames our intuitions about justice. Many ordinary people have embraced the image of the social contract as a figuration of the kind of society they want to live in, and politicians routinely appeal to this mythical social contract to rally support for their views. I myself think that this figuration has gained too much control over our moral and political imagination (for related discussion, see Held, 1987). Nevertheless, its history has proven it to be a durable image that has sometimes functioned effectively to voice egalitarian aims. In short, the social contract is a figuration that has survived the test of experience, and social contract theorists are indebted to that social testing process.

Pointing out that professional philosophers are deeply dependent on their cultural milieu and on the activities and judgments of people who are not generally considered philosophers in no way belittles or demeans what professional philosophers do. Discerning unnoticed connections or conflicts between intuitions, organizing and expounding complex and subtle ideas, and marshalling sustained arguments for positions are not trivial contributions. Still, it is a mistake to regard the social processes that professional philosophers draw on as altogether extraphilosophical. To experiment with figurations and judge whether the results are beneficial is to probe, reconceive, reorder, and vindicate values—in other words, to philosophize. That dissident speech is a social practice with explicitly political aims in no way detracts from its philosophical standing. Indeed, I would venture that, insofar as professional philosophers remain aloof from communities of dissident speakers, their work on issues involving the dilemma of difference will probably suffer.

Identifying philosophy with foundationalism, Nancy Fraser and Linda Nicholson argue that effective social criticism entails jettisoning philosophy (Fraser and Nicholson, 1990, 21–26). Although my conclusions about the role of philosophy in social criticism differ from those that Fraser and Nicholson reach, I believe that we share similar aims and that the line of thought I have developed is compatible with both their underlying concerns and their recommendations regarding the future of feminist theory. Since philosophy need not be foundationalist, and since professional philosophy is neither likely to disappear from academic institutions nor entirely devoid of public influence, I have not urged that philosophy be deposed. Instead, I have introduced a less precious, more democratic view of philosophy. Dissident speech enlivens philosophical discourse, expands the philosophical community, and, in some respects, deprofessionalizes philosophy. Philosophizing includes contesting culturally entrenched figurations of socially excluded groups, proposing counterfigurations, and assessing the merits of these figurations. The philosophical community includes the community of dissident speakers—collectivities defined by varying degrees of solidarity among members of socially excluded groups. Since philosophy need not be stiff or elitist, there is no need to give up on philosophy.

6

Empathic Thought:
Responding Morally to Difference

Irene Opdyke, a Polish woman who hid 18 Jews from the Nazis during World War II and when they were discovered became a Nazi officer's mistress in exchange for their safety, explains her heroic altruism in modest terms: "We all have to reach out to know that we're not alone in the world" (Block and Drucker, 1992, 196). I find her remark deeply poignant and also highly suggestive for moral philosophy. Opdyke expresses an approach to moral relations that strikes me as eminently propitious with respect to resolving the dilemma of difference, yet the major traditional ethical theories cannot easily accommodate her counsel.

At first blush, utilitarianism's demand that we maximize social welfare might seem to compass her point of view. But on closer inspection, I think the differences between the two orientations stand out. Whereas utilitarianism commends advancing the good of all and incidentally the good of particular individuals, Opdyke's primary focus seems to be making contact with particular others. Also, utilitarianism would have us follow its precepts out of a generalized fellow feeling, but Opdyke identifies a more human motive—the need to know that we are not alone. Kantian impartial reason fares no better. Here, the rational imperatives of consistency and respect for humanity altogether supplant concern with people, whether taken individually or in the aggregate. Moreover, this approach to moral reflection plays on people's defensive reflexes—think of being treated in such-and-such a fashion before you treat others that way. In contrast, Opdyke appeals to the wretchedness of isolation from others and the solace of human companionship.

Though traditional moral philosophy cannot plausibly interpret Irene Opdyke's explanation of her bravery and self-sacrifice, there can be no doubt that she expresses a profoundly moral view. Opdyke's life is a standing reproach to conformity and submissiveness, as well as to egotistical self-assertion. She does not rule out self-sacrifice—she endured fearsome danger and appalling sexual abuse for the sake of the people she protected. But neither does she urge people to maintain human connection by effacing themselves or suppressing their opposition to prevalent beliefs and practices. Asked about her life in the United States today (she immigrated after the war), she describes her work speaking out against racism in the public school system (Block and Drucker, 1992, 196). A fine balance between self and other is manifest in her choices and in her characterization of them. While ascribing fundamental importance to reaching out to others, she does not altogether neglect her own needs, for she links responsiveness to others to the reassurance of knowing one is not alone in the world.

In trying to make sense of Opdyke's moral view, and in searching for an empathy-friendly account of moral reflection, I have found it helpful to look to the psychoanalytic feminist theories of Nancy Chodorow and Jessica Benjamin. While they differ in some respects, Chodorow and Benjamin concur in stressing the fundamental sociality of subjectivity. In conjunction with Chodorow's account of the role of empathy in the emergence of subjectivity, I believe that Benjamin's theory of mutual recognition provides the rudiments of an apt gloss of Opdyke's moral view.

In this chapter, I shall draw out the implications of Chodorow's and Benjamin's work with regard to the problem of moral reflection. Properly understood, mutual recognition is a relationship in which empathic understanding of others comes together with self-understanding to sustain moral judgment. Not only is empathy with the other necessary for mutual recognition, but also, I shall argue, self-recognition is necessary for mutual recognition. Accordingly, if moral reflection is to take full advantage of the insights derivable from broad empathy, moral subjects fashioning moral responses must recognize themselves while recognizing others (for discussion of broad empathy and its contribution to moral reflection, see Chapter 2, Section 4).

I believe that the key to this sort of moral reflection is the concept of individual moral identity. One's moral identity includes a conception of what kind of person one aspires to be—a collocation of values that one seeks to realize in making decisions and living a life. This ideal is conjoined with one's understanding of one's moral capabilities—an assessment of one's past performance as judged against the ideal as well as one's expectations for the future. In my view, self-recognition involves both cultivating one's moral identity and enacting one's moral identity, and both of these activities are inseparable from empathy with others. Through the concept of moral identity, then, the link between moral judgment and empathy can be forged.

Finally, it is important to underscore the connection between Irene Opdyke's moral outlook and the problem of difference and social exclusion (see Chapter 1, Section 1). Her Polish ethnicity spared her from Hitler's concentration camps but not from forced labor. A captive Pole who saved Jews, she resolved the dilemma of difference in her own life, and she did so under the most harrowing circumstances. Her actions during the Nazi regime, as well as her vocal opposition to racism today, attest to her refusal to see people through entrenched cultural figurations. Whether because circumstances threw her together with a group of Jews and their overwhelmingly needy presence made it possible for her to break through anti-Semitic figurations, or because she came from a background in which these dominant cultural figurations were expressly repudiated, or perhaps a combination of the two (the brief biography in Block and Drucker does not provide sufficient detail to form an opinion), Opdyke was able to empathize with the Jews she encountered. But grasping their humanity and their need posed a dire conflict between her own safety and right to sexual self-determination, on the one hand, and their peril, on the other. I believe that her ability to resist the Nazis and to save eighteen people from their genocidal policies can best be explained by assimilating her moral thinking to the approach to moral reflection I have sketched. Geared to the perception and appreciation of human diversity while endowing the individual with powers of critical judgment, I shall urge, this approach to moral reflection is capable of addressing those variants of the dilemma of difference that resist resolution through impartial reason (see Chapter 2, Section 2).

1. Empathy, Recognition, and the Emergence of Moral Subjectivity

Chodorow and Benjamin see people as social in two respects. On the one hand, every infant is cared for by an adult or adults, and every person is shaped for better or worse by this nonvoluntary experience. However, that people are deeply influenced by their social context does not have any direct moral consequences—that I grew up imbued with certain values does not entail that I should favor them, let alone hew to them, now (Friedman, 1989, 280–282). On the other hand, Chodorow and Benjamin regard people as social in a second sense that is itself morally significant and that they attribute to *adequate* nurturance. For Chodorow, empathic capacities are social inasmuch as they enable one to understand people who are different from oneself. Moreover, they prefigure moral choice and action, for they prepare one to respond to people's needs. For Benjamin, the need for recognition propels people into social relations since individuals are dependent on others to satisfy this need. Moreover, recognition has a moral complexion, for it cannot be gained unless it is reciprocated, and thus it is constitutive of respectful relations between equals. Chodorow and Benjamin see empathy and recognition as necessary for living a rich and rewarding life, and they regard these capacities as basic (for discussion of moral philosophy's indifference to these capacities, see Chapter 1, Section 3B). To lack empathic capacities or to be incapable of mutual recognition is to have had a defective upbringing.[1]

Chodorow's account of moral relations turns on her account of the relationship between caregivers and their children. A caregiver who is experienced as warmly solicitous is internalized as a "good internal mother" (Chodorow, 1980, 10). The "thereness" of a good caregiver, says Chodorow, becomes an "internal sense of another who is caring and affirming"—a sense of "self-in-good-relationship" (Chodorow, 1980, 10). Children consolidate a sense of their own identity and worthiness—that is, they gain a sense of "confident distinctness"—by internalizing the nurturance they receive and directing it toward themselves (Chodorow, 1980, 10). But their assimilation of nurturance is not exclusively egocentric, for, according to Chodorow, Freud was wrong to claim that people are originally affective narcissists (Chodorow, 1978, 63–64). If infants cathect (that is, invest psychic energy in) their relationship with their caregivers, as Chodorow claims they do, and if they receive adequate care, it is to be expected that they will readily learn to respect and to respond to other people by directing their internalized experience of nurturance toward others (Chodorow, 1980, 11). Since Chodorow attributes caregivers' ability to nurture children to empathy (Chodorow, 1978, 87), we can surmise that children internalize empathic skills and eventually learn to use them in conducting their interpersonal relationships. On Chodorow's view, then, empathy is the concerned attention that an individual who has a sense of "confident distinctness" but who values human connection extends to others.

Benjamin's theoretical assumptions differ from Chodorow's in several notable respects. Benjamin is critical of Chodorow's reliance on internalization theory (Benjamin, 1988, 43). Although she grants that children are profoundly influenced by the interpersonal environment that caregivers create, she denies that the infant is a blank slate and stresses the caregiver's responsibility for bringing out the infant's innate potentialities (Benjamin, 1988, 44).[2] Also, she rejects Chodorow's assumption that the child's primordial experience is one of fusion with the mother. According to Benjamin, the infant is "primed from the beginning to be interested in and to distinguish itself from the world of others" (Benjamin, 1988, 18; for discussion of the dangers of the myth of fusion with an archaic mother, see Kristeva, 1986, 205; Irigaray, 1993b, Part 3). Consequently, differentiating from the mother is not the child's sole developmental task. On Benjamin's view, the infant faces the dual task of establishing a distinct identity and making contact with others (Benjamin, 1988, 18). Despite these differences, I find it useful to read Benjamin and Chodorow as complementary thinkers.

For Benjamin, recognition is the key to the development of an independent identity in early childhood. She characterizes recognition as the "response from the other that makes meaningful the feelings, intentions, and actions of the self," that is, the response in which "we find ourselves" (Benjamin, 1988, 12, 21). Recognition takes a variety of forms—affirming, validating, acknowledging, knowing, accepting, understanding, empathizing, taking in, tolerating, appreciating, seeing, identifying with, finding familiar, and loving (Benjamin, 1988, 15–16). A person is not a self-sustaining, self-defining system. To know who one is, one must receive recognition from others.

On Benjamin's view, early childcare has two main aims—to facilitate the infant's expression of needs, desires, and other states of mind and to validate the infant's emerging personality. Caregivers accomplish the former aim by providing an environment in which the child feels safe and at ease. Neither intruded upon nor deprived, children are emboldened to try out new activities, and they experience their feelings and actions as originating in themselves or, in other words, as authentically their own (Benjamin, 1988, 42, 126–128; also see Chodorow, 1978, 60). But, according to Benjamin, unless they receive an affirming response from their caregiver, this incipient sense of authenticity dissipates. Specifically, children need "emotional attunement, mutual influence, affective mutuality, sharing states of mind"—in short, they need their caregiver's sympathy (Benjamin, 1988, 16; for the distinction between empathy and sympathy, see Chapter 2, Section 3). By sharing their charges' feelings and intentions, caregivers validate this experience and reinforce its authenticity, for they link these feelings and intentions to the pleasure of interpersonal harmony (Benjamin, 1988, 30–31). Moreover, sharing experience in this way allows the child to stop trying to gain control over the caregiver and to trust other people (Benjamin, 1988, 39–40).

But if the sympathy of caregivers is to have the desired effect, Benjamin maintains that they must resist the temptation to merge with the child and that they must maintain their status as independent subjects (Benjamin, 1988, 24). Ironically, capitulating to children and giving them everything they want makes them feel abandoned (Benjamin, 1988, 35, 39). Promiscuously catering to a child deprives the child of recognition, for the child cannot find a recognizer. But if caregivers go to the opposite extreme, invariably withholding validation and refusing to meet any of the child's demands, the child will feel overpowered. Forced to submit to someone else's choices, the child suppresses his or her own inclinations for fear of losing all connection with others (Benjamin, 1988, 39). Unless caregivers balance sharing experience with setting limits—that is, unless they present themselves as individuals who are like the children they care for in some respects yet different from them in others—children will be deprived of recognition (Benjamin, 1988, 30, 47). Deprived of recognition, children's capacity for full receptivity and attention to others will be stunted (Benjamin, 1988, 42).

Neither selfishness nor selflessness can relieve isolation. People need *mutual* recognition—the child needs to recognize the caregiver, as well as to be recognized (Benjamin, 1988, 23).[3] But caregivers cannot be seen as recognizers unless they are and are perceived to be subjects (Benjamin, 1988, 24; also see Chodorow, 1980, 6–8).

The virtue of Benjamin's account is the stress she places on the need for mutual recognition. Subjectivity requires intersubjectivity, and intersubjectivity requires two distinct subjects. Still, Benjamin's view is troubling, for she identifies intersubjectivity with "co-feeling" (Benjamin, 1988, 48) and subjectivity with resistance to the other. Thus, she perpetuates the polarity between sympathetic fusion and conflictual separation. This polarity ensures the impossibility of concomitant recognizing and being recognized. When one is recognizing another by sharing that person's feelings or intentions, one's independent identity is submerged. Only when one reasserts oneself and opposes the other can one be recognized as an independent subject. Thus, recognizing and being recognized alternate, and a struggle for recognition ensues (for discussion of Benjamin's treatment of the deplorable impact that this struggle has on women, see Chapter 4, Section 2A).

In contrast, Chodorow understands nurturance as the ability to "regress . . . to the psychological state of [infantile fusion]" and thus to grasp an infant's feelings and needs "while remaining adult" (Chodorow, 1978, 87). Requiring both that one imaginatively enter into the child's world and also that one not surrender one's own identity as a responsible adult agent, Chodorow places empathy, rather than sympathy, at the center of adequate caregiving. Indeed, she dismisses the psychoanalytic claim that mothers must totally identify with their babies as a case of theorists instating infantile desires as psychological truths (Chodorow, 1978, 82).

Now, I believe that there is good reason for Benjamin to give empathy a more prominent position in her theory. Indeed, I would not be surprised to learn that her neglect of empathy was simply an oversight. She mentions empathy when she enumerates various forms of recognition, but then she shifts her focus exclusively to sympathy. Moreover, she writes, "In recognition, someone who is different and outside shares a similar feeling; different minds and bodies attune" (Benjamin, 1988, 126). If this is so, it must be possible for recognizing and being recognized to occur simultaneously. In empathy, this is roughly what happens.[4] Empathy is a subjectivity-preserving form of intersubjectivity, for empathy requires one to reconstruct the other's experience in imagination (to imaginatively share it?) and thus to understand it, but it necessitates neither joining in nor endorsing the other's experience (for an account of empathy, see Chapter 2, Sections 3 and 4).

Of course, empathy is rarely an end in itself. In fact, empathic understanding of the other can persuade one that sympathy is called for. Throughout life, situations arise in which people need to know that others not only understand them but also share their point of view. Nevertheless, as Benjamin insists, it does not help to find oneself in a chamber of emotional mirrors—that is, surrounded by unrecognizable recognizers. Only when sympathy is forthcoming as a result of the other's judgment that it is warranted does sympathy allow one to be recognized while recognizing one's recognizer. If the "vital tension" (Benjamin, 1988, 132) between self and other is not to go slack, and if this tension is not to instigate a struggle for recognition, Benjamin must rest her account of mutual recognition primarily on empathy and only secondarily on sympathy.

Seeing mutual recognition based on empathy as integral to subjectivity enables Chodorow and Benjamin to diagnose certain pathologies stemming from exclusively female parenting in the nuclear family. These childrearing practices prevent children from recognizing their mothers, and this lack of recognition is harmful to women. As Chodorow observes, mothers are typically treated as "narcissistic extension[s] . . . whose sole reason for existence is to gratify one's own wants and needs" (Chodorow, 1980, 7–8). This instrumental view of mothers as all-purpose nursemaids who should always be on call damages the subjectivity of children, too. Unable to recognize their mothers, children are deprived of recognition.

Yet, Chodorow and Benjamin seem to be so preoccupied with subduing the individualist threat and so determined to secure social ties that neither of them gives more than cursory attention to the problem of how one is to maintain a distinct identity within one's relationships. Chodorow scarcely addresses this issue. She advocates coparenting as the solution to this problem but asks us to take it on faith that coparented children will achieve the proper balance between distinctness and relatedness. Benjamin takes this problem seriously, but she resorts to women's nonmaternal interests—mainly their careers outside the home—to give them an identity apart from their children. Still, I detect the germ of an intriguing line of thought in their efforts to come to grips with this issue, and in Section 2 I shall attempt to develop it.

2. Self-Recognition, Moral Identity, and Moral Subjectivity

Recall Benjamin's account of mutual recognition. Each individual recognizes the other while being recognized by the other. In recognizing another person, one gives that individual one's concerned attention; one seeks to understand that individual's circumstances and state of mind; and one validates that individual's feelings and actions when it is appropriate to do so. For Benjamin, recognition is defeated if one merges with the other and indiscriminately applauds everything this person thinks, feels, or does. Recognizers must be recognizable, and they will not be recognizable unless they exercise discernment and judgment. The salutary interplay of mutual recognition rests on the independent subjectivity of the parties to this relationship.

Chodorow's observation that there are fundamental continuities between one's relationship to oneself and one's relationships with others suggests an account of how independent subjectivity is sustained (see Section 1 above; but for Chodorow's failure to exploit this insight, see Meyers, 1992, 138–141). Although we think of the skills needed for caregiving as other-directed, it is clear that they can also be used reflexively. To empathize is to empathize with another person. Yet, in crafting autobiographical memoirs, writers turn their concerned attention on their own lives and reconstruct their past experiences in imagination. Also, in everyday life, people use the selfsame skills to revisit and think over their conduct. Similarly, although we think of nurturance as something that one person does for another, people can also nurture themselves, and, although we do not normally call it that, people are in fact expected to nurture themselves. When we are young, if we are fortunate and they are able, adults care for us—foster our growth, protect us from harm, and try to instill sound values in us (see Ruddick, 1986, 341–342). But realizing one's potential, securing one's physical and psychic equilibrium, and living up to one's ideals are lifelong concerns, and maturity shifts the burden of responsibility for pursuing these aims to the individual. To care for oneself, one must turn empathic and nurturing skills to the purposes of self-understanding, self-development, and self-validation.

To the best of my knowledge, Benjamin never uses the term "self-recognition." However, there is an empty niche in her theory of mutual recognition, and I shall adapt her terminology to fill it. *Self-recognition* is the self-directed care that consolidates independent subjectivity. The tragedy of peremptory, domineering parenting and, indeed, of all sorts of oppressive social environments is that they undermine and may even suppress self-recognition, and, when they do, they deprive individuals of others' recognition, as well.[5] To receive recognition, one must recognize the other, and to recognize the other, one must recognize oneself. Adequately nurtured in childhood, people become self-recognizers who both give recognition to others and receive recognition from them.

Although self-recognition concerns all aspects of a person's identity, I want to underscore its moral component. Among other things, self-recognition involves endorsing sound values, developing one's moral capacities, and living up to one's ideals. There is nothing particularly controversial about this claim since hardly anyone would deny that moral sensitivity and moral decency are conducive to human flourishing. Still, I want to advance the further claim that Benjamin's theory of mutual recognition would make no sense without this moral component. Since she holds that recognition is impossible in relationships based on domination and subordination, the discernment and judgment needed to recognize another cannot echo prevailing social norms to the extent that those norms mandate inequitable relations. To recognize one another, then, people must be capable of assessing the merits of social norms, and they must be capable of resisting these norms insofar as they prescribe domination and subordination and interfere with mutual recognition.[6] Independent moral subjectivity, that is, moral self-recognition, is required for mutual recognition.[7]

Our moral vernacular directly links self-recognition to moral reflection. Parents and other caregivers use the question "Do you want to be the sort of person who would do that?" as a heuristic in teaching children how to make moral choices.[8] Though very much a part of everyday moral discourse, this way of thinking about morality has received scant attention from moral philosophers.[9] I believe, however, that it provides the key to an empathy-friendly approach to moral reflection.

The question "Do you want to be the sort of person who would do that?" is premised on the assumption that people should be cultivating a moral identity—that is, they should be refining their moral sensibilities and strengthening their ability to give practical expression to their moral beliefs. Likewise, the admonitory corollary "Think what sort of person that would make you!" is premised on the assumption that the individual to whom it is addressed has a moral identity that should not be betrayed and that would be betrayed by behaving in a certain way. Sometimes people justify their decisions by explicitly invoking their desire to cultivate their moral identity or their aversion to this sort of self-betrayal. They say things like "I have to do such and such if I'm going to hang onto my self-respect," or "I couldn't do that and live with myself." What underlies remarks of this kind is a moral identity that includes a conception of the sort of person one aspires to be—that is, a moral ideal. To act in a way that conflicts with one's moral ideal is to betray oneself; to act in a way that expresses one's moral ideal is to enact and reinforce one's moral identity. The better the fit between one's moral ideal and one's proposed conduct, then, the better the reason to act on it.[10] By cultivating one's moral identity, and by bringing one's conduct into conformity with one's moral ideal, one recognizes oneself.

Anyone who is not a sociopath grew up with a moral identity that includes a moral ideal. People do not create their moral ideals from scratch. As heirs to a cultural tradition, children assimilate its values and develop traits of character that facilitate the realization of these values. Traditional moral ideals are commonly defective in important respects—many countenance misogyny and other forms of bigotry. But they are never altogether worthless—they curb some forms of violence, and they promote some forms of kindness. In short, they provide a point of departure.

People are usually very attached to the moral ideal they assimilated when they were young and impressionable. Nonetheless, childhood acculturation does not finalize one's moral ideal once and for all. Many modern societies are comprised of diverse cultures, and this setting affords opportunities to meet people from different backgrounds. Moreover, novels, nonfiction books and magazine articles, movies, and television programs expose people to the moral views of cultures with which they have no personal contact. The give-and-take of cultural pluralism and global media confronts people with values different from the ones they grew up with and encourages people to examine and reexamine their values.

Here, it is worth reiterating broad empathy's potential contribution to the evolution of one's moral ideal, a potential that is greatly enhanced in culturally pluralistic settings (Chapter 2, Section 4). By disclosing the values that are achievable in virtue of another person's distinctive constellation of beliefs, desires, capacities, limitations, and so forth, broad empathy may lead one to reconsider one's moral ideal. One may see the need to add values one had not previously taken seriously; one may come to doubt the soundness of a value one had previously held dear; one may decide to reorder one's priorities. Thus, self-recognition in the context of mutual recognition is not static. It prompts people to review the ideals they embrace and to renew or revise their commitments in light of their insights into others' lives. Informed by empathy, self-recognition enriches the moral ideals people conceive for themselves and protects against distorted judgments of value.

That people's moral ideals reflect their cultural backgrounds and their personal social histories entails that these ideals are not uniform. The circumstances and aims of individuals further diversify their moral ideals. Since a moral ideal would be otiose if it set standards that far outstripped one's ability to live up to them, a moral ideal must incorporate the values one embraces in a form that takes into account a realistic appraisal of one's strengths and weaknesses along with sensible expectations about one's capacity to improve. Also, people have commitments to family members and friends, and they have values and personal projects that they weight in distinctive ways. Moral ideals must allow for these dimensions of people's lives, as well (for related discussion of moral particularity, see M. Walker, 1987, 174–180; for related discussion of character, see B. Williams, 1981, 14–15; Kupperman, 1991b, 143–145, 153). Moral ideals are individualized conceptions of a good person.[11] A virtue of this individualization is that it ensures that self-recognition validates moral subjects *qua* unique individuals, not *qua* instantiations of a universal human nature.

Still, not every set of aims that someone might concoct can count as a moral ideal. Moral ideals do not merely authorize people to follow their inclinations, nor do they permit people to pursue every ambition that might attract them. Others' needs and desires place constraints on moral ideals, as does one's own need for recognition. Although mutual recognition dictates no single moral ideal—moral ideals may include diverse values and order them differently—a moral ideal must articulate a conception of a person who is capable of sustaining relationships that instantiate the good of mutual recognition. Broadly, one must aspire to be a kind of person who gladly recognizes others and who welcomes their recognition. Though individualized, moral ideals cannot be self-centered or self-erasing.

The basic need for mutual recognition establishes a presumption in favor of concern for and appreciation of other people. Yet, it cannot prescribe concern and appreciation at the price of self-abnegation. People sometimes behave in ways that rupture connection and enforce isolation despite ongoing relationship. They become so absorbed in their own projects that they fail to notice anyone else's needs, or they seize decision-making power and ignore dissenting voices. When this is so and cannot be changed, tolerating it is counterproductive as judged by the standard set by the need for mutual recognition. To continue in such a relationship would be to soldier on vainly trying to recognize the other while being deprived of that benefit oneself. The overzealous self-sacrifice with which some commentators have tarred the ethic of care is alien to mutual recognition.[12]

Furthermore, taking pity on others in a way that leaves them diminished in one's eyes is incompatible with mutual recognition. Condescending to people emotionally isolates one from them, severs human connection, and blocks recognition. When one knows another person well, one cannot help but be aware of that person's weaknesses. Still, the need for mutual recognition precludes dismissing people for weaknesses that pose no threat to mutual recognition.

The need for mutual recognition rules out egoism and egotism, as well as self-destructive altruism. In Benjamin's words, people do not "grow *out of* relationships;" they "becom[e] more active and sovereign *within* them" (Benjamin, 1988, 18). Moral ideals anchored in mutual recognition must secure self-recognition along with recognition of the other and recognition from the other.

3. From Empathy to Moral Judgment

Chapter 3 closed with an unsolved problem: how can moral reflection make use of empathic understanding of people who are different from oneself? Simply to acquiesce to the other's demands is to abrogate responsibility for moral judgment, but empathically obtained insight into cherished or intractable difference jams the gears of Kantian impartial reason. Are we to conclude that empathy sets people adrift on a sea of random empathic encounters—drawn to some people's values and projects, repelled by those of others, incapable of critical moral judgment? Plainly, what is needed is a way to move from empathic understanding of difference to deciding how best to respond to the different individual while keeping the empathic infrastructure intact. The theory of self-recognition in the context of mutual recognition that Chodorow and Benjamin adumbrate suggests a view of moral reflection that sustains individual judgment without severing interpersonal connection. In this section, I shall lay out this view; in Section 4, I shall defend it against several objections; and in Section 5, I shall present an extended example of how it might work in practice.

There is a tendency among philosophers to think of moral reflection as beginning with a ready-made inventory of options which are then measured one by one against an ultimate criterion of right and wrong. Which maximizes utility? Or which is universalizable? By a process of elimination, one of the options is chosen. In important respects, this picture is misleading.

There are no pre-existing lists of candidate actions, nor does it make any sense to start moral reflection by trying to think of everything one might do. People feel their way into difficult moral choices little by little. They think of a course of conduct; they become troubled by it in one way or another; they try to fix it up; they cast about for alternatives; they reconsider an option they had previously set aside, and so forth. If they have time, they sometimes generate lists of options and sort through the pros and cons. But these lists are never exhaustive, and considering a list often leads people to hit on a new possibility, which then opens up unexpected avenues of thought. Moral decision-making owes a lot to extemporaneous muddling along that is not particularly amenable to philosophical formalization.

Still, it is important to recognize that, however morally perplexed one may be, one is never at a total moral loss. People completely ignore many options because it is obvious that they are ineligible, or they almost instinctively modify a proposed course of conduct because it does not "feel" quite right. I would like to suggest that one's empathic understanding of those who will be affected by one's action joins forces with one's sense of one's moral identity to sustain this improvisational process and that one interprets the moral significance of a situation by seeking an enactment of one's moral identity that takes into account one's empathic insight into others.

The range of options one will consider is demarcated by one's grasp of the situation one is in—one's perception of the circumstances, one's empathic understanding of the other people who are involved, and one's understanding of one's own position with respect to them. Even the most rudimentary empathy with others gives one some awareness of the moral significance of their predicament and carves out a range of responses for serious consideration, while definitively excluding others as irrelevant, awkward, or even despicable. Incident-specific empathy with a background of broad empathy further narrows this range (for discussion of these types of empathy, see Chapter 2, Sections 3 and 4). As one's empathic understanding increases, so does one's ability to rule out inappropriate courses of action and to identify appropriate ones.

Still, the range of plausible options is not ordained by others without input from the deliberator. Although one could never fully articulate the stock of knowledge and experience that one draws on or the moral ideal that shapes one's intuitions, these materials together with the reasoning, imaginative, and communication skills one brings to bear on them constitute one's distinctive moral identity. Innumerable options never enter one's mind, for one's moral identity deems them beyond the pale; other options are adjusted straightaway out of an implicit realization that they do not quite accord with one's moral identity (for a Kantian view of this process, see Herman, 1991, 789–791). Needless to say, there is usually a great deal of overlap between the options that empathy identifies as candidates and the ones that an individual's moral identity picks out. In fairly routine situations, it is not uncommon for moral reflection to go no farther, for empathy and the agent's moral identity often converge on a single option.

In difficult situations, however, empathic insight is out of alignment with the deliberator's moral identity, and moral reflection must go forward (for an example, see Section 5 below). Moral quandaries often elicit more explicit appeals to empathic understanding of others and to one's own moral identity. One may solicit detailed information about the other's concerns or try to enlarge the scope of one's imaginative reconstruction. One may adopt counterfigurations proposed by socially excluded groups (see Chapters 3–5) in the hope of ridding one's empathic understanding of prejudicial distortion. Puzzling over whether one can take up a particular option in good conscience, one may enlist a friend to play devil's advocate—to survey and probe the values that define one's self-concept and to assess more precisely the fit between one's sense of one's self and a possible plan of action. One may negotiate with the other hoping to find common ground or, at any rate, to split the difference. All of these strategies are commonplace (except, perhaps, invoking dissident speech, which I would argue should be more common), and all of them are designed to sustain human connection by reconciling the integrity of the individual moral subject with other people's needs, desires, values, and the like.[13]

Everything I have said about fashioning a moral response assumes that the deliberator genuinely wants to choose and act morally. It is well known that people who only want to promote their self-interest or who just want to "get it over with" often latch onto a generally accepted moral precept and cloak their actions in this rationale. But real moral reflection is not reducible to implementing handy rules. Rules have a part to play in moral reflection. They capture aspects of most people's moral identity, and they often function as reminders of morally relevant considerations. Still, morally complex situations, and everyday life is full of them, oblige us to improvise.

It is evident that the deliberative process I have been describing embeds self-recognition in mutual recognition. One fashions a moral response by improvising an enactment of one's moral identity in the context of empathic understanding of another's subjective state. To highlight the foundational role of empathy in this approach to moral reflection while stressing that moral judgment requires that the information obtained through empathy be considered in light of independent concerns and values, I shall call this form of moral reflection *empathic thought*. Empathic thought recognizes the deliberator while recognizing the other.

Whether in routine or difficult situations, I submit, people commonly understand the aim of moral deliberation as that of finding a workable continuation of a relationship based on mutual recognition. The improvisational process I have sketched is driven by the search for an answer to the question "How can I *best* respond to you?" This question can seldom be answered without inviting others to voice their understanding of their situation, and empathic access to the other's perspective discloses the values and disvalues that are at stake for the other. Informed by broad empathy, deliberation is eased away from habit and obtuseness. But since asking how one can best respond to another person is not equivalent to asking what that individual wants one to do, empathic insight must be filtered. People rely on the questions "What sort of a person would doing that (not doing that) make me?" and "Do I want to be the sort of person who would (would not) do that?" to establish a point of moral leverage. Answering these questions distinguishes empathic thought from surrender to others' demands irrespective of their merits, as well as from the pursuit of self-interest without regard for others' needs. A moral interpretation of a situation cannot be confined to the perspective of any one of the participants. Moving back and forth between their empathic understanding of others and their understanding of their own moral identity, people shape and dismiss options according to moral standards and find reasons to settle on one course of action rather than another. Coupled with empathic concern for the other, the guidance of one's moral identity gives this process its moral character.[14]

4. Three Challenges to Empathic Thought

There are three major objections that might be lodged against empathic thought. First, it might be argued that it construes morality too narrowly. Many moral decisions do not concern personal relationships. Should one donate money for famine relief? How much money should one give? Should one support welfare reform? Which policy is most fair? What about protecting the panda's shrinking habitat? And so forth. It is not obvious what mutual recognition has to do with these decisions.

Second, building on the first objection, it might be urged that empathic thought is merely a first step in moral reflection. It is a way of generating proposals for handling a subclass of moral issues, namely, those that arise in interpersonal relations. It does not, however, settle questions about the morality of actions, even in this limited subclass. To know whether an action is right or wrong, one must check it against an impersonal, objective standard. Does the action maximize aggregate utility? Would I agree to this principle in the original position? Or some other philosophically reputable test.

Third, it might be urged that unified moral identity is an illusion and a pernicious one at that. To preserve this illusion, moral subjects may freeze questionable moral beliefs in place along with sound ones and become rigid in their thinking. Or acknowledging the heterogeneity of their moral identities, they may find that their ideals provide no definite guidance and that they are better off reverting to an established criterion of right and wrong. I can only address these objections in a general way here, but I think they are considerably less telling than they initially seem.

A. Empathic Thought without Intimacy

While it is undeniable that many moral questions concern distant strangers, it would be inadvisable to take action with respect to distant strangers as the paradigm of moral relations. Doing so would reduce morality to a relatively crude instrument, for on this view morality would be based on meager understanding of the class of potential moral patients, and the range of issues classed as moral would shrink to comparatively paltry proportions. If there must be a paradigm, action among acquaintances seems a much more promising one. Many acquaintances are not intimates, but they are people who know each other, whose lives are to some degree intertwined, and whose actions therefore have a direct and sometimes significant impact on one another's well-being. This personalized model explains the subtlety and complexity we ordinarily associate with moral choice and action. Since acquaintances know quite a bit about each other, they can and often do calibrate their words and deeds to one another's exact needs. Moreover, acquaintances matter to one another. They do not all matter equally. But they do matter, and withheld recognition is experienced at least as a slight and sometimes as an injury.

Nevertheless, our understanding of moral reflection cannot be confined to relations between acquaintances. If empathic thought is a comprehensive approach to moral reflection, it must be able to handle issues that arise in wider contexts. Although it is undeniable that most people begin to acquire the skills needed for mutual recognition in family settings where they learn to empathize with and come to the assistance of loved ones, this form of recognition is just one point on a continuum (for related discussion of moral development, see Okin, 1989b, 232–233, 235–237). The scope of recognition is readily enlarged to encompass friends and a wider circle of acquaintances. It is not at all unusual for people who have heard news of an acquaintance's woe to take steps to ameliorate it. Office collections on behalf of co-workers who have been hospitalized succeed in virtue of people's ability to empathize with such misfortune and their disposition to alleviate it. Thus, empathy shapes people's responses to individuals to whom they have little attachment and whose troubles they are not experiencing directly. Moreover, people often apply recognition skills to more remote cases. They read newspaper reports about the deprivation or dislocation inflicted on people whom they have never met and whom they may even regard as enemies, and they sometimes respond to these hardships compassionately.

Still, it might be argued that it is inadvisable to rest rights on empathic thought because empathy is all too rare. Alvin Goldman cites evidence that empathy tends to be biased in two respects. Not only do people empathize better with others who are "familiar and similar to themselves," but also they are more apt to empathize with "someone's distress in the immediate situation than [with] distress they know is being experienced by someone elsewhere" (Goldman, 1992, 35). If this is so, impartial reason's stress on respect for person-hood as such and the incorruptibility of impartial reason's consistency imperative may seem a necessary antidote to the unreliability of empathy.

Of course, the fact that people's empathic horizons are presently quite limited does not entail that they could not be expanded. Childhood moral education and political rhetoric in U.S. society do little to nurture empathic skills, but moral development need not be arrested in this way. Moreover, if my call for dissident speech to displace prejudicial, culturally entrenched figurations of socially excluded groups and to replace these figurations with emancipatory counterfigurations were heeded, a further obstacle to empathy with strangers would be eliminated (see Chapter 5). Finally, in-depth documentaries could take advantage of the immediacy of television to compensate for geographic distance and the emotional disengagement it promotes.

More importantly, however, my experience does not confirm that, apart from most people's habitual compliance with a set of elementary moral rules that prescribe minimal respect for others, respect for persons *qua* persons and aversion to inconsistency are in any greater supply than empathy. When people confront situations that afford them some discretion, and when adherence to the tenets of impartial reason conflicts with their self-interest, neither the threat of inconsistency nor the inherent dignity Kant discerned in persons seems to deter many people from favoring themselves, their families, or their associates. Thus, I do not think that proponents of impartial reason can plausibly maintain that it draws on commonplace and ingrained moral capacities, nor do I think that there is reason to dismiss empathic thought as Polyannaish.

Though the strangers whom one hopes to benefit may not be able to return the recognition one accords them, the model of mutual recognition is not inapplicable. If one seeks to act in ways that are consonant with mutual recognition, even when one knows that reciprocal recognition will not be forthcoming, one will not go wrong. Of course, broad empathy with a stranger is seldom possible, and, as empathy becomes more attenuated, the moral deliberator must rely on generalizations about people and their needs. Still, modeling moral relations on mutual recognition does not allow one to complacently accept formulaic generalizations about human nature. This model presses moral subjects to take advantage of the arts and the media to enrich their empathic understanding of strangers and to adjust their moral judgments to take into account this enriched understanding. Furthermore, whether or not one is acquainted with the people whose circumstances occasion moral reflection, one's moral ideal provides guidance. Indifference to starvation halfway around the world would say something about the kind of person one is, as would leaving one's ailing parent to join the relief effort there. One's response, whatever it is, enacts or abrogates one's moral ideal. By treating mutual recognition as central to moral relations, moral theory enjoins moral subjects to be "finely aware and richly responsible," regardless of whether their beneficiaries are in a position to reciprocate (Nussbaum, quoting Henry James, 1990, 37).

B. Moral Reflection without Superordinate Moral Criteria

It might be thought that moral reflection should ultimately advert to some philosophically established criterion of right and wrong, for individual moral ideals are too idiosyncratic and too susceptible to self-interested manipulation to have the final say in moral judgment. There are two ways to conceive of the place of traditional philosophical criteria of right and wrong in the process of moral reflection. One account—the account that I shall defend—subordinates these criteria to people's moral identities. On this view, moral deliberators make use of traditional philosophical criteria to help them fashion moral responses that felicitously enact their moral ideals.[15] Thus, people whose moral ideals shun selfishness and parochialism and valorize benevolence and fairness do well to consider whether acting on an option would be best for everyone (utilitarianism) and whether they would want to be treated the way they are proposing to treat someone else (Kantianism). The other account holds that traditional philosophical criteria are independent of moral identity, and, where the two conflict, these criteria supersede the guidance one's moral identity gives. On this view, one develops a proposed course of action and then employs a philosophically sanctioned test to determine whether it is the right thing to do.

In my judgment, the latter view is all too reminiscent of the twilight of Ptolemaic astronomy. As data disconfirming the earth-centered picture of the universe accumulated, Ptolemaic astronomers resorted to embellishing the orbits of celestial bodies with rococo epicycles in order to save the phenomena without relinquishing their theory of the order of the universe. To require that moral subjects defer to a philosophical test of right and wrong over and above their moral identity is to tack an epicycle onto the theory of moral reflection. It is hard to see any reason for doing this, apart from securing the preeminence of philosophy.

A conspicuous difficulty for this view is that no single criterion of right and wrong enjoys philosophy's imprimatur. Currently, there are two major contenders, Kantianism and utilitarianism, and no rapprochement between these camps is in sight. Furthermore, within these camps, there is considerable controversy. Utilitarians disagree about how to interpret their own criterion. Some argue for promoting average utility and others for promoting total utility. Some support act utilitarianism, others rule utilitarianism. And they differ over how to conceptualize and measure happiness, too. Kantian theory is equally rife with debate over fundamental issues. Libertarians like Robert Nozick and welfare liberals like John Rawls both claim Kantian antecedents. Since the authority of every traditional philosophical test of right and wrong is open to doubt, it is baffling why a conscientious moral deliberator should regard any of these tests as superseding his or her moral ideal.

Suppose that, in the process of fashioning a moral response, one never applies the test of universalizability—that is, one never asks "What if everybody acted that way?" or "How would I like to be treated like that?" Only one's sense of what is worthy or unworthy of oneself and one's intuitions about what outcomes are good and bad guide one's thinking. The criterion of universalizability is external to one's moral identity. One's failure to make use of this criterion is not just an oversight. But suppose that nonetheless one is convinced of the validity and the supremacy of this criterion. Perhaps, one thinks that it is wise to have a final check on one's judgments that is independent of the prior process of arriving at them. Once one has a plan of action in hand, therefore, one submits it to the test of universalizability. What would using this test as an overriding criterion of right and wrong add to the process of fashioning a moral response? I believe that it would add nothing and that it would merely duplicate the moral judgment reached in fashioning a moral response using one's empathic understanding of others and the resources of one's moral identity.

To see why this is so, let us return to the problem of gender harassment I discussed in Chapter 2 in which some women students who are distracted and upset by their engineering professor's telling sexist jokes during lectures ask him to desist. If the professor sees these students as a bunch of hopeless wimps who will never survive in the engineering profession, he will be able to justify his jokes on Kantian grounds. He is weeding out unfit candidates, and his practice can be universalized. If he sees a bunch of wimps who can be toughened up by redoubling the joking, he will also be able to justify denying their request on Kantian grounds. He is helping to ensure equal opportunity for his students, and his practice can be universalized. But suppose instead that he sees a group of women who are vulnerable to this sort of humor but who bring to the classroom a spirit of cooperativeness that is helping other students to succeed. He might decide that it would be good for other engineers to have these women as colleagues and that it is worth eliminating his jokes from his lectures to keep them in the profession. But he could reach a different conclusion. He might decide that, however desirable it would be to recruit these women as engineers, deleting his jokes would compromise his academic freedom. Whichever he decides, he could universalize his proposed course of action. Everything hinges on how the professor perceives the students, on what he thinks he can accomplish and by what means, and on what sorts of behavior he regards it as fitting for him to undertake. Barring egregious irrationality, universalizability will ratify the results of the process of fashioning a moral response.

The way one formulates the maxim that characterizes one's intended action reflects one's understanding of what is morally significant about the situation and one's assessment of the relative importance of the morally significant factors. Unless one's moral ideal is strangely and alarmingly out of sync with the ultimate criterion of morality that one accepts, one will conceptualize situations and preferred courses of conduct in ways that conform to this criterion. It is to be expected, then, that one will consistently find that the maxims one presents are universalizable. A parallel argument could be made for utilitarian tests of morality.

Now, I am not accusing people of bad faith. It is true that people sometimes contrive devious characterizations of their conduct that will survive traditional philosophical tests, and they do so in order to gain authorization (albeit spurious) for morally deficient choices or to exculpate such choices in retrospect. But my claim concerns sincere, open-minded moral reflection. Both fashioning a moral response and applying philosophical criteria of right and wrong depend on the way one interprets situations, and the way one interprets situations depends on one's empathic understanding of others, on the moral concepts one has at one's disposal, and on one's moral ideal. If this is so, performing the universalizability exercise or the utilitarian calculus after one has fashioned a moral response is superfluous.

I suspect that the appeal of the claim that moral reflection is not complete until one has checked one's decision against a traditional philosophical criterion of right and wrong is heightened by the specter of the serial murderer or the war criminal. Since people of this kind cannot be trusted to adopt humane moral ideals or to live up to humane moral ideals if they have them, it seems to follow that some external check must be imposed. I think, however, that this line of thought confuses two different issues.

On the one hand, there is the problem of how we can be justified in morally condemning what these people do and in punishing or try-ing to reform them. These practices require that we reject individual relativism, and it might seem that empathic thought is a form of indi-vidual relativism. However, as I argued in Section 2, the content of tenable moral ideals is constrained by the need for mutual recogni-tion. Plainly, this constraint will not countenance the behavior of mass killers or torturers.

On the other hand, there is the problem of furnishing an adequate theory of moral reflection. In this connection, I must concede that empathic thought cannot guarantee that people will act in morally acceptable ways, but I would add that no theory of moral reflection can guarantee this. Showing serial murderers and war criminals that they cannot universalize their actions or that their actions send aggre-gate utility plummeting will not put an end to their reprehensible conduct. Unless they adopt moral ideals that commit them to com-plying with these standards or develop sufficient self-control to fulfill their moral ideals, their behavior is likely to persist. Abstract moral standards that have not been assimilated to a person's moral identity have little influence over the person's conduct.

Still, the moral ideals that guide empathic thought are individualized, and it is worth noting that this circumscribed individualization can be seen as an advantage. Any convincing moral theory must make sense of our tolerance for moral disagreement. I take it that all theories would say that we must make allowance for human fallibility, and therefore we must tolerate differences of moral opinion. But I have in mind a somewhat different orientation to this issue. Suppose that one thinks that diversity of moral judgment is a good thing, not just a consequence of the inevitability of error. Then it is necessary to focus on the accounts of moral permissibility that moral theories furnish, for it would be wrong not to tolerate different morally permissible views.

For utilitarians, actions are permissible if each of them will produce as much utility as the other and no other action will produce more utility. For Kantians, actions are permissible if the categorical imperative does not reject them. In contrast, for empathic thought, diverse moral opinion arises because different people have different moral ideals, and differing moral opinion deserves respect provided that it arises from a moral ideal that is capable of sustaining mutual recognition. I shall not argue this point, but I find the idea of linking tolerance to individuality and individual styles of interaction attractive —more attractive than the idea of linking tolerance to the coincidence that more than one action will yield the same amount of utility or to the happenstance that more than one maxim does not snare one in self-contradiction (for related discussion, see M. Walker, 1987, 179).

At the risk of belaboring the point, my position is certainly not that Kantian and utilitarian considerations have no place in moral reflection. What I am maintaining is that asking oneself whether one's action maximizes aggregate welfare or passes the test of universalizability is appropriate if one or both of these tests help one to figure out how to enact one's moral ideal. Since these tests are well ensconced in Western culture, and since many caregivers in this culture teach children to pause and consider whether what they want to do is best for everyone concerned and whether they would want to be treated the way they are planning to act, it is probable that many people have a moral identity that incorporates utilitarian and Kantian considerations. Thus, in fashioning moral responses these people will factor in these considerations. But if they comply with these standards, they do so, not because one of these tests is definitive of the moral point of view, but rather because they would betray their moral identity as well as their empathic understanding of others if they violated these standards.

C. Moral Identity without Unitary Subjects

The tenability of empathic thought rests on the assumption that people's moral identities are both sufficiently well-defined to provide clear practical direction and also sufficiently independent to protect moral reflection from noxious cultural influences. But postmodernists might object that such unity and such independence are neither possible nor desirable. Since the self is inescapably fragmented, coherent moral identity and critical moral reflection are will-o'-the-wisps left over from modernism (but for objections to postmodernist romanticization of decentered subjectivity, see Flax, 1987, 92–94, 106). In addition, there could be a modernist variant of this objection. Modernists might say that moral identity is too ill-defined and too molded by social norms to provide clear and independent practical guidance, but that, happily, people can turn to philosophically defensible criteria of right and wrong to make moral judgments. In Section 4B above, I argued that separating the authority of such moral tests from moral identity is misguided. In what follows, I shall argue that neither postmodernists nor modernists should endorse a view of inner diversity that disables moral identity, that the forms of inner diversity that some prominent feminist postmodernists have endorsed do not disable moral identity, and that, since socially situated, nonunitary subjects can engage in critical moral reflection, modernists should join postmodernists in endorsing these forms of inner diversity.

Inner diversity can take various forms. Let me begin by describing a form of nonunitary subjectivity that I think both modernists and postmodernists should eschew. Vladimir V. Zhirinovsky, the right-wing politician whose party captured an unexpectedly large vote in the December 1993 parliamentary elections in Russia, is reported to be a nonunitary subject (*New York Times*, December 28, 1993). Ten years ago, while Russia was still under Communist rule, he claimed to have a Jewish father and sought an application to immigrate to Israel. Today, now that Russia has undertaken democratic reforms, he is a nationalistic fascist who espouses anti-Semitic views and courts an anti-Semitic constituency. A fragmented self, to be sure. A Jew *and* an anti-Semitic fascist.

Zhirinovsky is an extreme case of a fairly common phenomenon. By deceiving themselves or repressing aspects of themselves, people become unabashedly opportunistic or complacently malign. The ability to protect oneself from moral scrutiny in this way seems to be part of our psychic endowment, and it may be inevitable that people will sometimes resort to this defense mechanism. However, that people should strive to avoid such dishonesty and that they should strive to confront it and extricate themselves from it when it occurs seem indisputable. No one should condone Zhirinovsky's inner diversity.

Still, there may be some difference of opinion between postmodernists and me over how to extricate oneself from such fragmentation. In a discussion of multiple personality disorder, Naomi Scheman maintains that the solution to this problem is neither "integrating all the personalities into one, nor making all but one go away" (Scheman, 1993, 103). Rather, the solution is to "creat[e] the possibility for respectful conversation among them, facilitating their mutual recognition and acceptance" (Scheman, 1993, 103). This may be the best that psychotherapists can do for those who suffer from multiple personality disorder, but it often proves to be a Sisyphean treatment. As communication is initiated between existing parts of the self, new and hostile parts begin to emerge and to subvert the rapprochement between the parts that are interacting (Elizabeth Hegeman, private communication).

Regardless of its therapeutic record, this conversational model is not always a morally tenable model of the intrapersonal life of a heterogeneous subject. I think it would be a travesty if Zhirinovsky, the Jew, were to lend himself to respectful dialogue with and acceptance of Zhirinovsky, the anti-Semitic fascist. I think it would be all to the good if Zhirinovsky, the anti-Semitic fascist, were destroyed. Zhirinovsky-style fragmentation needs to be addressed, not through the courtesies of mutually respectful conversation, but rather through the shock therapy of dissident speech (see Chapters 3–5).

In *The Company She Keeps,* Mary McCarthy describes a less morally objectionable form of inner diversity. Meg Sargent is reflecting on a dream in which she allows herself to be seduced by a loutish Nazi by closing her eyes and pretending that her lover is a Byronic hero. She recognizes that even in her sexual transports she never really forgot who her lover was, and she realizes that this residual lucidity must be preserved: "'Oh my God,' she said, . . . 'do not let them take this away from me. If the flesh must be blind, let the spirit see. Preserve me in disunity.'" (McCarthy quoted in Strouse, 1992, 17) Meg Sargent's dream together with her response to it exemplifies a guilty, ashamed, or embarrassed form of heterogeneity. Her conscience is in conflict with her effective motivation and her conduct (fortunately, confined to her dream). Unlike Zhirinovsky, she is not a hypocrite or a liar, though she is weak. Moreover, she retains a self-critical perspective and preserves a commitment, however vestigial, to a moral ideal. Plainly, it would be better from a moral point of view if Meg Sargent could resist the blandishments of Nazis, but she pleads to be preserved in disunity because her fragmentation makes her aware of her wrongdoing and makes her potentially amenable to change. She is not a moral wanton.

Sandra Bartky presents a similar, but slightly different type of inner diversity. Bartky's discussion of feminism and masochistic sexuality is similar to McCarthy's portrayal of Meg Sargent, for there is a discrepancy between the individual's moral ideal and her conduct. The masochistic feminist, whom Bartky ironically calls P., indicts masochistic desire as an internalization and eroticization of male dominance (Bartky, 1990, 47). Thus, like Meg Sargent, P. is estranged from her desire (Bartky, 1990, 51). But the two cases differ, for Meg Sargent's betrayal of her moral ideal stems from her personal failings, whereas the feminist who cannot extirpate her masochistic desires is caught in a patriarchal culture that she cannot overcome by herself (Bartky, 1990, 54–60). "P. is entitled to her shame" regarding her masochistic desires, yet her "sexuality is opaque and mysterious, seemingly unalterable because its meaning is impenetrable" (Bartky, 1990, 52, 61).

The solution seems to be to abandon either one's shame or one's desire, but both options pose insurmountable obstacles (Bartky, 1990, 60). To disavow one's shame would be to violate one's moral ideal, but it appears to be futile to try to transform one's desire. Alas, P. *is* both a feminist and also a masochist.

Now, it might seem that P.'s moral predicament resembles Zhirinovsky's. The components of their respective moral identities are irreconcilably at odds with one another. However, the differences between Zhirinovsky and P. are more significant than their similarities. First, P.'s conflict arises as a result of her feminist critique of unjust social relations, whereas Zhirinovsky's fascism is propelled by culturally normative prejudice. Second, P. is conscious of her conflict and deplores it, whereas Zhirinovsky, the fascist, takes the expedient of refusing to admit that his father was Jewish and thus denies the fragmentation within him. These differences are morally significant because P.'s consciousness enables her to use her fragmentation constructively. She may not be able to cure it. Still, understanding why she cannot cure it may undergird her social critique and strengthen her resolve as a feminist.

Finally, Maria Lugones portrays herself as an "ambiguous being" containing a "plurality of selves," and she argues that such fragmentation is politically fruitful (Lugones, 1987, 13–14, 17–18). Lugones' example is her own conflictual experience as a Latina and a lesbian. In the Latino community, Lugones declares, "[l]esbians are abominations" (Lugones, 1990, 142). If Lugones is ever to be able to affirm her identity as a Latina lesbian, she must participate in the evolution of Latino culture, but, to participate in the evolution of this culture, she must conceal her sexual orientation from other members of this community. Lugones sees this split as morally empowering, for by maintaining her dual identity she can help to dismantle heterosexism within a culture that in other respects nourishes her (Lugones, 1990, 143–144).

It seems to me that Lugones and Irene Opdyke have quite a bit in common. Their selves are fragmented, and they act duplicitously. Yet, their moral identities are intact and quite well-defined. Opdyke believes in reaching out to others, and she knows that anti-Semitism is wrong. Lugones values Latino culture, and she knows that homophobia is wrong. These women are neither ambivalent nor irresolute.

They are, however, committed to values that cannot be completely reconciled in any cultural context that is available to them. The tensions that this fragmentation creates prompt their social critiques and keep them alive to possibilities for social protest or amelioration. They are fragmented, but not in a disabling or opprobrious way. Living with such inner diversity can be an ordeal. Opdyke must often have been terrified, and sometimes she must have felt soiled. Lugones must sometimes feel frustrated and angry that there is no place where she can fully affirm both dimensions of her identity. Here is where Scheman's proposal for respectful conversation and mutual recognition among parts of the self belongs [in fact, Scheman cites Lugones (Scheman, 1993, 103); also see Lugones, 1990, 145]. By refusing to disavow any part of their moral identities and keeping the lines of communication open between these parts, Opdyke and Lugones are able to maintain the sorts of human relations they value while resisting cooptation by social environments that vigorously and systematically oppose their emancipatory social visions. In short, they enact their moral identities insofar as circumstances permit.

Social change seldom moves swiftly enough to alleviate the inner conflicts of dissenters. Yet, it is doubtful that social critics should eliminate their inner diversity through individual adjustment. To defend such a view, it would be necessary to conceive of intrapersonal integration as an extremely tight unity and to elevate intrapersonal integration to the status of a supreme value. I wonder if any contemporary philosopher would take this position. Surely, no one would hold that Opdyke ought to have become a Nazi collaborator. Would anyone hold that P. ought to learn to revel in masochistic pleasures if neither psychotherapy nor feminist consciousness-raising enables her to extirpate these desires? Would anyone hold that Lugones ought to exile herself from and attack Latino culture if she cannot immediately win it over to accepting gay and lesbian rights? Some people in similar positions might choose these routes. Still, they are not our moral exemplars, for there are compelling reasons not to capitulate to the repressive social forces that may tempt people to retreat from opposition.

Since the value of the critical perspectives that Opdyke, Lugones, and P. bring to their lives cannot be gainsaid, it seems to me that modernists should accept this form of inner diversity. Likewise, since Opdyke's, Lugones', and P.'s lives testify to the fact that inner diversity can support a moral identity that is definite enough to provide practical moral direction, modernists should acknowledge that moral subjects do not need superordinate philosophical criteria of right and wrong, and postmodernists should acknowledge that moral identity is compatible with nonunitary subjectivity.

5. Coparenting, Impartial Reason, and Empathic Thought

To round off my account of empathic thought, I would like to consider an application in some detail. Nancy Chodorow's main contribution to ameliorative gender theory is her recommendation that coparenting replace exclusive mothering—that mothers and fathers assume equal responsibility for all aspects of childcare. On

Chodorow's view, it is only through coparenting that male dominance can be overcome (Chodorow, 1978, 215; also see Chapter 4, Section 2B). If fathers are emotionally available to their sons, boys will not grow up dismissing emotional warmth as feminine, and masculine identity will be formed in the context of a close, ongoing relationship. More secure in their own identity, less troubled by intimacy, men will not need to define themselves by negating femininity, and they will cease to despise women as a group. Likewise, if fathers share the work of caring for their daughters and mothers go to work outside the home, girls will cease to worship men as symbols of freedom and independence and also will stop equating femininity with sequestered domesticity and unflagging devotion to others. Women, then, will not experience self-development as conflicting with feminine identity and will be emotionally free to pursue careers. Work outside the home and familial caregiving will be genuine choices for both women and men.

Many feminists support Chodorow's goal. Indeed, it can be seen as part of a solution to the dilemma of difference with respect to gender (see Chapter 1, Section 1). Since mothers have traditionally served as primary parents, daycare is regarded as a women's issue, and subsidizing high-quality, reasonably priced daycare seems like a special benefit for women who want to work outside the home. But if fathers took equal responsibility for childcare, the demand to make daycare available to all would no longer be stigmatized as a women's issue and a departure from gender neutrality. Men would benefit as much as women.

Still, some of Chodorow's critics have raised doubts that her psychology is compatible with this reform. If today's men grew up lacking warm, unbroken emotional bonds to a same-sex parent and defining themselves by negating femininity, as Chodorow claims (Chodorow, 1974, 49–51; 1978, 106, 175–176), then they do not have the nurturing skills that would equip them to share equally in the rearing of their children (Lorber et al., 1981, 485–486). Here, I want to point out that this apparent psychological dead end has moral parallels and that the moral dead end can be overcome only through empathic thought and dissident speech.

If Chodorow's account of masculine development is correct, it would seem that men's childhood experience prepares them to approach moral questions only using detached, universalist methods (for this reading of Chodorow, see Hartsock, 1983, 294–297; also see

Flax, 1983). In that case, it is possible for feminists to commend coparenting to men who resist taking on this responsibility only by appealing to impartial reason. Accordingly, the argument must be that all people are basically the same and that they share a common interest in participating in the upbringing of their children—that is, a parental interest.[16] However, few men accept this view of themselves. Most mothers who work full-time and who live with the fathers of their children must wage a ceaseless battle if they want to enlist fathers to "help" with childcare. In other words, if mothers and fathers do share a common parental interest, this interest is so deeply buried in many men's psyches that it would be very difficult to recover. Moreover, some single women who wish to have a child and to raise it on their own arrange to be artificially inseminated using the sperm of a male friend. To hold that such arrangements violate the biological father's fundamental parental interest would be to needlessly constrain women's reproductive options. Thus, arguments from impartial reason seem both futile and wrongheaded.

An alternative approach that has not been widely explored but that deserves serious consideration is empathic thought in concert with dissident speech. I doubt that reluctant men can be induced to coparent gladly until they empathically engage with caregivers, but I suspect that many men will not be able to empathize with female or male caregivers without the assistance of dissident speech. Culturally entrenched figurations of gender denigrate female caregivers as instinctual creatures and male caregivers as effeminate. Feminist dissident speech seeks to refigure both maternity and paternity (for relevant examples, see Chapter 4, Sections 2A–2D). Adopting these counterfigurations would facilitate men's ability to feel concern for caregivers and to imaginatively reconstruct caregiving experience. In other words, dissident speech would help to reduce distortion in men's empathic understanding of caregivers. In addition, dissident speech regarding masculinity provides positive images of male caregiving and thus would help to reduce many men's resistance to seeing themselves as caregivers. Broad empathy with caregivers would then enable fathers to discover that avoiding childcare deprives them of fascinating experiences and cuts them off from values that they might be loathe to forgo if they were aware of the consequences of their choices (for discussion of how broad empathy discloses value, see Chapter 2, Section 4). In sum, many fathers would discover that they would betray their moral identities if they scorned coparenting.

Still, there is good reason to doubt that all fathers (or, for that matter, all mothers) have a basic interest in taking a major role in parenting. Some might conclude that participating equally in childcare would interfere to an intolerable degree with other aims that are more compelling for them. Still, if this conclusion were reached through empathic thought, I believe that these fathers (and their female counterparts) would be disposed to see caregiving as a worthwhile life focus that does not happen to fit with their own moral identity. Consequently, they would shed the disdain that many of them now profess for caregiving activities, and they would accord caregiving the respect it deserves.

A further reason to base arguments for coparenting on empathic thought stems from impartial reason's difficulty accommodating the fact that some women (and some men) have no wish to divide childcare with their partners and prefer to take full responsibility for childcare themselves. It is hard to see how arguments for coparenting based on Kantian impartial reason could condone exclusive mothering (or fathering) in two-parent, heterosexual households. Although impartial reason permits interference with basic interests provided that the individual consents to this treatment, individuals who do consent are seen as making a major sacrifice. On this construal, then, it would be morally suspect for one parent to ask another to cede childcare responsibilities. But the fact that many people are not at all eager to be primary caregivers belies this strong presumption against exclusive mothering or fathering. Similarly, utilitarian calculations would probably leave no room for discretion. If children who are coparented are somewhat happier than children parented exclusively by a mother or by a father, and if parents who coparent are not utterly miserable, utilitarianism will dictate coparenting. But, again, this seems an unduly restrictive conclusion.

In contrast, empathic thought gives credence to individual preferences and imposes no universal rule. Empathic thought avoids what might be called the *tyranny of typicality*. Standardized interpretations of human interests leave little room for individual idiosyncrasy. It seems to me obvious that in a matter as personal as family relationships empathic thought's flexibility is highly desirable.

A problem remains for my contention that empathic thought provides the best way to address the issue of coparenting, for Chodorow's account of masculinity suggests that few men have the capacities that would enable them to engage in empathic thought.

Nevertheless, there is more reason to hope that adult men will develop the skills needed to empathize with mothers and reflect on their responsibilities as fathers than there is to hope that they will be persuaded to fulfill the abstract obligations that impartial reason posits. Although Chodorow herself maintains that "good-enough" mothering endows men with an empathic and nurturant potentiality, she maintains that this potentiality typically remains latent (Chodorow, 1978, 87–88). However, Carol Gilligan's research suggests that this potential is more developed and accessible than Chodorow seems to think. According to Gilligan, one-third of her male subjects switch back and forth between impartial reason and the ethic of care (Gilligan, 1987, 25). Furthermore, men who do not spontaneously think in terms of care are capable of constructing care-based arguments (Gilligan, 1987, 27–28). Since empathic thought is quite similar to Gilligan's ethic of care, her results are encouraging.

Finally, it seems to me that the expansion of one's repertory of interpersonal skills that empathic thought commends would be less threatening and potentially more rewarding than embracing primary parenting on principle. It is a singular virtue of empathic thought that it exhorts moral subjects to strengthen their empathic skills and connect with others, for I should think that most people would be highly motivated to follow this advice. Not only are the satisfactions of wide acquaintanceship and rich understanding of other people abundant, but also the potential satisfaction of gaining recognition from the people one gets to know furnishes an added incentive. In Irene Opdyke's memorable words, "We all have to reach out to know that we're not alone in the world," and surely we all need to know we're not alone.

7

Empathic Thought
and the Politics of Rights

Few, if any, societies are free of the problem of institutionalized
social exclusion based on group membership. By fastening on group
differences and magnifying their negative social and economic consequences, societies commit grievous injustices and snare themselves in
the double bind of the dilemma of difference (see Chapter 1, Section
1). If they belatedly extend equal rights to members of these groups
but ignore difference, existing social and economic divisions often
persist. Yet, if they focus on difference and create programs to meet
the distinctive needs of members of these groups, members of the
dominant group resent this special treatment and resist social change.
Again, justice is indefinitely postponed.

Let me briefly review the major reasons for regarding empathic
thought undertaken against a background of dissident speech as especially well-adapted to addressing the most vexing forms of the
dilemma of difference. Empathic thought's most obvious advantage
in this regard is that it is based on empathy, preferably broad empathy (Chapter 2, Sections 3 and 4). It requires people to attend to others in order to learn to see the world from their point of view—in
Elizabeth V. Spelman's apt phrase, to "apprentice" themselves to others (Spelman, 1988, 178).

Yet, empathizing with people from groups that are different from
one's own is often fraught with difficulties. De facto segregation in
education, employment, and housing minimizes opportunities for
friendship across group boundaries. Moreover, ubiquitous, prejudi-

cial, cultural figurations of socially excluded groups frame and distort perception (see Chapter 3; Chapter 4, Section 1). To overcome these obstacles, I have urged that moral reflection must be informed by dissident speech (see Chapters 4 and 5). Dissident speech produces emancipatory figurations that articulate a socially excluded group's sense of its own identity and that counteract culturally entrenched stereotypes. By adopting these counterfigurations and letting them structure perception, empathizers can rid their empathic reconstructions of others' experience of the taint of culturally normative prejudice. As Maria Lugones might put it, dissident speech facilitates "travel" to other people's "worlds" (Lugones, 1987, 3).

Such travel is invaluable. Since broad empathy makes moral deliberators aware of the values and the disvalues that are realizable for the other, it demonstrates the force of others' claims and keeps reflection from calcifying around egocentric categories that negate difference. In addition, by introducing deliberators to unfamiliar values or combinations of values, broad empathy with people from different social groups guards against narrow-minded, mean-spirited moral ideals. Empathic thought is dynamic inasmuch as it fosters both appreciation of others' aims and life choices and also enrichment of one's own moral ideal (Chapter 2, Section 4; Chapter 6, Section 2).

Still, empathic thought does not rely exclusively on empathy to ensure the soundness of people's moral ideals, for in addition the moral ideals associated with empathic thought must support mutual recognition (Chapter 6, Section 2). One's dependency on others for recognition militates against overhasty, misplaced contempt for others. Likewise, this dependency militates in favor of cultivating traits of character and interpersonal skills—including those needed to join in the production of dissident speech and those needed to benefit from emancipatory counterfigurations that others have produced—that deter impulses to dismiss others arbitrarily. But mutual recognition is incompatible with indiscriminate acceptance of others or subservience to their demands, for to recognize others one must also recognize oneself (Chapter 6, Section 2). Aspiring to recognize oneself along with others, one must assess the merits of others' claims.

Unlike impartial reason, however, empathic thought does not rest these assessments on a set of general principles that implicitly reinforce the status quo. The moral ideals associated with empathic thought provide a more supple basis for judgment (Chapter 6, Section 3). A moral ideal includes an assortment of values and concerns, and the relative weights of the components of a moral ideal are not fixed in a predetermined hierarchy. Moreover, since a single value can be enacted in countless ways, it is usually possible to devise a response that enacts a number of one's values. Most importantly, this flexibility allows moral deliberators to tailor their responses to their empathic grasp of other individuals.

The synthesis of mutual recognition and self-recognition that empathic thought effects sanctions an improvisational form of critical moral reflection geared to recognizing without penalizing difference (Chapter 6, Section 5). Although empathic thought relies on the deliberator's accumulated experience of people and human relations, it assumes no standard case. Rather, it pays attention to individuals and seeks to understand and respond to each individual's distinctive ensemble of strengths and weaknesses, hopes and fears. Whereas impartial reason relies on comprehensive moral categories and thus minimizes the number of moral categories, empathic thought allows moral categories to proliferate in proportion to one's perception of moral variation. Whereas impartial reason celebrates the value of universal humanity through fidelity to general principles, empathic thought celebrates the value of human diversity through concern for individuals. Difference is presumed to be the norm—every person is unique—and the task of moral reflection is to find a response that is gauged to particular persons. Thus, making allowance for difference carries no connotations of favoritism or exploitation. Relishing and honoring difference, yet guided by moral ideals, empathic thought licenses moral subjects to reinvent morality without setting them adrift.

At this point, however, a worry might arise about whether empathic thought can connect with political and legal discourse. In the United States, rights talk is the lingua franca in which we articulate our sense of justice, in which we set forth what we believe is our due and what we owe to others, and in which we seek access to those who wield political power and fight against injustice. Since rights have traditionally been associated with impartial reason, it might seem that displacing impartial reason would also displace rights. On the one hand, if the socially excluded cannot appeal to rights, they are likely to remain disempowered (P. Williams, 1991, 152–154, 159, 163). But, on the other hand, rights have hardly been an unalloyed blessing for the victims of unjust social exclusion. Since rights grounded in impartial reason are often treated as if they were timeless and absolute, they may threaten the interests of excluded groups by obstructing social change (Minow, 1990, 146–147, 308). From the standpoint of justification, though, it seems to me that rights are overdetermined—that is, derivable both from impartial reason and from empathic thought. Thus, I shall argue that rights are not alien to empathic thought and that empathically grounded rights can serve as vehicles for social change.

1. Political Discourse and Empathic Thought

Impartial reason furnishes the classic argument for basic rights. This reasoning assumes that the deliberator is a representative person, and it proceeds deductively. Having identified an urgent universal human need, one reasons that, since no one would want to live in a society that did not meet that need, everyone must be entitled to have it met. Depending on the nature of the need, this entitlement will ensure noninterference, positive benefits, or some combination of the two. To deprive a person of the goods that basic rights specify is unjust, for it denies the humanity of this victim. Everyone has an equal right to these goods.

The structure of this argument explains both why rights can be an important ally for the dispossessed and also why rights often fail them. The universalism undergirding this type of argument has supplied socially excluded groups with a powerful weapon. They can argue that they, too, are persons who share the very needs that ground basic rights and therefore that they have the same rights as everyone else. This argument played an influential part in the struggle to extend suffrage to women and to African-Americans and also in the struggle to enact legislation prohibiting discrimination against these groups and extending equal opportunity to them. Yet, recognizing the equal rights of all members of society does not eliminate injustice. We have seen, for instance, how equal opportunity disadvantages mothers who let their careers lapse in order to stay home and care for their young children and how equal opportunity can be compromised when free speech collides with demands from members of traditionally excluded social groups that professors stop making jokes at their expense (Chapter 1, Section 1; Chapter 2, Section 2). The generality of arguments based on impartial reason creates a presumption in favor of a single standardized conception of a right, and the claim that infringing a right violates a person's humanity creates a presumption against adapting rights to meet newly recognized social contingencies. In practice, these presumptions often prevent members of socially excluded groups from enjoying the benefits their rights officially confer.

Despite the historical link between rights and impartial reason, there is no reason to regard impartial reason as holding a monopoly over rights. Indeed, it is easy to see the seeds of rights in empathic thought within interpersonal contexts. For example, in conjunction with their moral ideals, parents' empathic understanding of their adolescent children typically leads them to the conclusion that they must grant these individuals greater decision-making power over their own lives. Parents begin to grasp their daughters' or sons' frustration at having decisions imposed on them and to appreciate their budding capacity for autonomous choice. Thus, parents who feel antipathy for an overbearing, authoritarian style of childrearing expand the sphere of liberty they accord to their teenagers and resolve not to meddle in or overrule the choices they make. Henceforth, when their kids tell them to back off, they regard this demand as legitimate and try to respect it. Parents use their intimate knowledge of their children's developing capacities and needs to increase their freedom commensurately. In so doing, they informally recognize rights that are sensitive to individual needs.

This kind of thinking can be transposed into the wider social arena. The questions I used to characterize empathic thought can be framed from a political standpoint, as well as from an individual one. Instead of asking "What sort of a person would doing that (not doing that) make me?" and "Do I want to be the sort of person who would (would not) do that?" polities can ask "What sort of a society would adopting that policy (not adopting that policy) make us?" and "Do we want to have the sort of society that would (would not) implement such a policy?" To answer these questions, political participants must grasp the social meaning of the options available to them. To that end, they must gain empathic understanding of those who will be affected by their choices. Moreover, they must articulate their society's moral identity—its historical antecedents in law and custom, the resources that are currently at their disposal, and their collective aspirations for the future. Although political actors may seek to clarify their individual views by asking whether they want to be the sort of person who would support the government's taking (or failing to take) a certain measure, political decision-making must ultimately confront social ideals and the match between those ideals and public policy. For empathic thought, the object of moral reflection at the social level is to bring public policy into alignment both with empathic understanding of the impact of alternative policies on people's lives and also with the best traditions and the enduring values of a polity.

This empathically based framework for addressing political issues can be applied to rights. Empathic thought starts from concrete cases—empathy with this person's distinctive potential and urgent needs, empathy with that person's distinctive potential and urgent needs, and so forth. It then asks, "What kind of a society would fail to meet these needs?" and "Is this the kind of society we want to belong to?" Suppose we judge that a society that subjected people to such-and-such a constraint (or privation) and that let many people's potential languish as a result would be repressive (or heartless), and we agree that we would want no part of a society of this kind. (I do not mean to suggest that a society's moral identity can be captured in a word or two; I am merely sampling the sort of considerations that might be adduced.) If we combine our aversion with our inductive grasp of people's various needs, we will conclude that we have a collective responsibility to find appropriate ways to meet those needs and therefore that people are entitled to whatever benefits are required for this purpose.[1] To withhold these benefits would be to commit a serious injustice, for mistreating individuals in this way would deny them recognition and betray our moral identity as a society.

2. Nonunitary Political Identity, Injustice, and Rights

Curiously, John Rawls presents a view of the metaethical status of his principles of justice that is quite similar to the view I have just outlined. He holds that his two principles of justice and the rights they guarantee constitute the "kernel of an overlapping consensus" that articulates the "basic intuitive ideas found in the public culture of a constitutional democracy" (Rawls, 1985, 246; 1993, 13–15, 175). In other words, justice as fairness expresses the moral identity of modern constitutional democracies. There are a number of major differences, however, between Rawls's view and mine. In my view, the moral identities of modern constitutional democracies are far more complex than Rawls acknowledges, and it is fortunate that they are, for complex moral identities are needed to address pressing social issues.

It seems to me that Rawls's analysis of the moral identity of the United States is empirically inaccurate. For Rawls, the public political culture of modern democratic societies "comprises the political institutions of a constitutional regime and the public traditions of their interpretation (including those of the judiciary), as well as historic texts and documents that are common knowledge" (Rawls, 1993, 13–14). Rawls believes that this characterization excludes a great deal. He consigns "[c]omprehensive doctrines of all kinds—religious, philosophical, and moral" to the "background culture" (Rawls, 1993, 14). Kantianism, utilitarianism, Islam, and Judaism all belong to the social, as distinct from the political, realm. Rawls expects individuals who believe in these and similar doctrines to find reasons drawn from them to join the "overlapping consensus" and support his conception of justice (Rawls, 1993, 15, 134, 141). However, he reduces the public culture of modern constitutional democracies to a monistic moral identity that is comprised of key ideas taken from impartial reason alone—the idea of a society as a fair system of cooperation over time, the idea of free and equal persons, and the idea of a well-ordered society (Rawls, 1993, 14). These ideas are rich veins, and Rawls demonstrates that a powerful theory of justice can be mined from them. Nevertheless, it is clear that rights-based, contractarian liberalism is but one strand of U.S. public political culture.

Articulating this moral identity in any detail would take us too far afield, but let me mention a few constituent themes that Rawls discards. Utilitarian calculations of social welfare and republican appeals to civic virtue are very much a part of U.S. legislative and judicial history. Likewise, major historical documents are laced with the Protestantism of the Founding Fathers. The ethic of care, though largely suppressed in public debate as a result of contempt for that which is identified as feminine together with the exclusion of women from positions of political leadership, has long been waiting to take its rightful place in political discourse. The moral identity implicit in a complex, pluralistic society's political institutions and documents is not reducible to a single canonical tradition. Nor would it be desirable to effect such a reduction, since doing so would radically constrict the moral resources available to address social problems and thus impoverish moral reflection.

Another difference between Rawls and me is that I envisage a democratic process of self-definition, whereas he seems to rely on historical scholarship and philosophical speculation to articulate a society's moral identity. Rawls looks backward for guidance and seeks to discover what values are "embedded in the political institutions of a constitutional democratic regime and the public traditions of their interpretation" (Rawls, 1985, 225). But, since any society's past is flawed, it is necessary to critically assess its political and legal heritage and also to turn to the future and consider what kind of society we should aspire to achieve. Intellectuals have a great deal to contribute to this discussion, but the process of political self-definition cannot claim legitimacy without the participation of a broad spectrum of society's membership.

Finally, empathic thought is grounded in empathy, whereas Rawls advocates an abstract, theoretical exercise in "self-clarification"— that is, the deduction from the original position (Rawls, 1985, 238; 1993, 22). I suspect that the source of this difference can be traced to a difference of opinion about the nature of the problems confronting moral and political philosophy today. Rawls's project is to justify a set of broad principles that are designed primarily to secure a set of basic rights and liberties and secondarily to alleviate chronic poverty and its bad social consequences. In my judgment, however, this project is something of an anachronism. Long ago, such questions as whether religious differences should be tolerated, whether slavery should be permitted, and whether women should have the vote sparked heated disagreement and stood at the center of political debate in Western societies. Novel philosophical defenses of basic rights can be fascinating. Still, from a practical standpoint, these questions about equal rights have been settled in liberal democratic states, and a new set of issues has come to the fore.

The problems that plague contemporary liberal democratic societies stem from a legacy of past wrongs that persists in the form of residual domination and oppression (for a helpful account of domination and oppression and the various forms they assume, see Young, 1990). These injustices take a variety of forms. Established institutions affect different groups differently. Minority men are rarely subjected to sexual harassment in the workplace; white women are seldom held back by racism. Poverty is often a factor in these injustices, but not always in the same way. Many women enjoy middle-class privileges until divorce forces them to provide for themselves and their children. The nature of the prejudices that sustain these wrongs is not uniform. Racists see African-Americans as lowlifes and criminals; misogynists see women as fools and harridans. The expression of these wrongs is to some degree localized. In some communities, taunting is a socially acceptable expression of homophobia; elsewhere, wry, supercilious humor among friends is acceptable, but taunts are not. Accordingly, there is no single wrong that a theory of justice can concentrate on righting.

The complexity of the contemporary problem of justice is compounded, moreover, by the fact that many of the victims insist on asserting their own different identities. Whereas in the past some excluded groups made it easier for the dominant group to accept them by disavowing their own difference, many of today's excluded groups are demanding that others learn to respect difference. This demand fractures the dilemma of difference into innumerable dilemmas of difference. Thus, many pressing social problems call for microsolutions.

Rights are not irrelevant to contemporary social issues. But the focus of controversy has shifted away from questions about whether there are any basic rights and how to demarcate the scope of the class of right-holders. Although foes of abortion and advocates of animal rights are now contesting the boundaries of the class of right-holders, these debates are peripheral compared to earlier debates in which respected thinkers denied the rights of the majority of humans, namely, all men of color and women. Currently, controversy centers on questions about what constitutes equal enjoyment of a right and how the class of basic rights should be expanded. Sweeping, principled accounts of justice underestimate the difficulty of these questions.

Rawls' discussion of fair equality of opportunity and the difference principle is the best-known attempt to address these new questions without abandoning the framework of impartial reason. By investing extra resources in the education of disadvantaged students and by redistributing income to the least advantaged members of society, Rawls seeks to answer critics of formally equal liberty by ensuring that the basic liberties of all members of society will have a minimally acceptable degree of worth—a degree of worth sufficient to enable all right-holders to exercise their liberties effectively (Rawls, 1971, 204–205). Thus, he breaches the traditional liberal barrier between the realm of rights and the laissez-faire realm of the distribution of economic goods, and he defends his redistributive principles as solutions to the wrongs that stem from systemic inequality.

Of course, it must be acknowledged that Rawls is concerned exclusively with ideal theory and he does not claim that his principles suffice to redress longstanding injustices. Nevertheless, it is evident that if the United States, for example, fully implemented his principles, it would not become a just society unless measures were also taken to curb sexism, racism, classism, homophobia, ethnocentrism, and the like. Discrimination does not stop, nor do social divisions disappear when members of excluded groups become better educated and more affluent. Cornel West recounts his appalling experience on the high ways of the Northeast United States:

> The cop peered into the car and said, "I see you going back and forth once a week; this is the fourth time I've seen you." That made him feel that I was dealing in cocaine. I said to him, "You've been seeing me that often because I teach at Williams College once a week. I'm a professor of philosophy and religion." "Yes," he replied, "and I'm the Flying Nun. Let's go, nigger." (West quoted in "The Public Intellectual," *The New Yorker,* January 17, 1994, p. 40)

Thus, the moral identity Rawls proposes for modern constitutional democracies—a moral identity dedicated solely to the value of implementing ideal principles derived from impartial reason—is out of step with social reality.

To address contemporary social issues adequately, rights must be anchored in empathy with members of different groups who are suffering different forms of injustice. Likewise, rights must be construed flexibly if they are to meet heterogeneous needs in suitably heterogeneous ways. Yet, if rights are not to lose their moral force—that is, if rights violations are grave moral wrongs and if right-holders are entitled to press demands based on their rights—a balance must be struck between the stability of rights and their adaptability to the needs of individuals with diverse backgrounds and circumstances.

Here, it is necessary to point out that there is no difference between impartial reason and empathic thought with regard to treating others' needs and desires as equal to one's own. Since bias commonly works unconsciously, good intentions and conscientious reflection may produce unfair judgments whether one reasons impartially or thinks empathically. Accordingly, neither impartial reason nor empathic thought can do without dissident speech to counteract culturally normative prejudice (Chapters 3–5). Still, a tenable approach to moral reflection must include some guarantee of equal consideration for others that takes over once unconscious bias has been addressed.

Deliberate nepotism is no more acceptable than unconscious discrimination. Kant's consistency requirement and Rawls's veil of ignorance are designed to rule out bias against others and bias in favor of oneself. Empathic thought relies on vivid and nuanced imagination of others' experience coupled with moral ideals that secure mutual recognition to neutralize unwarranted discrimination and favoritism (for helpful critique of the view that impartiality is best achieved through distance and abstraction, see M. Walker, 1991). The trouble with nepotists is not that they empathize, but rather that they empathize too little—their empathy is confined to relatives and does not extend to other people who are affected by their practices.

Incorporated into the pluralistic moral identity that shapes empathic thought, values that are traditionally associated with impartial reason, such as fairness and respect, do not bury other social values. It seems to me, then, that the only way a society can achieve the balance between the stability and the adaptability of rights that the dilemma of difference demands is to embrace a moral identity that encompasses the value of equal consideration along with values that are associated with empathy, such as delight in diversity and compassion. The deficiencies of impartial reason and empathic thought with respect to rights are complementary, as are their virtues. By itself, impartial reason resists customizing rights to fit actual people's diverse needs, for it focuses on the universality of certain needs (for discussion of impartial reason's inability to accommodate empathy with some types of difference, see Chapter 2, Section 5). In contrast, empathic thought's attention to the morally compelling features of the lives of particular individuals sets up resistance to generalizing to a broad pattern of need that would warrant the recognition of a right. However, if rights were understood as grounded in a nonunitary moral identity that fostered a collaboration between the values associated with impartial reason and the values associated with empathy, societies would secure rights that guaranteed benefits suited to the capacities and limitations of individuals— rights that would not substitute formal equality for substantive equality, rights that would not defeat the legitimate demands of socially excluded groups.

For example, it seems likely that empathic thought would certify a right to equality of opportunity. Yet, it seems altogether possible that empathic thought would call into question the absoluteness of the job applicant's right to be judged exclusively on the basis of those qualifications that demonstrably enhance expected job performance, for this policy perpetuates patterns of social exclusion that have had devastating effects on the life prospects of members of marginalized groups. However, empathic thought would not ignore the adverse impact of preferential treatment on young white males. Although their high expectations often assume a background of systemic injustice that shields them from fair competition, their disappointments are not morally insignificant, and it is important to develop programs that will relieve their suffering (for useful proposals, see Ezorsky, 1991, 84–88). Less preoccupied with issues of transgression, blame, and exact compensation than impartial reason, empathic thought could reconfigure the right to equality of opportunity giving due consideration to everyone's interests.

Likewise, one would expect empathic thought to endorse a right to freedom of expression, but one would also expect empathic thought to reconsider free speech in view of the damage done by hate speech as well as by pornography that glorifies violence against women (Meyers, n.d.). Leading liberal legal theorists who believe that the class of hate speech can be delineated clearly enough to block the slide down the slippery slope to tyranny nevertheless think that respect for persons requires that individuals be permitted to decide what they will view or read (Dworkin, 1992, 58, 62). Empathic thought would require that we empathize, as well, with women whose husbands' idea of a great Friday night is to pick up several sadistic pornographic videos and a case of beer on their way home from work and to spend the evening drinking and forcing their wives to join them in reenacting the video scenarios. Broad empathy with a sexually abused woman is likely to give one more vivid experience than one would care to have of chronic fear, intense physical pain, and shattered self-esteem that dim her memory of better times and crush her hope for the future. In *Butler v. Her Majesty the Queen* (1992), the Supreme Court of Canada embraced a moral identity that judged the harms to women caused by pornography to be more pernicious than the harms to the autonomy of the customers of video shops and magazine stands, and it authorized the government to suppress sexually explicit materials that harm women. It remains to be seen whether banning this sort of pornography will succeed in removing it from the market, whether men who use it as a prop will find some other excuse to attack their "lovers," and whether this censorship will pose a danger to artistic and political expression. If the

Canadian government remains alert to the possibility of malfunctioning policies and is prepared to correct defective policies as they come to light, the bold social experiment on which Canada has embarked will provide a dramatic practical vindication of empathic thought's viability as an arbiter of rights.

Empathic thought might well raise doubts about some tenets of rights interpretation that are held sacred by U.S. civil libertarians, for this approach to moral reflection calls into question interpretations of rights that betray empathic understanding of the members of socially excluded groups. Still, empathic thought does not authorize indifference to the members of other groups. Nor does it jettison rights insofar as they protect everyone from terrible harms. There is little reason, then, to worry that grounding rights in empathic thought would make them too vulnerable to the caprice of public outcry or the vagaries of political momentum and that abridgments of rights will be authorized too readily. It hardly seems likely, for example, that empathy-based moral reflection would permit military officers to torture insurrectionists in order to protect a brutal regime or authorize the restriction of suffrage to propertied white males. Indeed, I would hazard that expanded empathy could be counted on to lend support to emancipatory initiatives and to defeat repressive ones. In addition, since empathic thought does not pretend to give moral deliberators access to eternal moral verities, it does not deny the improvisational and experimental nature of some of its prescriptions. Thus, societies guided by empathic thought will not commit themselves to disastrous, but incorrigible and irrevocable policies. In sum, there is no reason to worry that empathic thought will strip rights of their moral force or bring right-holders under attack.

Still, I have maintained that contemporary issues of justice concern diverse groups and call for microsolutions, and this claim suggests that time constraints will severely limit the usefulness of empathic thought. Admittedly, no one has time to empathize broadly with members of all of the social groups that are victimized by the dilemma of difference. However, it seems to me that the right conclusion to draw from this limitation is not that we should give up empathic thought and resort to universal moral categories and abstract moral reasoning, but rather that we should give up the illusion of the omnicompetent citizen who is well informed about every social issue and who has well thought-out opinions about all of them.

It is necessary, I believe, to become more realistic and more modest about our moral capacities—that is, to acknowledge that we can be morally insightful only if we accept some degree of moral specialization. How can anyone know enough about welfare reform, the Russian economy, sexual assault law, euthanasia practices, South African politics, capital punishment, financing universal health care, Israeli-Arab relations, and so forth to have well grounded, well-developed views about all of these issues? Operating with a stock of general principles, people can generate judgments about almost any issue, but these opinions fail to take into account how carrying out those judgments would affect actual people. Moral specialization and the willingness to defer to conscientious, able associates whose moral ideals coincide with one's own and who have carefully studied a moral question are not abrogations of social responsibility. On the contrary, they take social responsibility far more seriously than glib opinion prattling.

Now, it is important to be clear that affirming that empathic thought can support rights claims does not entail that rights are the only type of moral consideration or that rights are the key to resolving all instances of the dilemma of difference. As Annette Baier has argued, we need justice, but justice is not enough (Baier, 1987). Thus, it would be foolish to elevate rights to the status of an all-consuming, all-purpose moral currency. But it would also be foolish to give up on the dynamic of rights-based social protest and litigation for fear of the stasis of rights-based judicial reinforcement of existing social hierarchies.

Grounded in impartial reason, traditional rights theories address the generic human unity discernible in the diversity of individuals and indirectly the diversity of individuals that flourishes within the unity of common humanity. Traditional liberal theorists justify basic liberties by appealing to universal human traits, but they expect individuality to thrive through the exercise of these liberties. The challenge that the dilemma of difference levels at contemporary rights theory is to extend this double perspective to a broader spectrum of rights and to the life prospects of the full spectrum of right-holders. This can best be accomplished through an account of rights that integrates the values and strategies of impartial reason into a pluralistic overarching moral identity—a societal moral identity that is receptive to empathic understanding of diverse individuals. Without empathic

thought, rights theory funnels moral reflection into universal categories that can nullify morally significant difference. With empathic
thought, rights theory can join in the process of moral revisioning
that is indispensable to coming to grips with the most recalcitrant
issues societies now face.

3. Dynamic Moral Reflection and Social Criticism

Throughout my discussion, I have used a problem from nonideal
moral theory—namely, the dilemma of difference—to highlight the
limitations of impartial reason. Whereas ideal theory asks what principles a perfectly just society would follow, nonideal theory asks how
a society that is to some degree unjust can be made more just.
Nonideal theory contends with moral problems in the real world of
culturally normative prejudice and institutionalized social exclusion.
In this context, a monistic view of the moral subject and moral
reflection founders. Rights derived from impartial reason are too
rigid to accommodate the needs of socially excluded groups. Often,
they undergird the status quo instead. To address the problem of
unjust, group-based social exclusion, moral subjects—individuals and
polities alike—need moral identities that embrace diverse values and
aims, and they need to call on comprehensive repertoires of moral
skills. The unidimensional rational deliberator of impartial reason
must give way to the pluralistic, heterogeneous, multiplex moral subject of empathic thought.

At this point, however, it might be objected that there is no guarantee that the eclectic resources of empathic thought will always converge on a single moral solution. Now, it is evident from what I have
said so far that the moral ideals and moral capacities involved in
empathic thought are not fatally conflicted. In many situations,
empathic thought is capable of providing straightforward and decisive guidance. In fact, in some situations, the moral judgments
reached through empathic thought are the same as judgments that
would be reached by a strict Kantian or utilitarian. I think, then, that
the possibility of diverse values leading in divergent directions is
nothing more than a pretext for rejecting empathic thought and the
nonunitary moral subject.

On one reading, this objection seems to rest on the assumption that
a satisfactory method of moral deliberation must rule out sabotage
and guarantee good results. But this standard is far too high. No

deliberative procedure that respects the autonomy of moral subjects can defeat cynical, malicious, or obtuse practitioners and obviate their morally deficient conclusions. Any form of moral reflection is vulnerable to self-deception and insincerity. If this is so, we should not be seeking airtight protection against mistakes and manipulation. Rather, we should be seeking methods that afford opportunities to correct moral misapprehensions and to discover better ways of doing things.

The ideal of a decision procedure that generates clear and incontrovertible prescriptions for action may seem attractive; however, no one has ever produced a plausible method of moral reflection that ensures consensus, let alone correctness. As we have seen, proponents of impartial reason often reach incompatible conclusions (Chapter 1, Section 2; Chapter 6, Section 4B). Surely, then, it is no objection to empathic thought that different dimensions of one's moral identity and different lines of thought may draw it in different directions. Quite the contrary, I should think this possibility a virtue.

Morally speaking, it is right to regard people as sharing a common humanity, as members of distinct social groups, and as unique individuals. It may not always be possible to reconcile all three of these viewpoints, and there is no reason to suppose that one of them should invariably prevail over the others. Thus, moral reflection must be prepared to balance rival understandings of the moral patient. Moreover, it is sensible to regard ourselves as liable to moral blindspots, yet amenable to moral improvement. Thus, moral reflection should beware of finalizing judgments prematurely, and it should seek to marshall as much insight as possible at any given time. If these aims are paramount, the moral subject—whether an individual or a society—is best conceived as a nonunitary subject.

In the context of ongoing dissident speech, empathic thought provides conscientious moral subjects with an invaluable safeguard against seductive, yet morally suspect, social orthodoxy. Indeed, without a nonunitary moral subject, we are deprived of an account of how established moral beliefs can be propitiously destabilized. When the principles one endorses create an impasse with respect to the dilemma of difference, that predicament may signal the need to suspend definitive judgment in order to reconfigure moral perception and reconceptualize the issues through dissident speech. Likewise, such an impasse may signal the need to improvise novel moral solutions through empathic thought. One's principles may mask prejudice or stifle imagination. In that case, they do not deserve one's unqualified support, and it is a bad idea to stick with them. In general, when one's moral position seems all too pat and unyielding, it may be a good idea to throw it into question. One might do well to explore the possibility that there are needs at stake that have not been articulated, and that will confound one's judgment as long as they remain suppressed, but that could enrich one's moral understanding if they were brought to light and incorporated into moral reflection.

Perhaps, there are more values than any society can simultaneously realize. In that case, every form of social organization entails some loss of value and enforces some sort of repression (Hampshire, 1983, 147). Still, there is no reason to assume that one's own society has hit on the best possible combination of values and the least repressive social scheme. Forced coherence locks error in place. When it does, the desideratum of stability degenerates into the evil of stagnation. Bigotry is never scrutinized and challenged. An antiquated inventory of values is never pruned or augmented. No fresh life possibilities are envisaged. Moral and social renewal is thwarted.

The subject of moral reflection is best construed as a nonunitary subject. Such a subject has a complex, evolving moral identity and is equipped with interpersonal skills that enable one to imagine the subjective experience of others and to join with others in contesting virulent culturally normative prejudice. Endowed in this way, moral subjects are capable of bringing disparate moral themes to bear on a single issue and are capable of profiting from tensions between the moral conclusions these themes suggest. This tolerance for ambiguity has two salutary consequences. Moral judgments do not harden into fixed, inviolable positions, and the prospects of moral innovation are enhanced. Fanatics and ideologues are not empathic thinkers.

Now, complicating our account of the moral subject as I suggest may alarm moral philosophers who believe we should rely on minimal empirical assumptions about people and that we should seek to establish a single overriding constraint on moral reflection. However, it seems to me that neither loss seriously damages the case for the nonunitary moral subject. Since moral reflection is mainly concerned with how we should treat other people, it should neither surprise nor trouble us that moral reflection requires attunement to other people through empathy. Just as people who lack the ability to abstract from their immediate preferences and engage in universalizability exercises or people who lack the ability to bracket self-interest and consider the common good lack a crucial moral capacity, so people who are oblivious to or indifferent to others' states of mind are morally impaired. Likewise, since our basic moral convictions amalgamate diverse social inputs over long periods of time, and since these convictions become emotionally entrenched often in mysterious ways, it should neither surprise nor trouble us that sorting out these moral beliefs requires the ministrations of dissident speech. Moreover, in view of the enormous variety of social situations that morality is supposed to shepherd us through, it would surely be astonishing if there were one ultimate moral arbiter. The value pluralism of the empathic thinker seems better adapted to meeting life's demands. Moral reflection is, I'm afraid, messier than many philosophers have heretofore thought.

Finally, I think that proponents of impartial reason foster a rather outlandish moral illusion—the illusion of homogeneity among moral subjects. Insofar as we are moral subjects, we are all the same, for we have the same rational faculty. But the considerations I have adduced, not to mention everyday experience, belie this homogeneity. Moral subjects are unique. They arrive at similar moral conclusions by different routes, and they disagree over moral conclusions. By replacing the unitary moral subject with the moral subject of empathic thought, we can capture this uniqueness in the distinctive blend of an individual's moral capacities and ideals or in the distinctive blend of a society's traditions, resources, and aspirations. Though it is necessary, of course, to set parameters of toleration for individuality (empathic thought restricts moral ideals to ones that can support mutual recognition), it is a mistake to seek a universal moral calculus. Not only is moral reflection messier, it is also more vital and more fascinating than many philosophers have heretofore thought.

Notes

Chapter 1

1. It is worth noting that Kantianism's leading rival, utilitarianism, fares no better as an ultimate moral arbiter. Different utilitarians often reach divergent conclusions about what social policy should be implemented, for there is controversy about how social utility should be calculated. Utilitarians disagree about how individual welfare should be assessed, which pleasures or preferences should be taken into account, and whether quality of pleasure or intensity of preferences should be factored in. Moreover, since estimating the probable consequences of alternative courses of action—especially when the alternatives are comprehensive, far-reaching public policies—is largely guesswork, utilitarianism leaves ample room for tinkering with one's mathematics to obtain the policy prescriptions one is inclined to prefer.

2. A second and subsidiary project of psychoanalytic feminism is applying psychoanalytic feminist theories of gender to other fields. Psychoanalytic feminist cultural critique ranges over literary theory, art criticism, film theory, and the history of ideas. Unfortunately, space will not permit me to consider these diverse applications.

3. Earlier, I mentioned the cultural narrowness of much psychoanalytic feminist theory—that is, its tendency to focus on the particular form that gender takes among white, affluent, heterosexual people who live in industrialized societies in the late twentieth century. Here, I want to stress that one implication of my account of dissident speech is that the question of whether women from other social groups find the psychoanalytic feminist counterfigurations that I survey emancipatory is a political question that can be addressed only by groups of women who stand in solidarity with one another (see Chapter 5, Section 3).

Moreover, it is worth noting that this politicization of dissident speech argues in favor of a multiciplicity of counterfigurations of gender, for dissident speech figures women who come from diverse backgrounds and who occupy different social positions, and dissident speech addresses diverse audiences (see Chapter 5, Section 4.

Chapter 2

1. It is interesting that opponents of gay rights in the recent Colorado and Oregon referendum campaigns have sought to cast guarantees of equal rights, such as bans on discrimination in housing and employment, as special rights—that is, as rights conferring benefits that other citizens do not enjoy.

2. I want to stress that my criticisms of Okin's dual paycheck proposal do not extend to her helpful suggestions about ensuring the economic well-being of women and children in the aftermath of divorce.

3. In saying that there are women who sincerely and freely embrace the traditional feminine role, I do not mean simply that there are traditional women who have not been physically or economically coerced into the role of housewife and mother. I mean that some traditional women are adept at using the skills that are needed to make autonomous decisions, that they exercised these skills in making their life choices, and that their life choices were made in a social environment that would not have penalized them severely for choosing a different course (Meyers, 1989, 42–59, 76–97). I would caution, however, that traditional women's life choices rarely meet these criteria, and, for this reason, I have urged that it is imperative that childrearing and educational practices be reorganized to nurture autonomy skills (Meyers, 1989, 170, 189–202).

4. I hesitate to say that one could assuredly fulfill these duties since it is arguable that behavior that is ordinarily unobjectionable can coerce a person with exceptional sensitivities, and since, in the absence of explicit warnings from the vulnerable individual or others who are familiar with the case, one would fail to notice such sensitivities unless one brought empathic capacities into play.

5. Patricia Williams recounts a disturbing parallel case. A Stanford University student descended from German Jews (called Fred in the university's official report) became embroiled in an argument with an African-American student (called Q. C. in the report) over whether Beethoven had black ancestors. The following night Fred and some friends drew stereotypical African-American features on a poster of Beethoven and

tacked it outside Q. C.'s room. Williams cites further details from the report regarding Fred's understanding of his own conduct:

> [Fred] described incidents that he called "teasing"—I would call them humiliation, even torture—by his schoolmates [in England, where he was educated] about his being Jewish. They called him miserly, and his being a Jew was referred to as a weakness. Fred said that he learned not to mind it and indicated that the poster defacement at Ujaama House had been in the spirit of this teaching. He wondered why the black students couldn't respond to it in the spirit in which it was meant: "nothing serious," just "humor as a release." (P. Williams, 1991, 111)

It seems to me that, despite (or, perhaps, because of) his own experience of persecution, Fred is unable to empathize with Q. C. and shares the moral obtuseness of the professor I have described.

6. The Rawls-Nozick debate is a well-known example of philosophical controversy regarding how to set the moral baseline for impartial reason. Whereas Rawls insists that impartial reason must assume the perspective of the least advantaged members of society, Nozick insists that impartial reason must assume the perspective of those whose income will be redistributed to help the least advantaged. The main lessons to be learned from this debate are that the moral baseline depends on how one conceives of the person and that impartial reason furnishes no conclusive arguments for either side (for related discussion of the way in which the dominant self-understanding can become entrenched as the moral baseline and skew impartial reason, see Calhoun, 1988). Apropos of Barbara Herman's suggestion that the moral baseline is the legacy of one's cultural heritage (Herman, 1985, 425), it is worth noting that the Rawls-Nozick debate and more generally the ongoing debate between liberals and conservatives suggests that on this point the U.S. cultural heritage is comprised of incompatible positions (for further discussion of the plural values that constitute the moral identities of liberal democratic societies, see Chapter 7, Section 2).

7. It is worth noting that according to my dictionary this distinction is also marked by two senses of the term "vicarious." Vicarious experience can take the form of sharing another's feelings and intentions or the form of imagining these feelings and intentions.

    It is worth noting, too, the distinction between empathy and compassion. Though empathy presupposes concern for the other, it does not presuppose a desire to alleviate the other's misfortunes, as compassion does. Moreover, one may empathize with another person's positive states, but one cannot feel compassion for them.

8. For those who are inclined to doubt that there is an important distinction between sympathy and empathy, it is worth observing that broad sympathy would be pathological, for it would completely subordinate the sympathizer's subjectivity to that of another. In contrast, broad empathy preserves the empathizer's subjectivity and agency.

9. It is surprising how difficult it is to think of traits of character about which there is much disagreement as to their desirability or undesirability, but there are some. For example, I think asceticism is generally regarded as undesirable, but in this era of ecological consciousness-raising it would probably find defenders. Perhaps, the loci of controversy are traits of character that have become peripheral to typical contemporary patterns of life and thus seem somewhat anachronistic.

10. Martha Minow's treatment of special education supplies striking examples of mutual acceptance through the empathic approach to the dilemma of difference. Her description of an elementary school class that coped with the enrollment of a deaf pupil by learning sign language illustrates this approach (Minow, 1990, 84). It is undeniable that the deaf child is different, but by entering her world the teacher and the other students succeeded in bringing her into their community, thereby enriching everyone's classroom experience and affirming the value of acquainting oneself with an unfamiliar point of view. But special education has sometimes had much more far-reaching consequences, for it has brought about a curious deconstruction of "difference" in some United States schools. Various statutory mandates have entitled a whole range of pupils to demand "appropriate" public education. Thus, as the types of pupils have multiplied—deaf, hyperactive, dyslexic, gifted, bilingual, and so forth—and as the numbers of "different" students have soared—in some school systems 80% of the student body is considered learning disabled!—difference has ceased to be deviant (Minow, 1990, 94). With empathic response to difference comes the normalization of difference. Teachers tailor pedagogical methods and educational services to meet individual students' needs. Mainstreaming is effected without homogenization, and delight in diversity supplants grudging tolerance of difference.

11. I formulate impartial reason in colloquial terms partly for the sake of parsimony and partly because I am primarily interested in real-life moral reflection, as opposed to philosophers' formalizations. However, I want to stress that the arguments that I shall give apply, as well, to philosophical treatments of impartial reason, such as those of Barbara Herman, John Rawls, Jean Hampton, and T. M. Scanlon.

12. A variant of this defense of impartial reason might concede that impartial reason has no systematic way of assessing the morality of re-

sponses to difference. On this view, people have an imperfect duty to promote others' happiness, and, since what contributes to happiness varies from individual to individual, empathy is needed to find out what will make others happy and hence how to fulfill this duty. Still, it seems clear that an account of moral reflection must say something about what are and what are not morally admissible forms of happiness—that is, forms of happiness that we might plausibly have a duty to promote. Preference utilitarianism relies on the intensity of one's own countervailing desires or on large numbers of countervailing desires to resist the silly or abominable, though stable and informed, desires of a few individuals. But this strategy is not available to Kantian impartial reason.

13. From this, it is clear why impartial reason has been so strongly associated with a public morality of noninterference and minimal aid. Since people all need physical security, sustenance, and a measure of freedom, impartial reason is well equipped to certify principles that guarantee these goods. But in the morality of interpersonal relations where subtle differences between people become prominent, impartial reason seems a rather cloddish instrument.

14. It is worth thinking about this point in the context of one of the objections that has been lodged against John Rawls's attempt to deduce the difference principle from his account of the original position in *A Theory of Justice*. As many commentators have pointed out, in claiming that rational deliberators in the original position would use the maximin rule to select a principle of distribution for income and wealth, Rawls begs the question. The way he designs the original position smuggles in the difference principle. Thus, the deduction from the original position ceases to be a justification of the difference principle and becomes instead an application of a maximin vision of distributive justice to the problem of economic inequality. For further discussion of this problem in Rawls, see Meyers (1993, Section 2).

Chapter 3

1. For helpful discussion of responsibility for sexist behavior, see Gauthier (1991).

2. It is, perhaps, worth noting that some feminists today would not be satisfied with this argument either. In regard to pregnancy leave policy, for example, it is debatable whether women's reproductive difference should be acknowledged and special provisions enacted to protect their interests or whether women's needs should be assimilated to the gender-neutral category of disabilities and the principle of equality thus be

saved. The maximin argument would rule out the former position, but it seems to be a position that is worth considering on its merits.

3. His position in this regard seems to have shifted a bit since *A Theory of Justice* was published. In *Political Liberalism,* Rawls asserts that the veil of ignorance hides information about their sex and gender from the parties to the original position (Rawls, 1993, 25). Perhaps, he is leaning toward ruling out classification by sex a priori.

4. Phyllis Schlafly spoke for many opponents of the ERA when she penned "The Right to Be a Woman"—a tract in which she argued that equal rights would destroy women's "right" to be supported and their freedom to stay home and keep house (Schlafly, 1972). Although I find it hard to believe that a woman informed both of the current probability that her marriage will end in divorce and also of current statistics regarding fathers' failure to make child support payments after divorce could prefer Schlafly's "right to be a woman" over equal rights, it seems that even today many women continue to find the illusionistic pedestal of femininity attractive. Furthermore, it is worth noting that Schlafly's argument conforms to the form Rawls prescribes for defending limitations of liberty—she advocates limiting women's liberty for the sake of their liberty.

5. At this point, it might be urged that utilitarian impartiality provides the corrective for prejudice that contemporary Kantian theory lacks. By calculating the benefits to be gained and the burdens to be imposed by opening politics to women's participation, an objective assessment of people's considered convictions could be made. Unfortunately, utilitarian calculations regarding controversial policy questions are never themselves uncontroversial. Since assessments of the benefits and burdens associated with different policies are amenable to inflation or underestimation depending on one's political predispositions, utilitarian calculations are susceptible to prejudice-based manipulation, as well.

6. Phyllis Rooney quotes a passage from John Locke's *An Essay Concerning Human Understanding* that is both insightful and alarming:

> all the art of rhetoric, besides order and clearness, all the artificial and figurative application of words eloquence hath invented, are for nothing else but to insinuate wrong ideas, move the passions, and thereby mislead judgment ... *eloquence,* like the fair sex, has too prevailing beauties in it to suffer itself ever to be spoken against. And it is vain to find fault with those arts of deceiving wherein men find pleasure to be deceived. (Locke quoted in Rooney, 1991, 84)

I agree with Locke's observation that the beauty of figurative language is seductive and protects it from rational critique. But, amazingly, in the same breath as he condemns the misleadingness of figurative language, he does not hesitate to use a simile analogizing the seductiveness of "eloquence" to the wiles of feminine charm (for more examples of philosophers relying on tropes to condemn figurative language, see Kittay, 1987, 1). Evidently, traditional gender imagery is *very* seductive.

7. It is sometimes maintained that stereotypes persist because those who are stereotyped often conform to the stereotypes and thus provide evidence for the truth of the stereotypes. This observation is often thought to justify blaming the victim—that is, people who believe in negative stereotypes should be excused since many members of socially excluded groups actually instantiate them. However, as I shall argue below, figuratively encoded negative stereotypes do not depend on empirical evidence for their survival. Nevertheless, once this observation is uncoupled from blaming the victim, it adds an interesting dimension to Piper's point about the dynamic of social exclusion. Whereas conforming to a prejudicial figuration merely comports with generalized cultural contempt for one's group, violating a culturally entrenched figuration provokes wrath that is directed specifically at oneself. Thus, it may seem safer to conform to the negative stereotype.

8. Piper holds that higher-order discriminators are well intentioned and that they unwittingly engage in discriminatory conduct; however, her account raises doubts about their protestations of innocence. In her earlier article, Piper attributes a rather noble flaw to higher-order discriminators. They are forced into denial by their commitment to an inclusive, egalitarian moral theory. In her later article, she offers a less indulgent portrait of higher-order discriminators. Their denial is simply self-serving, for it is motivated by their attachment to an honorific stereotype of their group as morally righteous (Piper, 1992–93, 220). I have no wish to provide an apologia for higher-order discriminators. I agree with Piper that there is always more behind higher-order discrimination than reverence for a cultural heritage. But I would like to suggest that higher-order discrimination may well be overdetermined and that allegiance to a rich cultural heritage is far less unconscionable than clinging to an honorific stereotype. That cultural traditions are both nourishing and poisoning is a theme that I shall return to in discussions of moral identity in Chapters 6 and 7.

9. Nancy Chodorow holds similar views about social repression. With regard to gender, Chodorow traces masculine contempt for women to anxieties and conflicts that arise as a result of father-absent parenting (Chodorow, 1980, 12–14). However, since she does not develop her views into a theory of social criticism, but rather recommends changes in childrearing practices as a remedy, I shall focus on Kristeva's theory.

10. Young's discussion of Kristeva is particularly valuable since Young distinguishes the social and economic mechanisms though which some groups become defined as other from the psychic mechanisms that link groups defined as other to powerful aversive emotions (Young, 1990, 145).

11. Kristeva's ethical notion of aesthetic practices rests on a grand synthesis of her linguistic philosophy and her account of psychoanalytic clinical practice. I think, however, that her elaborate theoretical apparatus creates a distraction that obscures a basically sound insight. Thus, I shall set aside her claim that language is comprised of symbolic and semiotic dimensions. Likewise, I shall not rest my claims on her version of psychoanalysis. The position regarding figurative language and moral reflection that I shall put forward is compatible with analyzing prejudice in terms of emotionally and cognitively entrenched schemas. For a model of the psyche that seeks to synthesize psychoanalytic insight into emotional life with work in cognitive psychology on schemas, see Horowitz (1988).

12. Of course, the values and norms that cultures figuratively encode include humane and fair ones along with opprobrious throwbacks. Thus, it is necessary to distinguish emancipatory imagery from repressive imagery, and I shall take up this topic in Chapter 5.

13. Richard Brandt also invokes a therapeutic approach to moral reflection; however, Brandt characterizes the form of therapy he advocates as "cognitive psychotherapy" and confines the project to exorcising false beliefs through reconditioning (Brandt, 1979, Chapter 6). Brandt's account assumes that people can readily identify which of their beliefs are false and that their emotional commitments need only the simplest causal interpretation. But experience with ingrained moral pathology or with deep moral perplexity suggests that this view does not do justice to the complexity or the intractability of the problem.

Chapter 4

1. For discussion of Freud's Victorian heritage and his reluctance to acknowledge women's sexual desire, see Millett (1969, 194, 195, 199).

2. Many feminists who might admire Morgan's subversive fictions will be reluctant to endorse the French performance artist Orlan's literalizing enactment. Orlan has made a career of using plastic surgery to make aesthetic and political points. Claiming to be a feminist artist engaged in "a critique of beauty and a critique of cosmetic surgery," she has had a series of operations performed in order to achieve a face with "the mouth of Boucher's Europa, the chin of Botticelli's Venus,

Gerome's Psyche, the forehead of the Mona Lisa, and the nose of an unattributed French sculpture of Diana" (*New York Times*, Sunday, November 21, Section V, p. 8). Her surgical procedures, which are performed in costume in elaborately decorated operating rooms, are transmitted via satellite to art galleries where they are witnessed by invited guests. "I think that since I've been doing the operations, I'm much less pretty than before," Orlan comments. But she adds, "I have given my body to art" (*New York Times*, Sunday, November 21, Section V, p. 8). Both because the artist is needlessly endangering her health, and also because she seems confused about whether her aim is to achieve a composite perfection or to demonstrate the absurdity of this aim, her art is problematic from a feminist point of view. Yet, the challenge Orlan's art poses to the reverence in which icons of feminine beauty are held and also to the secrecy in which feminine vanity is cloaked has attracted some feminist champions of her work.

3. Behind these narratives is the assumption that people share a sense of what it is to lead a healthy, satisfying life and that they want to lead such a life. They want to love and be loved, to sustain and enjoy friendships, to fulfill their potential, and to make a contribution that society recognizes and rewards. The narratives psychoanalytic feminists spin describe how the capacities needed to live a healthy, satisfying life evolve (or fail to evolve) and articulate figurations of these capacities that are (or are not) conducive to leading such a life. A constructive psychoanalytic feminist narrative, such as Luce Irigaray's substitution of feminine lips for the masculine phallus (see Section 2D below), tries to induce identification with a novel figuration and the vision of social relations it suggests. A critical psychoanalytic feminist narrative, such as Jessica Benjamin's account of sadomasochism (see Section 2A below), tries to induce disidentification with a set of culturally entrenched norms and figurations. Thus, the concept of a healthy, satisfying life together with the reader's ability or inability to identify with a psychoanalytic narrative provides an initial basis for judging figurations of gender emancipatory or repressive (for discussion of evaluating counterfigurations, see Chapter 5, Section 5).

    Construed in this way, psychoanalytic feminism can be defended against a criticism that would otherwise be telling. Many feminist commentators have objected to psychoanalysis' preoccupation with the nuclear family. Feminists have pointed out that many children do not grow up in heterosexual two-parent households, and they have decried the heterosexist bias implicit in psychoanalysis. On both empirical and moral grounds, locating development in the nuclear family is objectionable. However, if one construes psychoanalytic feminism as a form of dissident speech, the choice of the nuclear family as the setting of psychoanalytic theorizing about childhood development can be given a more sympathetic reading. This setting, it could be argued, ensures that figurations of both femininity and masculinity are implicated in everyone's psychic make-up. Consequently, this framework ensures that with respect to gender the other will be part of you—boys cannot escape the feminine and girls cannot escape the masculine. Thus, to embrace a narrative with a deformed image of the other and endorse the norms implicit in that narrative is to diminish your own ability to live a healthy, satisfying life. There is reason, then, to reject narratives like Freud's that feature deformed images of women.

4. In her early essays and in *The Reproduction of Mothering*, Chodorow expresses approval of exclusively female, but communal childcare (Chodorow, 1974, 63; 1978, 75). But in her contribution to a later symposium on her work, she disavows this view and declares that coparenting by at least one male and at least one female is best (Chodorow, 1981, 512).

5. Jessica Benjamin also holds that children have an innate potential for individuation and thus that they are predisposed to individuate (Benjamin, 1988, 18). For discussion of her view, see Chapter 6, Section 1.

6. Habermas seems to have something like this in mind when he maintains that psychoanalysis furnishes a "systematically generalized history" or a "scheme for many histories" (Habermas, 1971, 263). Habermas characterizes psychoanalysis' protagonists as examples stripped of their particularity. However, the iconic figures of psychoanalysis seem to have a linguistic status different from examples abstracted from their life context. Applying these iconic figures to one's own experience is not a matter of fleshing them out by adding on biographical details of time, place, and personality; it is a matter of seeing one's experience differently through these figures. They are tropes, not types.

Chapter 5

1. It is interesting to note the similarities between Kristeva's account of motherhood and Sara Ruddick's account of the practice of mothering. Kristeva describes caring for a child as a "delightful apprenticeship in attentiveness, gentleness, forgetting oneself" and argues that an ethic is implicit in maternal experience (Kristeva, 1986, 206). Ruddick's account goes far beyond these rudimentary remarks to exhibit a selection of values, such as holding, humility, resilient cheerfulness, and appreciability, that are implicit in mothering practice and to tie these values to social criticism (Ruddick, 1986, 343–345, 350). Nevertheless, the overlap between them is striking.

2. Judith Jarvis Thomson's influential article on abortion is another well-known instance of this form of philosophizing (Thomson 1971). Her scenario in which a person is abducted by a Society of Music Lovers, taken to a hospital, and hooked up to an ailing violinist for nine months is a figuration of pregnancy resulting from rape. In her essay, Thomson explores the implications of accepting this image, and much subsequent debate has been devoted to questioning or defending its aptness.

Chapter 6

1. Both Chodorow and Benjamin are clear, however, that a defective upbringing is often a consequence of social structures, not of the failings of individual mothers and fathers.

2. It is wise to be cautious about innateness claims, and Benjamin does not clarify what she means by hers. If she means simply that infants are endowed with a predisposition to sense themselves as distinct and with some broad, open-ended potentialities, I have no quarrel with her view. However, if she means anything more definite than this, I would question her view. For discussion of this issue, see Meyers (1989, 27–29, 40–41, 45).

3. A child's ability to recognize caregivers is relative to its cognitive and emotional development, but Benjamin stresses that a baby gains rudimentary recognition capacities in the first few months of life (Benjamin 1988, 26–28).

4. Benjamin seeks to address the problems I have attributed to her reliance on sympathy by introducing the subjectivity conferring process of identificatory love (Benjamin, 1988, 100–107; also see Chapter 4, Section 2C). It seems to me, however, that it would be much more economical to rely on empathy as the foundation of caregiver-child relations.

5. Jill Johnston identifies a genre that she dubs "plebeian autobiography" in which ordinary people—that is, people who are not generally regarded as accomplished or influential—undertake to tell their stories, and she connects autobiographical narrative to self-recognition. For those who have been marginalized, autobiography is both an act of self-constitution and also an act of political defiance: "when we write the life, we are making it up (not the facts but the ways of seeing an organizing them), and this is a political act of *self-recognition*" (Johnston, 1993, 29; emphasis added).

6. This claim brings into relief one of the horrors of emotionally or physically abusive parenting. Young children lack the intellectual and emotional skills necessary to critique and resist practices of domination

—that is, they are not yet capable of moral self-recognition. Thus, when parents systematically suppress the development of these very skills, their children may be altogether deprived of the possibility of participating in relations of mutual recognition—that is, they may never be able to give recognition to others and enjoy the recognition of others. It is evident, then, that luck with respect to the household one is born or adopted into is crucial to the emergence of moral subjectivity.

7. Let me head off a possible misunderstanding here. Self-recognition does not require that one exercise a form of free will that transcends one's social context. Most people are born with the potential for empathy and nurturance, but empathic and nurturing skills are developed through social interaction. Likewise, one's social environment furnishes the values that one intially adopts and tries to live up to. Still, the skills involved in self-recognition enable people to test and criticize these values and to adjust their commitments in view of this experience. Self-recognition is a socially situated, socially indebted, yet independent form of subjectivity. For related discussion of autonomy competency, see Meyers (1987, 1989).

8. Of course, parents and other caregivers rely on additional questions for purposes of moral education, including "How would you like to be treated that way?" and "Do you think this is best for everyone?" These queries informally articulate the methods of Kantian impartial reason and utilitarianism, respectively.

9. Among the few moral philosophers I have come across who treat this approach to moral reflection as central are Stanley Cavell (1979, 312), Richard Rorty (1986, 12), Margaret Walker (1987, 173), and Charles Taylor (1991, 29). In view of Jill Johnston's linking of self-recognition to autobiography (see note 5 above), it is interesting that Rorty links moral identity to narrative. For Rorty, the aim of moral reflection is not to ascertain the moral implications of an essential human nature. Rather, moral reflection answers the question, "If I do this rather than that now, what story will I tell myself later?" (Rorty, 1986, 18)

10. For further discussion of this approach to deliberation and how it compares with impartial reason, see Meyers (1987b, 147–152).

11. A moral ideal should be distinguished from the concept of a good person in two respects. First, different people can reasonably decide to order the same set of values in different ways. Second, two different people who share identical views about what makes a person good will have different moral ideals if they have different strengths and weaknesses.

12. I disagree with criticisms of Carol Gilligan's ethic of care that claim that it is a morality of altruistic subservience that arises from condi-

tions of oppression and is likely to perpetuate women's oppression (J. Walker, 1983; Harding, 1987; Houston, 1987). At lower stages of development, exponents of the care perspective identify goodness with self-sacrifice. But at more advanced stages, these individuals stress caring for oneself as well as for others. Gilligan's interviews show that these women are concerned with issues of integrity, responsibility for self, and reciprocity and that they seek to reconcile these values with the value they place on caring for others (Gilligan, 1982, 99, 133, 149; 1986, 329–333). Nevertheless, one of the reasons I have coined the expression "empathic thought" (see Chapter 6, Section 3) rather than adopting Gilligan's terminology is that it is extremely difficult to extricate the latter from unwanted and misleading connotations of feminine selflessness and maternal self-sacrifice.

13. There are important connections between the line of thought I am developing and the literature on integrity and self-respect. Feminist discussions of these issues are especially pertinent since they construe integrity and self-respect in dynamic terms (Davion, 1991; Dillon, 1992; Herman, 1983; M. Walker, n.d. a; Meyers, 1989, 210–246).

14. It might be objected that empathic thought's preoccupation with cultivating and enacting one's own moral identity makes it too narcissistic to qualify as an approach to moral reflection. However, this objection rests on a misunderstanding of empathic thought. First, empathic thought is not an account of moral motivation. It is an approach to moral reflection. Just as asking "How would I like to be treated this way?" and asking "Would doing this be best for everyone?" are strategies for moral thinking and prompts for moral understanding that could be linked to various motives for carrying out the decision, so too asking "What sort of a person would doing that (not doing that) make me?" and "Do I want to be the sort of person who would (would not) do that?" is a strategy for moral thinking and a prompt for moral understanding that could be linked to various motives for carrying out the decision. Second, empathic thought explicitly incorporates empathic concern for and empathic understanding of others into the process of moral reflection. Thus, to the extent that one's motivation for acting echoes one's mode of moral reflection, empathic thinkers will be motivated as much by a desire to recognize others as by a desire to recognize themselves—recall Opdyke's motive (pp. 119–120 above).

15. A person could adopt an extremely constricted moral ideal that is coextensive with Kantianism or utilitarianism—that is, the sole content of one's moral ideal could be the value of adhering to principles deduced from the Categorical Imperative or the value of carrying out the dictates of utilitarian calculations. I think that this is a very unreal-

istic possibility. But it seems to be the view that John Rawls adopts, and I shall take it up in Chapter 7, Section 2.

16. I leave aside impartialist arguments based on fairness to women since these are notoriously easy to dodge. Pressed to do their share of child-care, fathers frequently point out that they were reluctant to have children in the first place and only went along with the plan to propitiate their female partners. Surely, the parent who insisted on having children despite the other's resistance should assume most of the burden of caring for them. It would be unfair to expect a parent who has merely acquiesced in the other's wishes to do an equal amount of this work. Furthermore, many fathers accurately point out that they shoulder the lion's share of economic responsibility for the family. Their jobs pay more, and some of them work longer hours outside the home. Again, equity seems to argue for mothers' assuming a larger share of domestic responsibility. Now, I do not think that these are persuasive arguments. But, as long as one accepts impartial reason's concern with consent and proportionate contribution, there is enough truth in them to make them formidable obstacles to equalizing childcare.

Chapter 7

1. If this view of the foundations of rights is tenable, it follows that the temptation to divide the moral realm between issues of rights and liberty and issues of welfare and aid, with impartial reason governing the former and empathic thought confined to the latter, should be resisted. Not only can sensitization to others' distinctive needs supply ample grounds for not interfering with them, but also, as we saw earlier, impartial reason can come to the defense of welfare programs, such as the Social Security system (Chapter 2, Section 1). Moreover, since commitments to liberty constrain welfare initiatives, and since welfare-enhancing programs impinge on liberty, this dichotomous pairing of moral issues and moral capacities is bound to break down. Impartial reason and empathic thought do not hold sway in conveniently separate domains, nor are their normative prescriptions invariably rivals.

Bibliography

Abel, Elizabeth. 1990. "Race, Class, and Psychoanalysis? Opening Questions." In *Conflicts in Feminism*. Eds. Marianne Hirsch and Evelyn Fox Keller. New York: Routledge.

Addelson, Kathryn. 1991. *Impure Thoughts*. Philadelphia: Temple University Press.

Baier, Annette C. 1987. "The Need for More than Justice." In *Science, Morality, and Feminist Theory*. Eds. Marsha Hanen and Kai Nielsen. Calgary: The University of Calgary Press.

Bartky, Sandra. 1990. *Femininity and Domination*. New York: Routledge.

———— n.d. "Self, Sympathy, and Solidarity: Reflections on the Problem of Difference in Feminist Theory." In *Feminists Rethink the Self*. Ed. Diana Tietjens Meyers. Boulder CO: Westview, Forthcoming.

Beardsley, Elizabeth Lane. 1982. "On Curing Conceptual Confusion: A Response to Mary Anne Warren." In *"Femininity," "Masculinity," and Androgyny*. Ed. Mary Vetterling-Braggin. Totowa NJ: Littlefield Adams.

Benjamin, Jessica. 1985. "The Bonds of Love: Rational Violence and Erotic Domination." In *The Future of Difference*. Eds. Hester Eisenstein and Alice Jardine. New Brunswick NJ: Rutgers University Press.

————. 1988. *The Bonds of Love: Psychoanalysis, Feminism, and the Problem of Domination*. New York: Pantheon.

Block, Gay and Malka Drucker. 1992. *Rescuers: Portraits of Moral Courage in the Holocaust*. New York: Holmes and Meier.

Blum, Lawrence A. 1980. *Friendship, Altruism, and Morality*. London: Routledge and Kegan Paul.

————. 1991. "Moral Perception and Particularity." *Ethics* 101: 701–725.

Brandt, Richard B. 1979. *A Theory of the Right and the Good*. Oxford: The Clarendon Press.

Brennan, Teresa. 1989. *Between Psychoanalysis and Feminism*. New York: Routledge.

Butler, Judith. 1990. *Gender Trouble: Feminism and the Subversion of Identity*. New York: Routledge.

————. 1993. *Bodies That Matter*. New York: Routledge.

Calhoun, Cheshire. 1988. "Justice, Care, Gender Bias." *Journal of Philosophy* 85: 451–463.

Cavell, Stanley. 1979. *The Claim of Reason*. New York: Oxford University Press.

Chodorow, Nancy. 1974. "Family Structure and Feminine Personality." In *Woman, Culture, and Society*. Eds. Michelle Zimbalist Rosaldo and Louise Lamphere. Stanford: Stanford University Press.

————. 1978. *The Reproduction of Mothering*. Berkeley: University of California Press.

————. 1980. "Gender, Relation, and Difference in Psychoanalytic Perspective." In *The Future of Difference*. Eds. Hester Eisenstein and Alice Jardine. Boston: G. K. Hall.

————. 1981. "On *The Reproduction of Mothering*: A Methodological Debate." *Signs* 6: 500–514.

Chodorow, Nancy and Susan Contratto. 1982. "The Fantasy of the Perfect Mother." In *Rethinking the Family*. Eds. Barrie Thorne and Marilyn Yalom. New York: Longman.

Cornell, Drucilla. 1991. *Beyond Accommodation*. New York: Routledge.

Crenshaw, Kimberle Williams. 1993. "Beyond Racism and Misogyny: Black Feminism and 2 Live Crew." In *Words That Wound*. Eds. Mari J. Matsuda et al. Boulder, CO: Westview.

de Beauvoir, Simone. 1989. *The Second Sex*. Trans. H. M. Parshley. New York: Vintage.

Davion, Victoria M. 1991. "Integrity and Radical Change." In *Feminist Ethics*. Ed. Claudia Card. Lawrence, KS: University Press of Kansas.

Dillon, Robin. 1992. "Towards a Feminist Conception of Self-respect." *Hypatia* 7: 52–69.

Dworkin, Ronald. 1992. "The Coming Battle over Free Speech." *The New York Review of Books* 39: 55–64.

Ezorsky, Gertrude. 1991. *Racism and Justice: The Case for Affirmative Action*. Ithaca, NY: Cornell University Press.

Feldstein, Richard and Judith Root. 1989. *Feminism and Psychoanalysis.* Ithaca, NY: Cornell University Press.

Firestone, Shulamith. 1970. *The Dialectic of Sex.* New York: William Morrow.

Flax, Jane. 1983. "Political Philosophy and the Patriarchal Unconscious: A Psychoanalytic Perspective on Epistemology and Metaphysics." In *Discovering Reality.* Eds. Sandra Harding and Merill B. Hintikka. Dordrecht, Holland: D. Reidel.

———. 1986. "Psychoanalysis as Deconstruction and Myth: On Gender, Narcissism and Modernity's Discontents." In *Crisis of Modernity.* Eds. Gunter H. Lenz and Kurt L. Shell. Boulder, CO: Westview.

———. 1987. "Re-membering the Selves: Is the Repressed Gendered?" *Michigan Quarterly Review* 26: 92–110.

Fraser, Nancy. 1989. "Talking about Needs: Interpretive Contests as Political Conflicts in Welfare-State Societies." *Ethics* 99: 291–313.

———. 1992. "The Uses and Abuses of French Discourse Theories for Feminist Politics." In *Revaluing French Feminism.* Eds. Nancy Fraser and Sandra Bartky. Bloomington, IN: Indiana University Press.

Fraser, Nancy and Sandra Bartky. 1992. *Revaluing French Feminism.* Bloomington, IN: Indiana University Press.

Fraser, Nancy and Linda J. Nicholson. 1990. "Social Criticism without Philosophy: An Encounter between Feminism and Postmodernism." In *Feminism/Postmodernism.* Ed. Linda J. Nicholson. New York: Routledge.

Freud, Sigmund. 1966. *The Complete Introductory Lectures on Psychoanalysis.* Trans. James Strachey. New York: W. W. Norton.

———. 1990. *Freud on Women: A Reader.* Edited by Elizabeth Young-Bruehl. New York: W. W. Norton.

Friedan, Betty. 1974. *The Feminine Mystique.* New York: Dell.

Friedman, Marilyn. 1989. "Feminism and Modern Friendship: Dislocating the Community." *Ethics* 99: 275–290.

Gallop, Jane. 1982. *The Daughter's Seduction.* Ithaca, NY: Cornell University Press.

———. 1985. *Reading Lacan.* Ithaca, NY: Cornell University Press.

Gauthier, Jeff. 1991. "Sexist Agency, Morality, and Self-Ignorance." *Michigan Feminist Studies* 6: 109–118.

Gilligan, Carol. 1982. *In a Different Voice.* Cambridge, MA: Harvard University Press.

———. 1986. "In a Different Voice: Women's Conceptions of Self and of

Morality." In *Women and Values*. Ed. Marilyn Pearsall. Belmont, CA: Wadsworth.

————. 1987. "Moral Orientation and Moral Development." In *Women and Moral Theory*. Eds. Eva Feder Kittay and Diana T. Meyers. Totowa, NJ: Rowman and Littlefield.

Gilman, Sander L. 1985. *Difference and Pathology: Stereotypes of Sexuality, Race, and Madness*. Ithaca, NY: Cornell University Press.

Goldman, Alvin I. 1992. "Empathy, Mind, and Morals." *Proceedings and Addresses of the American Philosophical Association* 66: 17–41.

Grimshaw, Jean. 1986. *Philosophy and Feminist Thinking*. Minneapolis: University of Minnesota Press.

Habermas, Jürgen. *Knowledge and Human Interests*. Boston: Beacon.

Hampshire, Stuart. 1983. *Morality and Conflict*. Cambridge, MA: Harvard University Press.

Harding, Sandra. 1987. "The Curious Coincidence of Feminine and African Moralities: Challenges for Feminist Theory." In *Women and Moral Theory*. Eds. Eva Feder Kittay and Diana T. Meyers. Totowa, NJ: Rowman and Littlefield.

————. 1991. *Whose Science? Whose Knowledge?* Ithaca, NY: Cornell University Press.

Hare, R.M. 1981. *Moral Thinking*. Oxford: Clarendon Press.

Hartsock, Nancy C. M. 1983. "The Feminist Standpoint: Developing the Ground for a Specifically Feminist Historical Materialism." In *Discovering Reality*. Eds. Sandra Harding and Merrill B. Hintikka. Dordrecht, Holland: D. Reidel.

Held, Virginia. 1984. "The Obligations of Mothers and Fathers." In *Mothering*. Ed. Joyce Trebilcot. Totowa, NJ: Rowman and Allanheld.

————. 1987. "Non-contractual Society." In *Science, Morality, and Feminist Theory*. Eds. Marsha Hanen and Kai Nielsen. Calgary: The University of Calgary Press.

————. 1989. *Rights and Goods*. Chicago: University of Chicago Press.

————. 1993. *Feminist Morality*. Chicago: University of Chicago Press.

Herman, Barbara. 1983. "Integrity and Impartiality." *The Monist* 66: 233–250.

————. 1985. "The Practice of Moral Judgment." *Journal of Philosophy* 82: 414–436.

————. 1990. "Obligation and Performance: A Kantian Account of Moral Conflict." In *Identity, Character, and Morality*. Eds. Owen Flanagan and Amelie Oksenberg Rorty. Cambridge, MA: The MIT Press.

———. 1991. "Agency, Attachment, and Difference." *Ethics* 101: 775–797.

Hill, Thomas, Jr. 1987. "The Importance of Autonomy." In *Women and Moral Theory*. Eds. Eva Feder Kittay and Diana T. Meyers. Totowa, NJ: Rowman and Littlefield.

hooks, bell. 1984. *Feminist Theory: From Margin to Center*. Boston: South End Press.

Horowitz, Mardi J. 1988. *Introduction to Psychodynamics: A New Synthesis*. New York: Basic Books.

Houston, Barbara. 1987. "Rescuing Womanly Virtues: Some Dangers of Moral Reclamation." In *Science, Morality, and Feminist Theory*. Eds. Marsha Hanen and Kai Nielsen. Calgary: The University of Calgary Press.

Irigaray, Luce. 1981. "And One Doesn't Stir without the Other." *Signs* 7: 60–67.

———. 1985a. *Speculum of the Other Woman*. Trans. Gillian C. Gill. Ithaca, NY: Cornell University Press.

———. 1985b. *This Sex Which Is Not One*. Trans. Catherine Porter. Ithaca, NY: Cornell University Press.

———. 1991. *The Irigaray Reader*. Ed. Margaret Whitford. Oxford: Basil Blackwell.

———. 1993a. *Je, Tu, Nous*. Trans. Alison Martin. New York: Routledge.

———. 1993b. *The Ethics of Sexual Difference*. Ithaca, NY: Cornell University Press.

Johnston, Jill. 1993. "Fictions of the Self in the Making." *The New York Times Book Review* April 25, 1993, pp. 1, 29–33.

Kittay, Eva Feder. 1984. "Womb Envy: An Explanatory Concept." In *Mothering*. Ed. Joyce Trebilcot. Totowa, NJ: Rowman and Allanheld.

———. 1987. *Metaphor*. Oxford: Clarendon Press.

———. 1988. "Woman as Metaphor." *Hypatia* 3: 63–86.

Kraditor, Aileen. 1965. *The Ideas of the Woman Suffrage Movement, 1890–1920*. New York: W. W. Norton.

Kristeva, Julia. 1980. *Desire in Language*. New York: Columbia University Press.

———. 1986. *The Kristeva Reader*. Ed. Toril Moi. New York: Columbia University Press.

———. 1987a. *Tales of Love*. Trans. Leon S. Roudiez. New York: Columbia University Press.

———. 1987b. *In the Beginning Was Love: Psychoanalysis and Faith*. New York: Columbia University Press.

———. 1988. Interview. In *Women Analyze Women*. Eds. Elaine Hoffman Baruch and Lucienne J. Serrano. New York: New York University Press.

———. 1991. *Strangers to Ourselves*. Trans. Leon S. Roudiez. New York: Columbia University Press.

Kundera, Milan. 1984. *The Unbearable Lightness of Being*. Trans. Michael Henry Heim. New York: Harper & Row.

Kupperman, Joel. 1991a. "Ethics for Extraterrestrials." *American Philosophical Quarterly* 28: 311–320.

———. 1991b. *Character*. New York: Oxford University Press.

Kuykendall, Eleanor H. 1984. "Toward an Ethic of Nurturance: Luce Irigaray on Mothering and Power." In *Mothering*. Ed. Joyce Trebilcot. Totowa, NJ: Rowman and Allanheld.

Leland, Dorothy. 1989. "Lacanian Psychoanalysis and French Feminism: Toward an Adequate Political Psychology." *Hypatia* 3: 81–103.

Lloyd, Genevieve. 1993. *The Man of Reason,* 2nd Edition. Minneapolis: University of Minnesota Press.

Lorber, Judith, et al. 1981. "On *The Reproduction of Mothering:* A Methodological Debate." *Signs* 6: 482–519.

Lugones, Maria C. 1987. "Playfulness, 'World'-Travelling, and Loving Perception." *Hypatia* 2: 3–19.

———. 1990. "Hispaneando y Lesbiando: On Sarah Hoagland's *Lesbian Ethics*." *Hypatia* 5: 138–146.

Lugones, Maria C. and Elizabeth V. Spelman. 1986. "Have We Got a Theory for You! Feminist Theory, Cultural Imperialism and the Demand for 'The Woman's Voice.'" In *Women and Values*. Ed. Marilyn Pearsall. Belmont, CA: Wadsworth.

MacKinnon, Catharine. 1989. *Toward a Feminist Theory of the State*. Cambridge, MA: Harvard University Press.

Meyers, Diana Tietjens. 1987a. "Personal Autonomy and the Paradox of Feminine Socialization." *The Journal of Philosophy* 84: 619–628.

———. 1987b. "The Socialized Individual and Individual Autonomy: An Intersection between Philosophy and Psychology." In *Women and Moral Theory*. Eds. Eva Feder Kittay and Diana T. Meyers. Totowa, NJ: Rowman and Littlefield.

———. 1989. *Self, Society, and Personal Choice*. New York: Columbia University Press.

———. 1992. "The Subversion of Women's Agency in Psychoanalytic Feminism: Chodorow, Flax, Kristeva." In *Revaluing French Feminism*. Eds. Nancy Fraser and Sandra Bartky. Bloomington, IN: Indiana University Press.

———. 1993. "Moral Reflection: Beyond Impartial Reason." *Hypatia* 8: 21–47.

———. n.d. "Rights in Collision: Injustice, Empathy, and Respect." Unpublished manuscript.

Mill, John Stuart. 1986. *The Subjection of Women*. Buffalo, NY: Prometheus Books.

Millett, Kate. 1969. *Sexual Politics*. New York: Avon Books.

Minow, Martha. 1990. *Making All the Difference*. Ithaca, NY: Cornell University Press.

Morgan, Kathryn Pauly. 1991. "Women and the Knife: Cosmetic Surgery and the Colonization of Women's Bodies." *Hypatia* 6: 25–53.

Mulvey, Laura. 1989. *Visual and Other Pleasures*. London: Macmillan.

Nagel, Thomas. 1994. "Freud's Permanent Revolution." *The New York Review of Books* 51: 34–38.

Nozick, Robert. 1974. *Anarchy, State, and Utopia*. New York: Basic Books.

Nussbaum, Martha C. 1990. *Love's Knowledge*. New York: Oxford University Press.

Nye, Andrea. 1987. "Woman Clothed with the Sun: Julia Kristeva and the Escape From/To Language." *Signs* 12: 664–686.

Okin, Susan Moller. 1989a. *Justice, Gender, and the Family*. New York: Basic Books.

———. 1989b. "Reason and Feeling in Thinking about Justice." *Ethics* 99: 229–249.

Piper, Adrian M. S. 1990. "Higher-Order Discrimination." In *Identity, Character, and Morality*. Eds. Owen Flanagan and Amelie Oksenberg Rorty. Cambridge, MA: MIT Press.

———. 1991. "Impartiality, Compassion, and Modal Imagination." *Ethics* 101: 726–757.

———. 1992–93. "Xenophobia and Kantian Rationalism." *The Philosophical Forum* 24: 188–232.

Pinckney, Darryl. 1992. *High Cotton*. New York: Penguin Books.

Rawls, John. 1971. *A Theory of Justice*. Cambridge, MA: Harvard University Press.

————. 1985. "Justice as Fairness: Political Not Metaphysical." *Philosophy and Public Affairs* 14: 223–251.

————. 1993. *Political Liberalism*. New York: Columbia University Press.

Rooney, Phyllis. 1991. "Gendered Reason: Sex Metaphor and Conceptions of Reason." *Hypatia* 6(2): 77–103.

Rorty, Richard. 1986. "Freud and Moral Reflection." In *Pragmatism's Freud*. Eds. Joseph Smith and William Kerrigan. Baltimore: Johns Hopkins University Press.

Rose, Jacqueline. 1986. *Sexuality in the Field of Vision*. London: Verso.

Ruddick, Sara. 1986. "Maternal Thinking." In *Women and Values*. Ed. Marilyn Pearsall. Belmont, CA: Wadsworth.

Sachs, David. 1989. "In Fairness to Freud: A Critical Notice of *The Foundations of Psychoanalysis*." *The Philosophical Review* 98: 349–378.

Scheman, Naomi. 1993. *Engenderings: Constructions of Knowledge, Authority, and Privilege*. New York: Routledge.

Schlafly, Phyllis. 1972. "The Right to Be a Woman." *The Phyllis Schlafly Report* 6.

Scott, Joan W. 1992. "'Experience'." In *Feminists Theorize the Political*. Eds. Judith Butler and Joan W. Scott. New York: Routledge

Smith, Alexis. 1991. "Interview with Alexis Smith." In *Alexis Smith*. Ed. and introduced by Richard Armstrong. New York: Whitney Museum of American Art and Rizzoli.

Spelman, Elizabeth V. 1988. *Inessential Woman*. Boston: Beacon.

Spence, Donald P. 1982. *Narrative Truth and Historical Truth*. New York: W. W. Norton.

Stanton, Domna C. 1986. "Difference on Trial: A Critique of the Maternal Metaphor in Cixous, Irigaray, and Kristeva." In *The Poetics of Gender*. Ed. Nancy K. Miller. New York: Columbia University Press.

Stein, Edith. 1989. *On the Problem of Empathy*. In *The Collected Works of Edith Stein,* Vol. 3, 3rd Rev. ed. Trans. Waltraut Stein. Washington DC: ICS Publications.

Strouse, Jean. 1992. "Making the Facts Obey." *The New York Times Book Review* Sunday, May 24, Section 7, pp. 1 and 16–17.

Taylor, Charles. 1991. *The Ethics of Authenticity*. Cambridge, MA: Harvard University Press.

Thomson, Judith Jarvis. 1971. "A Defense of Abortion." *Philosophy and Public Affairs* 1: 47–66.

Trebilcot, Joyce. 1982. "Two Forms of Androgynism." In *"Femininity," "Masculinity," and Androgyny.* Ed. Mary Vetterling-Braggin. Totowa, NJ: Littlefield Adams.

Walker, James C. 1983. "In a Diffident Voice: Cryptoseparatist Analysis of Female Moral Development." *Social Research* 50: 665–695.

Walker, Margaret Urban. 1987. "Moral Particularity." *Metaphilosophy* 18: 171–185.

———. 1989. "Moral Understandings." *Hypatia* 4: 15–28.

———. 1991. "Partial Consideration." *Ethics* 101: 758–774.

———. 1992. "Feminism, Ethics, and the Question of Theory." *Hypatia* 7: 23–38.

———. n.d. a "Responsibility and Integrity." Unpublished manuscript.

———. n.d. b "Pictures of the Human Soul: On Moral Graphics." Unpublished manuscript.

Whitford, Margaret. 1991. *Luce Irigaray: Philosophy in the Feminine.* London: Routledge.

Williams, Bernard. 1981. *Moral Luck.* Cambridge: Cambridge University Press.

Williams, Patricia. 1991. *The Alchemy of Race and Rights.* Cambridge, MA: Harvard University Press.

Wiseman, Mary Bittner. 1978. "Empathetic Identification." *American Philosophical Quarterly* 15: 107–113.

Wollheim, Richard. 1984. *The Thread of Life.* Cambridge, MA: Harvard University Press.

Young, Iris Marion. 1984. "Is Male Gender Identity the Cause of Male Domination?" In *Mothering.* Ed. Joyce Trebilcot. Totowa, NJ: Rowman and Allanheld.

———. 1990. *Justice and the Politics of Difference.* Princeton, NJ: Princeton University Press.

Young-Bruehl, Elizabeth. 1990. "Introduction." *Freud on Women: A Reader.* Ed. Elizabeth Young-Bruehl. New York: W. W. Norton.

Index